PRAISE FOR
WHAT WORKS IN COMMUNITY NEWS

"A valuable reference book for entrepreneurs and a compelling read for anyone interested in saving and reviving local news."

—PENELOPE MUSE ABERNATHY, author of *Saving Community Journalism: The Path to Profitability*

"Pulls together in one place innovative approaches from across the country to stave off growing 'news deserts.' You can't help but find this book nourishing if you care about preserving local news—and our democracy."

—GREGORY L. MOORE, former editor of *The Denver Post*

"Crackling with insights and richly detailed, this sharply written book is essential reading for anyone interested in journalism's future and the democracy it serves."

—VICTOR PICKARD, author of *Democracy Without Journalism? Confronting the Misinformation Society*

"A comprehensive history and analysis of major news ecosystems in the emerging digital media landscape."

—ANNE GALLOWAY, *VTDigger* founder and editor at large

WHAT
WORKS IN
COMMUNITY
NEWS

WHAT WORKS IN COMMUNITY NEWS

MEDIA STARTUPS, NEWS DESERTS, AND THE FUTURE OF THE FOURTH ESTATE

ELLEN CLEGG AND DAN KENNEDY

BEACON PRESS
BOSTON

BEACON PRESS
Boston, Massachusetts
www.beacon.org

Beacon Press books
are published under the auspices of
the Unitarian Universalist Association of Congregations.

27 26 25 24   8 7 6 5 4 3 2 1

This book is printed on acid-free paper that meets the uncoated paper
ANSI/NISO specifications for permanence as revised in 1992.

Text design and composition by Kim Arney

*Library of Congress Cataloguing-in-Publication
Data is available for this title.*
Paperback ISBN: 978-0-8070-1648-0
E-book ISBN: 978-0-8070-1019-8
Audiobook: 978-0-8070-1466-0

For our families and friends

CONTENTS

THE LOCAL NEWS CRISIS WILL BE SOLVED ONE COMMUNITY AT A TIME

Friday, August 12, 2022, was a terrible day for Gannett journalists and the communities they served. A week earlier, the country's largest newspaper chain reported it had lost $54 million on revenues of $749 million during the previous quarter. The company's response was to lay off employees, just as it had so many times before.[1] Though Gannett would not release exact numbers, many who lost their jobs took to social media to share their bad news. By the end of the day, it was apparent that the cuts were broad and deep, from Worcester County in Massachusetts, where several small weekly newspapers were shut down and their staff members let go, to the chain's national flagship, *USA Today*.[2] For perspective, *Los Angeles Times* reporter Jeong Park observed that, after the cuts, Gannett's more than two hundred daily newspapers and other publications employed fewer journalists than the combined newsrooms of just three national papers—*The New York Times*, *The Washington Post*, and *The Wall Street Journal*.[3] And the downsizing continued, with another two hundred or so jobs eliminated before the end of the year.[4]

In some respects, the layoffs were just another sign that the business model for local news is broken. According to a 2022 report by Penny Abernathy of Northwestern University, the country has lost more than a quarter of its newspapers—about 2,500—since 2005.[5] Technological changes are responsible for part of the decline, but that's not the only explanation. Chain ownership by corporations

1

and hedge funds has compounded the challenge by draining revenues from newspapers in order to enrich the folks at the top.

Given that the economic prospects for the news business have been in decline for the past quarter-century, it is fair to ask why investors who are mainly concerned about revenues and profits would want a piece of the action. The answer is that newspapers can still be lucrative for owners who are willing to cut expenses deeply enough. For instance, Gannett may be a money-loser, but that is not so for its top leaders. Michael Reed, Gannett's chair and chief executive officer, was paid more than $7.7 million in 2021 in the form of salary, stock awards, and other compensation. Gannett's eight part-time board members received more than $200,000 apiece.[6] The second-largest newspaper owner, the hedge fund Alden Global Capital, which controls more than one hundred papers, does not report earnings, but internal documents obtained by media analyst Ken Doctor showed that Alden's holdings produced an unconscionably high 17 percent profit margin during the 2017 fiscal year. As the headline of Doctor's column in *Nieman Lab* put it: "Alden Global Capital Is Making So Much Money Wrecking Local Journalism It Might Not Want to Stop Anytime Soon."[7] Moreover, both Gannett and Alden borrowed vast sums of money in assembling their empires and then gutted their newsrooms to pay down the debt.[8]

By contrast, independent local and regional news organizations are serving their audience by providing them with the news and information they need in a self-governing democracy. Some are thriving; others are just getting by. Many are digital startups; some are legacy print newspapers. There are hundreds of examples across the country, serving urban centers, affluent suburbs, and rural communities. In these pages, you'll learn about some of these projects, which we chose because they reflect a variety of business models, geographic areas, and demographic profiles. For instance:

- In New Jersey, *NJ Spotlight*, a nonprofit digital startup, merged with NJ PBS, the state's public broadcasting outlet. The new entity, *NJ Spotlight News*, offers deep coverage of state politics and policy in the form of text-based stories on its

website and a half-hour newscast that viewers can watch over
the air, on cable, and on the operation's digital platforms.
- In Minnesota, a former reporter for Minnesota Public Radio
  and the *Star Tribune* of Minneapolis launched the all-digital
  Sahan Journal to cover the immigrant communities that are
  transforming the culture and politics of a state that is 80 percent white. By 2022, the *Journal* had expanded its staff and
  coverage areas and booked grants from major funders.
- In Colorado, ten staff members left *The Denver Post* following extensive cuts at the hands of Alden Global Capital—and
  then started a for-profit digital news organization, *The Colorado Sun*, which covers both the city and the state. After the
  owners of a media group comprising twenty-four weekly and
  monthly newspapers in the Denver suburbs retired, the *Sun*
  was brought in to help oversee them in return for an ownership share, thus staving off a corporate takeover.

We would be the first to acknowledge that what critics sometimes
call "vulture capitalism" is not solely responsible for the hard times
that have befallen community journalism. When news began moving
from print to the web starting around 1995, many publishers believed
technology would be their salvation, as they would make money from
interactive online advertising and cut costs by not having to pay for
printing and distribution. It's no wonder that nearly all newspaper
websites offered their journalism for free. The optimism of those
early years, however, soon gave way to a bitter reality. Classified ads,
which once accounted for as much as 40 percent of a typical daily
newspaper's revenues, were wiped out by mostly free online services
such as Craigslist.[9] Moreover, about two-thirds of all digital advertising now goes to three internet giants: Google, Facebook, and Amazon.[10] Many newspapers cut their staff to the bone in order to offset
plunging ad revenues.

Gradually, though, newspapers whose owners were willing to in-
vest in the future began to find a way forward. As payment technology improved, many started to charge for digital subscriptions, thus
offsetting at least in part the precipitous decline in advertising. They

stopped cutting and began modestly rebuilding on the not especially esoteric theory that readers wouldn't pay unless you gave them journalism that mattered. They improved their websites and apps, cutting down on the pop-ups, pop-unders, and slow loading and scrolling speeds that had been the bane of online news. By the late 2010s, not only the national papers but also large regional for-profits like *The Boston Globe*, the *Star Tribune* of Minneapolis, and *The Seattle Times* were back on their feet. What they had in common was committed local owners who were willing to be patient as their papers progressed toward profitability.

The corporate chain owners, meanwhile, kept cutting, then cut even more as readers and advertisers spurned their hollowed-out papers. The result of this downward spiral was the spread of "news deserts," a term that was apparently coined in 2011 by the blog *Chicago Is the World*. The term refers to communities lacking a reliable source of news and information.[11] Some news deserts have neither a local newspaper nor a digital outlet. Some have "ghost newspapers," Penny Abernathy's phrase for papers that are filled with wire-service copy and articles from distant parts of the chain with little in the way of local content.

This is a book about democracy. Local news is essential to self-governance. Meaningful participation in civic life is impossible without it, as we depend on journalism to decide whom to vote for and to be informed about what's going on in municipal government, the school system, law enforcement, development, road repairs—the list is endless. Studies show that voter participation is lower and corruption more pervasive in places that lack reliable coverage.[12] Ideologically motivated media websites with murky funding, designed to look like legitimate outlets, pop up to fill the vacuum. These sites, known as "pink slime," are mostly but not exclusively on the political right, and they poison local discourse by pretending to be something they are not.[13] Communities try to make up for the lack of news coverage by forming groups on Facebook and Nextdoor, sometimes providing useful information but more often than not trading rumors and spreading misinformation.

A healthy local news ecosystem is vital to community life, whose very existence is in danger as our culture becomes increasingly nationalized. We are immersed in Big Media, from *The New York Times* to Instagram, from the Fox News Channel to Netflix. Yet our most important relationships are with our families, our friends, our neighbors, and the places where we live. All these connections are held together by news and information that have little to do with Tucker Carlson's racist outbursts, who might win the next presidential election, or the latest must-see viral video. This nationalization is being driven by technological advances, and there is nothing novel about it. Nearly 170 years ago, Henry David Thoreau lamented, "We are in great haste to construct a magnetic telegraph from Maine to Texas; but Maine and Texas, it may be, have nothing important to communicate."[14] Perhaps not to each other, but surely among themselves.

In the early part of the twentieth century, the philosopher John Dewey pushed back against the journalist Walter Lippmann's anti-democratic assertion that an increasingly complex society would best be served by a government of experts. The media's role, in Lippmann's view, was "the manufacture of consent" aimed at persuading an uninformed public to go along. Dewey, by contrast, articulated a vision of community life in which members of the public could inform themselves well enough to engage in self-government. We can only imagine how a commitment to such small-d democracy might have warded off the alienation that led to the populist authoritarianism and dark conspiracy theories afflicting American society in recent years. The journalism scholar Jay Rosen of New York University summed up Dewey's faith in public participation by writing, "Democracy for Dewey meant not a system of government but a society organized around certain principles: that every individual has something to contribute, that people are capable of making their own decisions, that given the chance they can understand their predicament well enough to puzzle through it, that the world is knowable if we teach ourselves how [to] study and discuss it."[15] But that hopeful outlook is not possible without reliable and comprehensive local news.

We believe that at a time when many Americans are highly engaged with national news, especially with the divisive talk shows that are carried on cable outlets, local journalism can be a way to bring us together. We all want quality schools, a police department that keeps us safe while respecting individual rights, and a health system that serves everyone. And yes, even these issues have gotten caught up in ugly rhetoric driven by the national blue-red divide. But community journalism, at its best, can be a way to bring people of different viewpoints together so they work toward common goals. The challenge is to find ways of providing such journalism at a time when technological, economic, and social forces make that more difficult than ever.

This book is an anti-manifesto. You won't find grand pronouncements here or proposals that the government act to save local news by approving this spending bill or enacting that tax credit. We believe that any approach can work depending on the dedication and experience of those who are on the ground, putting in long hours to serve their communities. Thus we take no sides on such matters as print versus digital or nonprofit versus for-profit, although most of the projects we write about here are nonprofit. Our one animating belief is that independent local leadership of such projects is crucial. We hope that the stories of these journalist-entrepreneurs will provide guidance to others and inspire them to start local news ventures in their own communities.

Our emphasis is on the folks actually doing the hard work of building news organizations in the places where they live. There are a number of nonprofit foundations that provide financial assistance to news startups, and they are doing good and important work. The John S. and James L. Knight Foundation has helped many local and regional media outlets. The National Trust for Local News is working to find (and fund) buyers for legacy newspapers that might otherwise close or fall into the grip of chain ownership. The Institute for Nonprofit News provides assistance through its NewsMatch program, which matches money raised at the local level. These organizations, though, are one step removed from the challenges of covering the news—and covering payroll—on a day-to-day basis.

What Works in Community News is divided into nine chapters, each focusing on one local or regional independent news outlet. In all of the places we've reported on, we also examine the broader media ecosystem, so that, in addition to learning about our principal subjects in some detail, you'll also be introduced to other news outlets in those regions. The COVID-19 pandemic delayed us for a year. Dan was in Northern California to report on *The Mendocino Voice* during the first week of March 2020, just before the national shutdown. Nevertheless, we persisted, spending time in each of the nine locales. The majority of our reporting took place between mid–2021 and mid–2022, although we've attempted to capture a few important developments that unfolded in the second half of 2022. Ellen is responsible for the chapters on Memphis, Minneapolis, Texas, and Storm Lake, Iowa. She also edited the four "Conversations" interviews, drawn from our podcast. Dan is responsible for the chapters on Bedford, Massachusetts; New Haven, Connecticut; Denver; Mendocino County, California; and New Jersey.

It's important to note that most of the projects we've written about offer their journalism without charge to the people they serve. Over the past decade or so, free news on the internet has given way to a media landscape dominated by paywalls, which has led to concerns about who has access to quality news and who doesn't. The media scholar Nikki Usher has warned that the need for reader revenue to support news has led to the rise of journalism aimed at "the rich, white, and blue"—that is, "news for those who can pay, news from white institutions that fail in comprehensive and inclusive coverage, and news read by liberals who still trust mainstream media."[16] We believe this concern, though real, is somewhat overwrought. For example, *The Boston Globe*, by all accounts the most expensive regional newspaper in the US, charges a dollar a day for a digital subscription. When adjusted for inflation, that's hardly out of line with what it cost in the early 1980s, when the price of a weekday edition was twenty-five cents. Nevertheless, with just a few exceptions, the news organizations we write about here do not have paywalls, although all of them, nonprofit and for-profit alike, ask for voluntary contributions. Of equal importance is that several of the news organizations we visited serve urban communities of color and less-than-affluent rural areas.

In the pages that follow, you will find news organizations that we describe as "regional," "local," and "hyperlocal." We confess that we use these mainly as terms of art, and we are unaware of any specific definitions. In general, though, we regard a regional news organization as one that covers multiple communities and focuses on news of interest to that region or to an entire state; such organizations generally do not report on city council meetings, neighborhood zoning issues, school controversies, and the like unless they are of interest to a broader audience. An example of a regional news organization would be a large or medium-size daily newspaper or a digital news site that covers state government. Where we have used the term "hyperlocal" to describe a media outlet, it is meant to convey the idea that its coverage is devoted to a single locale, though we have tended to use "hyperlocal" interchangeably with "local."

We come to this project with many years of experience. Ellen spent much of her career as a top editor at *The Boston Globe* and for several years was closely involved in directing coverage at Sunday supplements that covered the city's neighborhoods and suburbs. Thus, her experience comprises both regional and local journalism. Dan began his career in community news at *The Daily Times Chronicle* in the Boston suburb of Woburn, which—as of this writing—is still owned by the Haggerty family, who founded the paper in 1901. Dan's previous two books, *The Wired City* (2013) and *The Return of the Moguls* (2018), are both about the fate of local and regional journalism in an age of technological disruption. We are passionate and, as you'll see, optimistic about the future of local news.

As befits a topic that is changing so rapidly, *What Works in Community News* is not just a book but is also the hub of a larger enterprise. On our podcast, *What Works: The Future of Local News*, we interview entrepreneurs, academics, and others involved in charting the future. We also keep up with developments in local news at our website. We hope you will follow us through our various channels.[17]

In the past decade, a broad consensus has formed that local news is in a serious crisis. A number of ideas are floating around to address the issue, including federal tax credits, direct subsidies by state governments to news organizations, and attempts to force the technology giants Google and Facebook to pay for the news that they make use of on their platforms. Such top-down approaches may prove worthy. What is certain, though, is that the bottom-up growth of locally based news organizations has already provided communities with news that would otherwise go unreported. It's a hit-or-miss, imperfect process. News deserts will persist and may even expand. Yet, here and there, some communities and regions are being extraordinarily well covered. If we can understand why—what combination of founders, funders, and audience has come together in those places to make for a successful news organization—then we can begin to chart a way forward and apply those lessons to other communities and regions.

The local news crisis will be solved one community at a time. Let's get started.

CHAPTER ONE

NEW JERSEY

*A Digital Innovator Joins Forces
with a Public Television Powerhouse*

Most news executives would not regard the proliferation of warehouses as the sort of issue that would engage their audience. But that didn't stop *NJ Spotlight News* from organizing a virtual event on that seemingly somnolent topic. On a late afternoon in March 2022, a panel of speakers gathered on Zoom to discuss the environmental, social, and racial effects of the state's boom in warehouses. And though most of the program centered around the sort of bureaucratic arcana that only policymakers could love, there was also an important corrective to some overly sanguine coverage that had recently appeared in the real estate section of *The New York Times*.

According to the *Times*, the township of Robbinsville had emerged as a thriving, prosperous community on the strength of a "warehouse hub" that had been built on the outskirts, thus generating tax revenue that paid for a new high school, a municipal building, and a police training facility.[1] But according to the keynote speaker at the *Spotlight* event, Micah Rasmussen, director of the Rebovich Institute for New Jersey Politics at Rider University, Robbinsville's success came at a high price. "What the profile didn't mention was that Robbinsville residents enjoy all the tax benefits of those warehouses with none of their impacts," Rasmussen said. "Because what they've managed to do is outsource them completely to Allentown and Upper Freehold, where they've dumped them on their border. The traffic, air pollution, crime, and noise that are all centered on the residential areas of two communities that derive exactly none of their benefits that don't stop at the municipal border. It's a nice trick if you can manage it."[2]

Rasmussen offered exactly the sort of context that is a hallmark of *NJ Spotlight News*, a digital nonprofit that's part of NJ PBS, the state's public broadcasting network. For *Spotlight*, the event had significant multiplier effects. It was a live forum featuring newsmakers, drawing nearly 250 viewers in real time and still more on the site's YouTube and Vimeo channels. It was a news story, as highlights from the speakers' remarks were published on the website. And it was an exercise in civic engagement. Steven Shalit, *Spotlight*'s director of business development and event producer, told the audience that about a hundred questions had been submitted beforehand. Viewers were encouraged to continue submitting questions, which were forwarded to the panelists after the seventy-five-minute session had concluded. And though this particular forum, arcane as the topic was, did not attract any paying sponsors, many of *Spotlight*'s events, on COVID-19, public education, wind power, and the like, are a significant source of income. Attendance is free, with businesses involved in those fields paying to promote their services.

"Our charter is to produce news reporting," Shalit said in an interview. "On the business side, our job is to generate revenue. In the health-care space, or in energy, there's a lot of money floating around for sponsorships. In things like affordable housing, warehousing, or stormwater management, there's not a lot of money. But that doesn't mean we shouldn't do those topics. So what we've done is we've looked at the entire group of events as an aggregate, because some of them will be very lucrative, others not so much. But overall, the whole thing is in the black by a wide margin." What Shalit calls "earned revenue"—event sponsorships as well as advertising on the website and in its newsletters—brings in about $300,000 to $400,000 a year, with the remainder of *Spotlight*'s annual $1.2 million operating budget comprising donations and grants.[3]

Like many other local and regional news startups, *NJ Spotlight News*—originally *NJ Spotlight*—was born amid the turmoil that beset legacy newspapers as they failed to adjust to changes in technology and media consumption. John Mooney, who covered education for *The Star-Ledger* of Newark, the state's largest daily, took a buyout in 2008 amid massive cuts that eliminated 151 positions from a newsroom staff of about 330 people.[4] "It was a bigger risk to stay than to leave" is how he described it during an interview at his home in Montclair. He and another reporter who left *The Star-Ledger* put together a business plan and raised $10,000 in seed money. Mooney's would-be partner ended up taking a job with Bloomberg instead, but Mooney plowed ahead. With three journalists and a business manager, *NJ Spotlight* launched in May 2010 under the auspices of the nonprofit Community Foundation of New Jersey.[5]

Spotlight hit its stride journalistically about three to four years after its founding, Mooney said, but it fell short of breaking even, losing about $20,000 to $30,000 annually. The original understanding was that the project would remain affiliated with the Community Foundation for three years, but that stretched to nine years. The foundation, Mooney said, was growing impatient. Sometime around the late 2010s, executives at the WNET Group in New York—the largest public broadcaster in the country and the parent organization of NJ PBS (then called NJTV)—began talking with Mooney about an acquisition. The deal was consummated in 2019 and led to some significant changes.[6] The name of the website became *NJ Spotlight News*, and the daily half-hour newscast that is produced by NJ PBS took the same name. The newscast is posted on the *Spotlight* website, both in full and with individual stories broken out. *Spotlight* reporters—"digital reporters," in NJ PBS lingo, to distinguish them from the broadcast-side journalists—regularly appear on the newscast to talk about their stories. Both the broadcast and digital sides take part in news meetings so each knows what the other is working on.

For Mooney, who's the executive director of *Spotlight* as well as its education reporter, the merger may have saved the news outlet he founded. "The pandemic threw everything for a loop, but even before that it definitely was getting harder," he said. "It seemed we were struggling more and more to end a little bit in the red as opposed to a lot in the red. There's no doubt we did this to stay alive. And what I say to our folks is there's a decent chance we wouldn't have been here."

Neal Shapiro, the president and CEO of WNET, told us that his interest in acquiring *Spotlight* was to provide New Jersey with deeper coverage than NJ PBS could offer on its own. He described a situation unique to New Jersey that virtually everyone we interviewed echoed—that the state, despite its sizeable population (nearly 9.3 million, making it the eleventh-largest in the country[7]), is stuck between the media markets of New York and Philadelphia, leaving it without a media identity of its own. "NJ PBS is the only telecast that serves the entire state," he said. "And *NJ Spotlight* was and is one of the leading digital news-gatherers in the country. I was interested in the capacity to put things together that achieve economies of scale that can appeal to consumers—that calls for more ways for broadcasting and digital to play together." His hope, he added, was that "we will be stronger together than we were apart."[8]

The story of NJ PBS and *NJ Spotlight News* suggests that public broadcasting can play a role in bolstering coverage of regional and statewide news. What's needed to make it work is to bring together different newsroom cultures in a way that serves the audience rather than the bureaucratic imperatives of protecting turf and resisting change. As the journalism researcher Elizabeth Hansen Shapiro has written, "Public media can absolutely help fix market failures in local news, but it will take a simultaneous process of building on its traditional values and dismantling the legacy structures of the current system to create a new local journalism service worthy of 'the public' in public media."[9]

The merger of NJ PBS and *Spotlight* is not the only example of such a partnership. Colorado Public Radio acquired the digital outlet *Denverite* a few years ago. Likewise, *Billy Penn*, a mobile-first news outlet that covers Philadelphia, is now part of public radio station WHYY, and Chicago's number-two daily newspaper, the *Sun-Times*, has merged with WBEZ, also a public radio station. What's taking place in New Jersey, though, is among the more ambitious of these mergers in the way that two news organizations of roughly equivalent stature are working together on television and online. As for the cultural challenges identified by Hansen Shapiro, progress has been made—but folks on both sides of the digital-broadcast divide told us that more needs to be done.

In addition to being stuck between two major out-of-state media markets, New Jersey's journalistic landscape was shaped by the state's rapid move toward suburbanization in the decades after World War II. It was during these years when suburban living became the ideal for white middle-class America. The trend was particularly strong in New Jersey. For instance, in 1950 about half the state's population lived in its six largest cities—Newark, Jersey City, Paterson, Elizabeth, Trenton, and Camden. By the mid-1980s, only one-eighth of the state's residents lived in those cities, with suburbs dominating the corridor connecting New York City and Philadelphia.[10]

The shift from city to suburb reshaped the newspaper environment as well. Although overall circulation at papers across New Jersey increased and new dailies were founded, those serving the state's urban centers did not fare as well; four shut down. One of those, the *Newark Evening News*, had been regarded as the best in New Jersey. Its fatal mistake was to build a new printing plant in the 1960s next to its existing plant, in the center of the city, making it nearly impossible for delivery trucks to distribute the paper as the roads and highways became increasingly choked with traffic. The paper folded in 1972 amid a strike by its employees. By contrast, the *Newark Star-Ledger* constructed a new facility in nearby Piscataway, next to a major highway, enabling statewide distribution. It dropped "Newark" from its nameplate in the 1960s and grew into the state's largest newspaper by far, with weekday circulation in the early 1980s of more than 430,000—and 631,000 on Sundays.[11]

Those years were marked by scandal, sensationalism, and fierce competition. A 1977 exposé by the magazine *New Jersey Monthly* found that reporters at the *Hudson Dispatch* and the *Jersey Journal* took cash from politicians and other news sources, held no-show government jobs, and were paid to write press releases. New Jersey was also the setting for what *Washington Post* publisher Katharine

Graham once called "my Vietnam." In the 1970s, the *Post* owned the *Trenton Times*, which competed with *The Trentonian*. The *Post* failed to make inroads, favoring national news over local coverage and spurning *The Trentonian*'s working-class readership. Conceding defeat, the *Post* sold the *Times* in 1981 to one of its ancient rivals— Joe L. Allbritton, whose holdings included *The Washington Star* for a time and whose son, Robert, would later found *Politico* with the help of three former *Post* journalists.[12] *The Trentonian*, meanwhile, achieved tabloid infamy in 2002 when it published perhaps the most notoriously offensive headline in New Jersey newspaper history: "Roasted Nuts," about a fire at Trenton Psychiatric Hospital. No one was injured or killed in the blaze, but it was a stunning example of insensitivity, with the National Alliance for the Mentally Ill expressing "shock and outrage."[13]

In New Jersey, as elsewhere, the newspaper scene today is much diminished. *The Star-Ledger* remains the largest paper in the state, with a weekday print and digital circulation that averaged nearly 125,000 and a Sunday circulation of about 140,000. Next up is *The Record*, which covers northern New Jersey (35,000 on weekdays, 40,000 on Sundays) and the *Asbury Park Press* (27,000 on weekdays, 39,000 on Sundays), both of which are owned by Gannett.[14] Observers we spoke with gave those papers reasonably high marks for the quality of their reporting, but the breadth of their coverage was regarded as lacking. *The Star-Ledger*, owned by Advance Publications, is worth a closer look. Advance is a privately held company based in New York and controlled by the Newhouse family. It is best known for its magazine division, Condé Nast, which publishes prestige titles such as *The New Yorker* and *Vanity Fair*. But the company operates a number of daily newspapers as well, including *The Birmingham News* of Alabama, *The Plain Dealer* of Cleveland, and *The Oregonian* of Portland.

Advance runs its newspapers in regional groups, emphasizing paid digital subscriptions over print. In New Jersey, that means *The Star-Ledger* and two smaller dailies, *The Times* of Trenton and the *South Jersey News*, as well as a number of other Advance publications, are all part of NJ.com. A unified newsroom feeds stories to its digital hub and to its print newspapers. Some of those stories are specific to a particular region and might only run in one paper; others, more general in nature, might run statewide. All of them are posted at NJ.com, which, as of early 2022, was attracting about 1.5 million daily visits. What it means is that NJ.com is able to field the largest editorial staff in the state—about 115 journalists—as well as offer robust statehouse, investigative, and data reporting. The advantage is that Advance is able to provide its audience with strong statewide and regional coverage. The disadvantage is a shortage of day-to-day accountability journalism at the community level.

As was the case with many media outlets in the spring of 2022 (including *NJ Spotlight News*), the NJ.com newsroom was closed as a consequence of the COVID pandemic. We met Chris Kelly, NJ.com's senior director of news, features, topics, and innovation, who was serving as interim editor, at a restaurant near his home in Maplewood. (That fall he was promoted to NJ.com's vice president for content.)[15] He spoke animatedly about Advance's strategy for covering New Jersey. "My argument in the eight years that I've been here is that you've got to basically become a statewide news outlet and almost move from man-to-man coverage to zone coverage," he said. "We just simply cannot sustain a reporter covering Maplewood, covering Millbrook. I'm not unaware that doesn't come without the downside of, yeah, we cannot cover every council meeting, we are going to miss things. But that's been the strategy that mostly seems to be working and has allowed us to kind of sustain at the level we're sustaining." He also lauded Advance's commitment to enterprise journalism, telling us: "The one thing that I can say is, if we've got a story that we've got to get, we're going to get it, and we're going to keep doing it. That level of commitment, the financial support, the legal support has been unwavering since I've been there."[16]

NJ Spotlight News and NJ.com are not alone in providing news coverage at the state and regional level. Gannett has grouped some of its papers into a digital entity called NorthJersey.com, taking a regional approach that's similar to what NJ.com is doing. And there are at least three news organizations in addition to *Spotlight* that specialize in deep coverage of state politics and policy.

One of those organizations is *Politico*'s New Jersey operation, which is well staffed compared to many of that outlet's other regional bureaus. According to Katherine Landergan, who was the bureau chief when we spoke (she later moved on to *The Atlanta Journal-Constitution*), the bureau employs five full-time reporters and publishes a free morning newsletter as well as a variety of free and high-priced subscriber-only content. The audience, she said, comprises inside players—government officials, lobbyists, policymakers, and the like. "I think we're more incremental than *Spotlight*," she said. "There is a lot of overlap in readership, but we're tracking legislation very closely. *Spotlight*'s strengths are that they have really strong institutional knowledge and excellent reporters who've been covering the state for a really long time."[17]

Another is the *New Jersey Globe*, a robust and gossipy website started by David Wildstein, well known in the state's political and publishing circles, who ran afoul of the law as "the mastermind of the Bridgegate scandal," as *Politico* once put it, while serving as a top official in the administration of Governor Chris Christie.[18]

Finally, there is the *New Jersey Monitor*, a relatively new digital nonprofit that's part of States Newsroom. Begun in 2017, States Newsroom aims to offset the decline in statehouse coverage across the country—on the wane for years, although there was a modest uptick in 2022.[19] "State government and politics and policy have the most impact on people's lives and it's covered the least," director and publisher Chris Fitzsimon told *The Washington Post*. "That's really why we exist."[20] By mid-2022, States Newsroom had affiliates in twenty-eight states.[21] The *Monitor*, Landergan told us, got off to a fast start by hiring experienced people and homing in on under-covered issues such as social justice and the criminal justice system.

But if New Jersey residents have a number of options for informing themselves about what's going on in their state, the opposite is the case for keeping up on city hall, school boards, law enforcement, and local businesses. Over the past decade, New Jersey has been a center of activity around the future of local news. Scholars have studied the problem. Solutions have been proposed. New business models are being tried. The state has even pioneered the use of government funding to bolster community journalism. The challenges, though, are enormous, and it's far from certain that all this activity will be enough to offset the market failure that has left many parts of the state without quality journalism.

Unlike many states, where county and regional officials oversee multiple communities, New Jersey is home to 564 municipalities, each with its own individual governing authorities. This presents a monumental challenge for journalism. Each locale needs its own source of news coverage. Some areas are well served. Some are truly news deserts.

Keeping track of this is Stefanie Murray, the director of the Center for Cooperative Media at Montclair State University, which has been offering support, training, and advocacy for hyperlocal news since its founding in 2012, a substantial commitment aided by state funds. She and three staff members work out of spartan headquarters on the university's campus, devoting their energies to solving the local news crisis. (None of the four teach regularly.) Murray, a former journalist whose credentials include a stint as executive editor of *The Tennessean* in Nashville, said the existence of so many local entities that need coverage is a major impediment. "You throw a rock and you're in someone else's police jurisdiction, school district jurisdiction, local government," she said. "When I drive from work to home, I drive through seven, eight different towns. We've got this very dense state, and there are a lot of places that don't have anything, or what they do have is hit or miss. And, so, a lot of people get most of their news through Facebook groups or Nextdoor groups or WhatsApp groups or word of mouth, chamber of commerce papers, that sort of thing."[22]

Dispiriting but unsurprising, she added, is who gets adequate coverage and who doesn't: "Wealthy white people who live in suburban New Jersey are generally very well served. They are reflected in most of the coverage from the major news organizations. Their needs and thoughts and desires are centered. Decisions on news coverage will often end up being made by virtue of what an editor thinks might appeal best to that audience, because that's the audience that their advertisers want."

Murray's assessment is supported by a report that the center published in February 2021 that surveyed news sources in each of the state's municipalities. Written by the center's director of research, Sarah Stonbely, the report showed that suburban areas were better served than rural ones, and that mostly white communities were less likely to be news deserts than those with substantial Hispanic populations. The data showed there was some indication that Black communities were not well covered either.[23]

The heart of Stonbely's work is a database and map showing that there were 779 local news providers in New Jersey as of April 2020. There are, however, some limitations to that optimistic-sounding number. Consider Montclair, an affluent suburb. According to the database, there were forty-two outlets covering Montclair, nineteen of which were "local news originators." But that included a large number of media outlets providing little in the way of community-based journalism, such as *The Star-Ledger* and a plethora of radio and television stations.[24] In fact, Montclair has perhaps four or five truly local news outlets, the most important of which is a highly regarded nonprofit startup, *Montclair Local*. Stonbely acknowledged that the raw numbers told only part of the story and said she was in the process of conducting a content analysis with the help of the Internet Archive, using key phrases such as "city council," to determine how many of the media outlets in the database were actually providing local coverage.[25]

The center also serves as a resource for local news outlets across the state. News organizations can join the center's New Jersey News Commons, which provides training and collaboration resources as well as a newsletter that highlights what others are reporting. The producer of that newsletter is Joe Amditis, the assistant director for products and events. But Amditis, who started his own hyperlocal before joining the center in 2014, told us he believed his main value was in serving as a resource on technology questions and other issues. "One of my favorite things is that I just have conversations with these folks on a regular basis and just maintain those relationships," he said.[26]

The newest staff member, Cassandra Etienne, who joined in 2021, oversees the News Commons in her capacity as the assistant director for programming and membership. The Commons, she said, comprises about three hundred journalists and member organizations. Her role, she added, is to create "a sense of community," explaining: "We encourage people to share their work, to interact with one another, hopefully build collaboration among different newsrooms—especially the smaller ones that can achieve potentially more through collaborating. It's our way of really helping to support the local news ecosystem here and helping to foster those connections."[27]

The most innovative program with which the center is involved is the New Jersey Civic Information Consortium, which provides state government funding to local news outlets and other community-based organizations. The program is hosted at Montclair State, and Stefanie Murray is involved in administering it, although her center is not officially part of the consortium. The law that created the nonprofit consortium was passed by the state legislature in 2018 after a considerable amount of advocacy work by public-interest organizations, led by Free Press, a media-reform group. Over the past few years, the state has appropriated increasing amounts of money to the consortium, growing to $3 million for the fiscal year that began on July 1, 2022. Organizations apply for grants to pay for specific reporting and information projects, with funding decisions made by a sixteen-member board. Projects that have received money include a plan to expand news coverage across Jersey City, an online radio program in Creole for the Haitian community, and an oral history on efforts to clean up drinking water in Newark.[28]

The New Jersey model has served as an inspiration in other states. The most wide-ranging, by far, is in California, where $25 million was appropriated in 2022 to fund forty reporting fellows in underserved communities. The funds, which were to be administered by the Graduate School of Journalism at the University of California at Berkeley, will pay those fellows $50,000 stipends over a three-year period.[29] Nevertheless, government funding of journalism remains controversial because of the potential threat it poses to independent news coverage. Though government has always provided subsidies for journalism, from special postal rates in the early days of the republic to the tax advantages enjoyed by nonprofits today, direct funding represents a step beyond that. For instance, National Public Radio, one of our largest and most respected news organizations, relies almost entirely on nonprofit tax benefits, foundation grants, fees paid by member stations, and individual donations; less than 1 percent of NPR's funding comes from the federal government.[30] Murray, though, said she believed the New Jersey consortium's independent board was sufficiently insulated from government pressure. "My personal opinion is that it's sticky, but it can be done," she said. "And I disagree with people who say, 'That's just a red line I'm not going to cross.' It's state money, but it goes to this nonprofit. There's a good firewall there."

During its first few years, the consortium's funding decisions were project-based rather than organization-based. A news outlet could apply for money to pay for a specific need, but the consortium was not providing support for operating costs. That could change. Murray said the consortium was working to raise at least $25 million in private contributions that could be used to assist organizations that operate in underserved communities. And Molly de Aguiar, a longtime media activist who's a member of the board, said it seemed likely that the consortium would move in the direction of ongoing payments to local news outlets. "We're trying to make the barrier to entry to get those grants pretty low, and it's so early," de Aguiar told us. "At least some of the people on the board are very much in favor of operating support. It's just that it's not well-established enough yet, I think."[31]

The Center for Cooperative Media and the Civic Information Consortium are working to solve the local news crisis in New Jersey from the outside. Others are working on the inside, creating new sources of community journalism. Two, in particular, are worth examining.

The first is TAPinto, a network of nearly a hundred hyperlocal websites, most of them in New Jersey, that employs an innovative franchise model. The network was begun in 2009 by Michael Shapiro, who back then was a New York lawyer looking to spend more time with his young son after he underwent open-heart surgery (he made a full recovery). Shapiro started a website that he called *The Alternative Press* in New Providence, where he lived, because he was dissatisfied by the lack of coverage in the local newspaper. As Shapiro tells it, he soon heard from residents of other communities asking him to expand, and a network was born. (The "TAP" in TAPinto stands for "The Alternative Press.")

Although Shapiro is not a journalist, he said in an interview and on the *What Works* podcast that he takes journalistic objectivity seriously and requires his franchisees to adhere to the Society of Professional Journalists' Code of Ethics. The way it works is this. For a fee of $5,000, a franchisee can set up shop with what is essentially a turnkey operation: a website based on a ready-made template with backend and technical support, training, and everything else they might need to begin covering local news and selling advertising. Publishers keep 80 percent of whatever ad revenues they're able to earn, with 20 percent going to TAPinto. Advertising can also be shared across sites, and some editorial content is shared as well. Publishers are required to produce at least one original piece of journalism each day; stories typically cover such topics as neighborhood development issues, feel-good features, and public-safety news. A common arrangement, Shapiro said, is for a businessperson to become a franchisee and employ a journalist either full- or part-time.[32]

Access to TAPinto sites is free, and Shapiro said the $5,000 franchise fee is far lower than what it would cost for a local media entrepreneur to get started on their own. "I think we've been able to demonstrate that you can have profitable local news sites that are 100 percent advertising-based, and that, to me, is really important," he said. "People who are economically distressed shouldn't have to choose between putting food on the table or buying medicine and finding out what's going on in their town. So that's very fundamental to us. And it's also fundamental on the ownership side. In a lot of these situations, you have to be wealthy to start an online local news site if you want to have the technology and the functionality and stuff we offer."

Observers we spoke with gave Shapiro generally high marks but said the sites tend to be of uneven quality, which is not surprising given the inexperience of many of the franchisees. Nevertheless, TAPinto represents a genuinely new way of providing local news and bears watching—particularly if Shapiro is able to build out his network nationally or inspires imitators.

The other local news project that deserves some attention is less innovative than TAPinto but of tremendous value to the residents of one community—*Montclair Local*, a nonprofit weekly newspaper and website begun in 2017 that is largely funded by a software entrepreneur named Heeten Choxi.[33] Montclair is exactly the sort of community that ought to be able to support a project like the *Local*. Its forty-one thousand residents enjoy a median household income of about $134,000, well above the state average of $85,245. Nearly 70 percent of residents earned a bachelor's degree or higher. And the community has a reputation for having a high concentration of residents who work in New York media, from *The New York Times* to Stephen Colbert, a major benefactor of the Montclair Film Festival. As such, it's not surprising that Montclair wouldn't have been considered a news desert even before the founding of the *Local*. It is also the home of *Baristanet*, a pioneering hyperlocal blog; the weekly *Montclair Times*, part of the Gannett chain; a TAPinto outlet; and a Patch site, which gathers news from Montclair and surrounding communities. But the *Local*, whose full-time staff of five as well as part-time contributors gives it considerably more resources than its competitors, stands as the town's preeminent news source.

The *Local* also has some high-powered friends—including Stephen Engelberg, the editor in chief of the nonprofit investigative news organization *ProPublica*, who serves on the governing board, and Jonathan Alter, a well-known author and television commentator, who's on the advisory board. (Also on the advisory board: Stefanie Murray and John Mooney.) Over dinner at a pub in downtown Montclair, Engelberg and Alter told us how they got involved in the project and about their hopes for cutting their dependence on Choxi's generosity. "We have said from the beginning, if it doesn't work in Montclair, it can't work anywhere," Engelberg said. "And I will tell you, if it works in Montclair it will be because of backbreaking hard work." Both of them were firing off ideas, with Alter suggesting the *Local* needs edgy columnists ("The right kinds of local voices can pull a community together") and Engelberg opining that the paper should concentrate on raising money in large chunks rather than small individual donations ("If you try to go and win this thing subscription by subscription, you're really walking in molasses"). Access to the *Local*'s website is free; paid members receive the weekly print edition, which Engelberg jokingly referred to as "our tote bag." (In April 2023, the *Local* and *Baristanet* announced they would merge and that the *Local*'s print edition would be discontinued.)[34]

The editor in chief and CEO of the *Local* was Lou Hochman, who was recruited from a commercial radio station in the Philadelphia area (not long after our interview, Hochman left to take a job at WNYC in New York). Engelberg had told us that the *Local*'s annual budget was $800,000, with about $600,000 coming from various fundraising initiatives and Choxi making up the rest. How to close the gap? "We're figuring out a lot of it as we go," Hochman said. "Membership's part of it. It will never take us the whole way. I hope somebody figures it out, because we're not sustainable yet in a town where everything lines up. And not every town is Montclair."[35]

From the beginning, *NJ Spotlight News* has focused on news about state policy, the budget, the governor's office, and the legislative process in a manner aimed at political and governmental insiders. When we asked John Mooney to list some high-impact stories that *Spotlight* has published over the years, he turned the question around. "I think our impact comes in a slower, more methodical way in terms of informing folks and in terms of informing legislators and their staff," he said. "I can give you a lot of examples of legislators or staff who've come to me and said, 'We didn't know that.' And that's part of watchdog journalism. It's not sexy, and it makes it very hard, because you're not the first to ask that. Grantmakers always ask that, and I have to go through the explanation of where I think we do have our impact."

Because of *Spotlight*'s emphasis on explanatory journalism, much of its coverage can come across as not especially challenging to those in power. Molly de Aguiar, who was involved in a number of media efforts in New Jersey over the years as the program director of the

Geraldine R. Dodge Foundation's Informed Communities initiative, told us that's why Dodge cut off funding. "I don't want to speak ill of *Spotlight*," said de Aguiar, who later became president of the Independence Public Media Foundation in Philadelphia. "They're the only outlet that was really focused on the statehouse, so obviously they're a very important organization. But overall, what I found frustrating about them, challenging, was that they really were trying to serve the legislature more than they were trying to hold the legislature accountable. At the end, I said to John, whom I admire and like very much, 'We're not here to fund journalism that only serves powerful people. That's just not what we want to do.'"

It's a criticism that Mooney takes seriously—to a point. Fundamentally, he believes that what strikes de Aguiar as an excessive deference to power is a reflection of *Spotlight*'s mission to report on the inner workings of government. "Not tough enough? Yeah, I think we could be," he said. "I'm not saying she's not right. We're not vicious, and we don't go willy-nilly. These policy discussions aren't typically going to be that kind of confrontational thing. But, yeah, we could be harder."

Mooney lays out *Spotlight*'s strategy in terms of threes—three pillars to its business model, three sources of income, three types of audiences. The business model, he explained, was based on having a diverse range of revenues, an experienced staff so that the project's journalism would be credible, and collaboration with other media outlets. He lamented that the revenues were out of whack, with about a quarter coming from events and advertising, a quarter coming from individual donations, and half from grants. His ideal, based on *The Texas Tribune*'s model, would be for each to account for about a third. The site was roughly break-even, he added, although he cautioned that *Spotlight* received administrative support from NJ PBS that made it difficult to know for sure. As for collaboration, any news outlet is free to republish *Spotlight*'s content with permission. In mid-2022, Mooney was in content-sharing discussions with two major public radio stations, WNET in New York and WHYY in Philadelphia, and was hoping to put together a network with various hyperlocal sites as well. On the audience side, Mooney identified three concentric circles: state government insiders at the center; on the next ring out, those who closely follow state policy, such as local school officials, hospital executives, and people working in clean energy, utilities, and the like; and, on the outer circle, people who simply care about having a deep understanding of public affairs—what Mooney described as "the public media crowd."

By the spring of 2022, Mooney said, the *Spotlight* website was attracting a little under two hundred thousand unique visitors each month—down from the height of the COVID pandemic, when traffic could reach as high as five hundred thousand. Those who signed up for *Spotlight*'s free newsletters received a morning news roundup, evening updates that began as a COVID-centered email and was later expanded to include other topics, and a Saturday wrap-up of the week's top news. There were about thirty thousand newsletter subscribers, Mooney said, with 25 to 30 percent of those subscribers actually opening those emails. The staff comprised about ten full-timers, ranging from some of the most experienced journalists in the state to a young Report for America corps member who had been assigned to cover mental health in the rural parts of southern New Jersey.

Mooney is essentially the publisher of the site, spending anywhere from half to three-fourths of his time on business issues. The managing editor is John McAlpin, a veteran of the Associated Press and of *The Record* in Bergen County who got out in the face of cuts by Gannett, the paper's owner. "I'm the story person," McAlpin said. "I talk to you about your stories. I help the reporters refine the assignments. I essentially sign off on the assignments. I coordinate the coverage."[36] Others on the digital side include a projects editor, Colleen O'Dea; an energy and environment reporter, Tom Johnson; a health-care reporter, Lilo Stainton; and a budget and finance reporter, John Reitmeyer. Stainton drew the enormously challenging assignment of covering the pandemic, an experience she called exhausting and emotional, adding: "I was just interviewing someone about how we're too tired of this pandemic to do the right thing."[37] Reitmeyer, whose specialty is digging into the arcana of taxes and spending, described his role as illuminating a process that even government officials don't always fully understand. "A lot of times in New Jersey, what happens is we do things because we've always done it that way," he said. "Well, is that a good way to do it? Is there a better way to do it? Is this actually the best way to do it? So I'm kind of a policy wonk at heart, I think."[38]

According to Bob Feinberg, a former federal prosecutor who's vice president and general counsel of WNET, the merger of *Spotlight* and what was then known as NJTV took place after a slow buildup. *Spotlight* had been collaborating on the daily newscast, and it seemed natural to seek a closer relationship. "You don't want to just jump into something like this without a sense of how the two sides are going to work together," he said, "and I thought, and I think John certainly agreed, that the editorial chops and focus of *Spotlight* would sync very well with what we were trying to do."[39] Three years later, NJ PBS and *Spotlight* were still working to meld the two operations and the two cultures. Perhaps the biggest challenge was how to bring the organizations together so that *Spotlight*'s ten journalists and NJ PBS's forty to fifty reporters, producers, and editors formed one unified newsroom. They were getting there—but, as with so many things, the COVID pandemic had slowed those efforts.

On a hot July day in 2022, Jamie Kraft, the senior managing editor of both the broadcast and digital arms of *NJ Spotlight News*, led us on a tour of the NJ PBS facilities, a short walk from Union Station in downtown Newark. That space had been nearly vacant during the pandemic, even as it was expanded to accommodate what he hoped would eventually become a vibrant in-person operation. The newsroom, which could hold several dozen people, was empty except for Kraft, senior editorial producer Julie Daurio, and news anchor Briana Vannozzi. Through a corridor on the other side of the newsroom was a large, comfortable shared workspace that Kraft hopes will someday entice the digital journalists to come in and work. It too was empty except for Mooney, who came in for part of the day. Kraft, who came to NJ PBS in 2019 after a long career at national outlets such as NBC News, CBS News, CNN, and MSNBC, had been presiding over an unusual newscast since the COVID-induced lockdown in the spring of 2020. Rather than going live, as is standard in the industry and as had been the case at NJ PBS before the pandemic, the program's segments were pieced together during the afternoon, recorded out of order and then edited into a coherent whole.[40]

The broadcast version of *NJ Spotlight News* is a half-hour newscast (twenty-six minutes, forty-six seconds to be precise) that is shown on multiple platforms. It gets its first airing at 5:30 p.m. on WNET, the mother ship, and then is shown on NJ PBS's various broadcast and cable outlets at 6, 7:30, and 11 p.m. It's also posted on YouTube and on the *Spotlight* website. That complexity makes it difficult to estimate the size of the audience, although Kraft put the size of the broadcast audience in the "tens of thousands." Like the digital version of *Spotlight*, the newscast takes a serious look at state issues, with stories clocking in at three to five minutes. "My whole goal is to give the people of New Jersey a voice in whatever issues are being decided down in Trenton by the legislators that everybody's elected," said Kraft, whose portfolio also includes three public-affairs programs and other projects. "Every story we do finds voices of folks that are affected or impacted by whatever is being passed or whatever is being proposed in terms of future legislation or future concepts or programs. The idea is to really try to humanize a lot of the programs that are being put in place by the state."[41]

It's a formula that Kraft, Mooney, and others are trying to broaden. As noted earlier, website metrics were down from the height of the pandemic, and Mooney told us he was concerned that *Spotlight* was not as good at appealing to the third concentric circle of his audience—ordinary people who care about public affairs—as it was to insiders. The person in charge of figuring out how to expand that reach is Joseph Lee, the vice president and general manager of NJ PBS. In a sparsely furnished office at the network's headquarters, Lee told us he was pushing in a number of different directions to expand the audience. "There is a bit of news burnout. There's a little bit of people tired of the serious problems, the issues," said Lee, who came to NJ PBS in 2021 after twenty-eight years of running the public radio operation at Syracuse University. "The question is, are we meeting the basic information needs of the people of New Jersey? What kinds of entertainment, cultural events, places, what's happening in the sports landscape? I mean, there's a lot of information out there that we could be serving to broaden our audience a bit. And that is the goal moving forward."[42]

Several months before our visit, *Spotlight* had unveiled its first podcast, *Hazard NJ*, a four-part investigative series on the state's hazardous-waste sites, a national story going back to the 1980s that just never seems to end. Lee said he was interested in developing more, possibly including a daily news podcast. Hosting debates in the state's twelve congressional districts as podcasts was also under consideration. "We as a media organization are faced with the fracturing of audiences in this heavily fractured media landscape," said Lee. "The question for us is how do we continue to serve our audiences, our constituents, in as many ways as possible. Wherever they're spending their time is where we want to be. So I think audio production, whether it's podcasting or whether it's audio stories on our digital platforms, is going to be an important part of how we move forward."

As with most news organizations, diversity has lagged at *Spotlight* and NJ PBS. Mooney told us he was acutely aware of the need to add people of color to his staff. "We have only recently started to address that with hiring, because basically we were white out of the gate," Mooney said. "I didn't pay enough attention to diversity. I will fully acknowledge that, and it shows in our coverage." By 2022, there was one Asian American journalist covering social-justice issues on the site's small staff but no Black or Latino reporters—although Mooney said the site had several Black contract employees. On the broadcast side, Lee is a visible Black leader, but most of the people who work for the network are white. "We are diversifying the applicant pool," Lee said. "We're trying to be serious about the people, the issues that we cover, because we want to be an attractive place for people of color to want to come work."

At about 2 p.m. on the day of our visit, Briana Vannozzi took her place in front of the green screen while we observed from the control booth. Coming in remotely was US Representative Bonnie Watson Coleman, a Democrat from the Trenton area. Watson Coleman and sixteen other members of Congress had been arrested a day earlier for protesting outside the Supreme Court following its decision to repeal *Roe v. Wade*, thus removing constitutional protections for abortion rights. Providing state and local context for national issues is a staple of *Spotlight*'s newscast and website, so Watson Coleman was an important get.[43]

"I'm glad to see that you're well, that you're no longer in custody," Vannozzi began. "Of course, that's what everyone's talking about. But, really, the question here is whether or not you feel the ideological makeup of this court is a threat to what some people would consider some basic rights."

"Absolutely. I think that this is a particularly politicized court," Watson Coleman replied. "I believe that their ideological embracement is detrimental to our privacy and the rights that have already been established." And, with that, they were off and running with a conversation that lasted nearly four and a half minutes.

Interviews are a key part of the evening broadcast; Vannozzi often talks with two or three newsmakers and journalists from *Spotlight* and other news organizations. It's an aspect of the newscast that has actually become easier during the pandemic, as fears that viewers would be put off by the lower video and audio production standards of Zoom have given way to a new reality. Both Kraft and Vannozzi said they believed there was no going back, even if COVID somehow magically disappeared. "We've found that we can include a much larger cast of characters in our pieces now," Vannozzi said. "When I was driving up and down the state to do interviews, every single one of them in person, just logistically, I only had time to get to maybe three people to put a story on the air for 5:30. Now we can interview three people within thirty minutes."[44]

Vannozzi generally arrives at work at about 9:15 a.m. By then she's already been in contact with Kraft and Julie Daurio. She spends the morning taking part in news meetings to find out what people are working on, to make suggestions, and to see how stories in the works from the digital side of *Spotlight* can be integrated into the broadcast. She and Kraft decide the order in which the stories should appear. She's in touch with reporters and writes the script, drawing on her long experience as a reporter in New Jersey to add background and context. Vannozzi has worked for the newscast in various capacities since 2012 and became the anchor in 2020.[45]

Very few public media operations offer a television newscast. When you think of public broadcasting and news, you think of radio, with national and international reports from NPR that are interspersed with local updates. In that regard, the *Spotlight* newscast is unusual. Vannozzi believes it fills an important void. "When New Jersey is covered, it's really 'it bleeds, it leads,'" she said. "We sat down when we did our merger and talked about how we wanted to revamp—everything, from how we go about selecting stories to how we cover them. We decided we may be first sometimes, but that's not going to be our goal. Our goal is to be right and to provide analysis that you're not going to find anywhere else."

NJ Spotlight News is a leading example of how a venerable public broadcasting station and a digital startup can come together to fill a vital need. *Spotlight* is not the only news organization in New Jersey to provide coverage of what the governor, the legislature, and other state agencies are up to. But it is the only free, nonpartisan service whose mission is to examine and explain the inner workings of government for insiders and a broader audience alike. *Spotlight* is not a solution to the local news crisis; a regional news outlet can't delve into what's taking place at the hyperlocal level. New Jersey has taken some steps to solve that problem, through research, government funding, and innovative community journalism projects such as TAPinto and *Montclair Local*. What *Spotlight* can do is serve as a beacon for other public broadcasters on how to provide high-quality regional and statewide news.

CHAPTER TWO

MINNEAPOLIS, MINNESOTA

How Heated Competition
Is Reviving Local News

On a hot July day in 2021, the air heavy with humidity from the nearby Mississippi River, visitors lingered outside Cup Foods at the intersection of East Thirty-Eighth Street and Chicago Avenue in Minneapolis, a crossroads now known to the world as George Floyd Square. Some took selfies with smartphones. Others silently read the tributes and manifestos posted on signs and walls.

Although Cup Foods was open for business, the square was quiet. It was a complicated quiet—the quiet of grief and contemplation, of reverence and rage—because this intersection marks the spot where a Black Minnesotan, George Floyd, was murdered on May 25, 2020, his life choked out of him under the knee of a white Minneapolis police officer. Floyd's death sparked demonstrations, anger, soul-searching, and demands for change. The city, a nexus of the largely white progressive Democratic-Farmer-Labor coalition forged by Hubert H. Humphrey in the 1940s, could no longer ignore the fault lines of race, class, and privilege that cut across it. (In 1940, African Americans made up only 0.9 percent of the Minneapolis population. Historically, Black Minnesotans faced structural racism in the Twin Cities, including restrictive covenants barring them from certain neighborhoods.)[1]

The murder of George Floyd also galvanized Twin Cities newsrooms. It brought home the essential value of having a robust local corps of reporters to cut through the chaos—a necessary step toward creating the kind of unadorned civic dialogue that is necessary to sustain a participatory democracy. Ultimately, the resurgent morning daily, the Minneapolis *Star Tribune*, won the Pulitzer Prize in 2021 for Breaking News Reporting.[2] Seventeen-year-old Darnella Frazier, a bystander outside Cup Foods that day and witness to history, received a special citation from the Pulitzer Board for recording a ten-minute video of the murder on her phone. Her video not only provided crucial context in the courtroom but also, as the board noted, highlighted "the crucial role of citizens in journalists' quest for truth and justice."[3]

SAHAN JOURNAL

The fledgling newsroom of the digital startup *Sahan Journal* was scrambling to adjust to the COVID-19 pandemic in the spring of 2020 when Floyd was murdered. "We were establishing our newsroom as things were exploding around us," editor and founder Mukhtar Ibrahim said in July 2021.[4] He had moved our in-person interview scheduled at *Sahan Journal*'s St. Paul office to a telephone discussion. As Ibrahim spoke on the phone from a spot outdoors, with the soft noise of traffic in the background, he explained that even though COVID infection levels in the Twin Cities were relatively stable (that month, Hennepin County, where Minneapolis is located, and Ramsey County, home to St. Paul, both reported a COVID positive test rate of 5.8 percent), he was limiting in-person contacts because he had vulnerable relatives in town for Eid al-Adha, the major Muslim holiday that honors the obedience of the prophet Ibrahim who was willing to sacrifice his son at Allah's command.[5]

A former reporter for Minnesota Public Radio and the *Star Tribune*, Ibrahim launched his all-digital *Sahan Journal* in August 2019 with an ambitious goal: to cover the immigrant communities from Somalia, Laos, and other countries that are transforming the culture and politics of a state that is 80 percent white.[6] The Minnesota Chamber of Commerce reported in 2021 that Minnesota has the largest Somali population in the United States.[7] Overall, the chamber reported, immigrants represent 8.5 percent of the state's population; the top four nations of origin for foreign-born residents are Mexico, Somalia, India, and Laos.

Ibrahim, who was born in Somalia, moved to Minnesota in 2005, part of a wave of immigration that began in 1992 when faith-based organizations and refugee resettlement nonprofits in Minnesota began sponsoring Somalis fleeing civil war. Although the Minnesota census counts fifty-two thousand Somalis living in the state, other sources estimate there may be as many as one hundred thousand.[8] The community is large enough that in July 2021, thousands of Somalis prayed during Eid al-Adha in the open-air Huntington Bank Stadium at the University of Minnesota.[9] White-clad Somali families could be seen walking through nearby neighborhoods to services. "[The Twin Cities are] the best place to be a journalist, but on the flip side, I was frustrated at the level of resources dedicated to covering immigrant communities," Ibrahim said. "As I launched the *Journal*, I wanted to fill that gap."[10]

Although he had only one salaried employee at the outset—himself—he had dreamed the dream long before. After obtaining a bachelor's degree from the Hubbard School of Journalism and Communication at the University of Minnesota in 2011, he realized that there wasn't any professional news publication—digital or print—that catered to the growing Somali and East African diaspora in Minnesota. By 2013, he had translated his idea for a side project into pixels, and an initial iteration of *Sahan Journal* had a presence on the web. "The idea was to highlight stories and cover what's going on in the world when it comes to Somali issues," he said. The site immediately filled a need, he added: "People were sending me content left and right. I barely had time to edit!"

He fielded opinion pieces about culture, history, and politics, both in Minnesota and in Africa. One of his first contributors was Mustafa Muhammad Omer, an activist and aid worker from the Somali Region in Ethiopia. In 2018, Muhammad Omer became president of the region.[11] "That was a moment," Ibrahim said, "that someone who used to write for the *Journal* emerged as a national leader."

The website remained a side project as Ibrahim married, welcomed a baby, and built his journalism career as a reporter at Minnesota Public Radio and the *Star Tribune*. But it was never far from his thoughts. He quietly plotted a potential path forward. He wanted to turn his work on *Sahan Journal* into a full-time job, and he wanted to focus it on Minnesota. "That's where I am, that's where my family is, that's where my kids were born. That's the place I call home," he said. His early website showed potential, but, without the support of an organization or wealthy donor, publishing out of his apartment in St. Paul on a voluntary basis got old.

In early 2019, he decided to take the leap. "I left the *Star Tribune* and dedicated all my time to making that the mission—telling the stories of immigrants in Minnesota and communicating their transformation, their challenges and successes. I wanted the site to be a home for content about immigrants, for immigrants."

Nancy Cassutt, Ibrahim's former boss and then executive director of news programming for Minnesota Public Radio, helped stoke the fires: MPR agreed to pay Ibrahim's salary for eighteen months to support *Sahan Journal*, and Ibrahim agreed to supply some stories for MPR. "I see Mukhtar as an incubator for the future of MPR News," she said in an interview at MPR headquarters in St. Paul just before the reboot in 2019. *Sahan Journal* fit her stated mission: to help diversify coverage to reflect a changing Minnesota. MPR had just seen a disproportionate number of journalists of color leave for jobs elsewhere.[12] "That's a blow to a newsroom of our size," she wrote in an "Inside MPR News" column, "one that's been nearly all white through its history. . . . I've got work to do. As a white woman from a Midwestern, middle-class background, I know I have blind spots. I have lots to learn about how news organizations can tell rich, nuanced and accurate stories about our indigenous people and communities of color; how we can strengthen our relationships in the community; and how our content can better reflect the state we serve." She noted that employees of color made up 15 percent of the MPR newsroom in a metropolitan area where about 25 percent are people of color.

Cassutt, who has since moved to California to take a job as managing director of news for American Public Media's *Marketplace*, added in an interview in her St. Paul office: "If we want to serve our audiences, we darn well better work really fast to change the face of the newsroom."[13] The Glen Nelson Center at American Public Media, an incubator for new ventures, provided a first office for the *Journal* and access to what Cassutt called "business brains" to help raise funds.[14] Ibrahim also connected with Kate Moos, a Peabody Award–winning journalist at MPR with a penchant for building things.[15] Moos later became managing director of the *Journal* and is now retired.

Ibrahim's three-year business plan was ambitious, targeting a broad audience, with a large enough reporting staff to dig deeply into the community, covering events, government, health care, education, mosques, and churches. "Basically, everyone in Minnesota," he said. "We want to educate the wider community about the immigrant population in their midst and the issues they face. I realized that the only way to do that would be to have a professional news outlet that could host high-quality journalism."

In an inaugural editor's note in August 2019, Ibrahim laid out ambitious goals: to chronicle how immigrant communities "are changing and redefining what it means to be a Minnesotan," to train young reporters from immigrant backgrounds and give them a platform, and to create a membership program for a baseline of support while also seeking philanthropic grants and underwriting sponsorships.[16]

Among the new stories he wanted to tell about Minnesota: the way that state and city government are changing. He explained, "Our state legislature is the most diverse state legislature in the history of Minnesota. What I'm trying to do coincides with how the state is changing in terms of demographics." In August 2020, *Sahan Journal* reporter Ibrahim Hirsi counted thirteen Black immigrant elected officials in Minnesota.[17] The one with the highest profile is US Representative Ilhan Omar, who was born in Somalia and fled to Kenya, then the United States. A Democrat, she became the first woman of color to represent Minnesota in Congress when she was elected in 2018—and the first African refugee to serve in the US House.[18]

There are numerous other barrier-breakers in the Somali community. In November 2020, Omar Fateh became the first Somali American and first Muslim to be elected to the Minnesota State Senate.[19] Fateh, an information technology specialist at the University of Minnesota and a member of the Democratic-Farmer-Labor Party, won in a landslide with 89 percent of the vote. His district in South

Minneapolis, with a population of eighty-three thousand, is richly diverse, home to Minnesotans who are white, Native American, Hispanic, African American, and Somali American, according to 2019 statistics.[20] It also is home to George Floyd Square.

Ibrahim's vision was ambitious. He wanted reporters to be embedded in the community, to be hunting for scoops and deeper takes at political meetings, cultural events, restaurants, churches, and mosques, with the kind of structured newsroom that he had been trained to lead at the Hubbard School and at Columbia University, where he received a master's degree in journalism. (Ibrahim's portrait was featured in a row of distinguished news alumni in the University of Minnesota's Murphy Hall in Minneapolis, and Columbia gave him its First Decade Award for "forging a path for the future of our industry" in 2022.)[21]

By the end of 2019, the *Journal* had raised nearly $500,000, a healthy number just four months after the launch. That amount included $25,000 from NewsMatch, a collaborative fundraising initiative available to members of the Institute for Nonprofit News (INN) that pools matching gifts from national, regional, and local donors to support nonprofit newsrooms.[22] He was gradually adding staff—and had just signed a full-time health reporter—when the COVID-19 pandemic hit in March 2020. "Reporters were meeting on Zoom with sources or conducting phone interviews," he said. "It was a different model than we had envisioned when we launched. It disrupted everything."

The small, intrepid staff persevered, however, and the *Journal* received more funding. Grants flowed in from the Knight Foundation, the Emerson Collective, and Borealis Philanthropy, and he added staffers who were corps members of Report for America. The *Journal* was one of five news outlets in the second cohort of the Sponsorship Lab, a partnership between Google News Initiative and INN. Thanks to strategic coaching from Blue Engine Collaborative, the *Journal* updated its messaging to potential sponsors and raised the newsletter sponsorship rate, plumping up year-over-year revenue in the process.[23] In January 2022, Ibrahim's newsroom received its largest grant to date: $1.2 million from the American Journalism Project (AJP) to help "change the news ecosystem in Minnesota and beyond." The award was the first time the AJP, a venture philanthropy initiative cofounded in 2018 by John Thornton of *Texas Tribune* fame and Elizabeth Green of *Chalkbeat*, funded a news organization in the North Star State.[24] In 2022, Ibrahim received a "Rising Star" Freedom of the Press Award from the Reporters Committee for Freedom of the Press.[25]

Ibrahim and his staff used targeted social media and a Somali show broadcast on Facebook Live to expand their reach. When a pioneering charter school serving Somali families was set to close, the *Journal's* education reporter, Becky Dernbach, wrote a news story for the website and began calling parents for comment. But many of the parents had not yet seen her story on the web. Dernbach and Ibrahim realized they couldn't just press publish and assume the story would automatically find an audience. *Journal* reporter Aala Abdullahi wrote a separate story about what happened next. "We had to find a creative, culturally relevant, and digestible way to communicate the months-long reporting that Becky had so diligently put together," Abdullahi wrote.[26]

The *Journal* recognized that there was a language barrier—parents spoke Somali, Spanish, Oromo, or Amharic as a first language. So the *Journal* experimented: it partnered with Somali TV Minnesota, a Somali-language channel on Facebook Live that reached a large Twin Cities audience and fielded live questions about the schools and other topics from online viewers. "Essentially," Abdullahi wrote, "we realized that we needed to create a version of this story that came to life through video or audio, produce it in a more familiar language, and publish it on a platform where our audience already existed." The Facebook Live event on May 27, 2021, had been viewed nine thousand times by mid-June. It was *Sahan Journal's* first Facebook Live event, and the staff hoped it would not be the last.

The most important lesson? Abdullahi explained: "We also recognize that one size does not fit all. That is to say, we expect that, with every community we want to develop deeper relationships with, there will be a specific avenue or method that works best. And we intend to keep asking the most important and relevant audience-centric questions—Who do we want to reach? Who is left out? What is the best way to connect them with news?—in order to get there."

When George Floyd's life was snuffed out under the knee of white police officer Derek Chauvin on May 25, 2020, protesters calling for racial justice poured into the streets. The *Journal*'s mission expanded. Floyd's murder served as a sobering reminder to the Somali community that Black men in Minneapolis—and more broadly in other parts of the state—were more likely to be subjected to police violence than white men, according to reporting by *The New York Times*.[27] Although 19 percent of the city's population of 429,954 is Black, according to the 2020 US Census, nearly 60 percent of people who face police violence are Black, the *Times* reported.[28] Out of 11,500 acts of force reported by police since 2015, the subject was Black in 6,650 cases.

"We knew we had to expand our coverage beyond immigration coverage to communities of color in general. We were encountering the fact that different communities [of color] were coming together and uniting around [Floyd's murder]," Ibrahim said, adding, "Indigenous people, the traditional African American community, and the new African American community, Somalis, Kenyans, Oromos, Haitians, were all gathered together. We were going out and gaining trust, observing events and verifying, but also engaging the community so people could tell their own stories and shape how they are being treated." The *Journal* staff was determined to provide sustained coverage of issues "instead of just coming to this community when something big happens," Ibrahim said. Its website offers coverage of policing and justice, climate and environment, education, health, culture and community, in addition to a robust "community voices" section with signed opinion pieces.

UNICORN RIOT

As Floyd's murder ignited protests across the country, *Unicorn Riot*, a free-ranging, nonhierarchical media collective, was providing video feeds from protests in a number of communities and continuously updating them with interviews from local residents.

Troy Patterson, writing in *The New Yorker*, commended the collective for "attend[ing] to this nationwide conflagration as a local news story."[29]

Dan Feidt, a reporter and producer for *Unicorn Riot* who helped launch the site in 2015, had seen the power of on-the-ground reporting that provided an alternative point of view during the Occupy Wall Street movement in 2011. Feidt, a web developer living in Boston, worked with others to set up live video streams from Occupy encampments. "The audio was a kind of murmuring buzz of activity—the sound was really intriguing, and putting it out live had a grip on people's attention, and it spread really fast," he said.[30] He was inspired. He wanted to take the lessons they had learned and expand into live video, written pieces, and investigations based on documents obtained under the Freedom of Information Act, a federal law enacted in the 1960s that gives the public the right to request access to records from any federal agency, with some exemptions. And, he told us, he wanted to make it "noncommercial and nonprofit." In 2015, *Unicorn Riot*, named by picking a slip out of a hat, was started on a shoestring. Its stated goal on its website: "*Unicorn Riot* engages and amplifies the stories of social and environmental struggles from the ground up. We seek to enrich the public by transforming the narrative with our accessible non-commercial independent content."[31] The site is up-front about its advocacy—there's no "both-sides-ism" to be found.

In 2019, revenue amounted to just over $115,000—which many founders would deem a good start—all from reader donations. (The website states: "Your Source for Independent Media. . . . We provide Creative Commons media that's publicly available for free without ads or paywalls. . . . Independently funded through contributions from our audience.")[32] Interest intensified after the outbreak of COVID-19 in March 2020 and again after George Floyd's murder in May that year. Donations poured in, and *Unicorn Riot* was able to see a sustainable path ahead and invest in new video equipment, as well as helmets and flak jackets to protect reporters from flash-bang grenades and rubber projectiles launched by police during protests. Feidt stressed the importance of security for reporters, recalling his own experience getting pepper-sprayed in the eye by police while filming at the Straight Pride Parade in Boston in August 2019.[33]

In 2020, the nonprofit reported revenue of more than $2 million.[34] Niko Georgiades, one of the *Unicorn Riot* founders, told Adam

Gabbatt of *The Guardian* that year, "[The influx of donations] shows our five years hasn't been in vain. But this newfound interest in us, this newfound love for our work, unfortunately came off of a black death. That's something we really need to be cognizant of, I don't take that lightly."[35]

Staffing levels are small. Freelancers are paid for contributions as events warrant, there is no paywall, and content is available for reuse under a license from Creative Commons, a nonprofit that facilitates sharing of creative work without charge. In a media-saturated culture, where audiences are used to packaged television broadcasts on the one hand, or the maddeningly fractal ecosystem of Twitter on the other, *Unicorn Riot* flexes its foundational principle: that there is value in watching a raw, live video feed of, say, activists putting their bodies in front of a giant drill bit to stop construction of a pipeline—as occurred on July 1, 2021, with *UR* videographers recording—and comprehending the conviction it must take to get in its way. In addition to local news from the communities where it has reporters, *Unicorn Riot* also includes coverage of international events, politics, and culture. In 2021, for example, a contributor who used the pseudonym EmiciThug conducted a Q&A with a Brazilian poet participating in Brazil's protests against then president Jair Messias Bolsonaro.[36]

Feidt would like to find "different ways to present things," building out panel discussions and community forums and continuing to make content available for free. "I take issue with the draconian nature of intellectual property," he told us. "Culture gets so continuously enclosed by this handful of huge media corporations that I think it's very harmful. It prevents remixing, it prevents a common cultural base, it increases the amount of ignorance in society by making things so unavailable."

MINNPOST

In the 1990s, under the visionary local publisher and CEO Joel Kramer, the *Star Tribune*—Minnesota's largest newspaper—possessed a considerable degree of regional panache. As editorial page editor, Susan Albright wrote high-impact progressive editorials that set the agenda for readers across the state—a vibrant but sometimes uneasy mix of rural burgs, a growing population of immigrants from Somalia, Laos, and other countries, struggling Iron Range towns, and the expanding urban centers of Minneapolis and St. Paul. She was steeped in the culture, politics, and potential of the region, from the blue strongholds of the Democratic-Farmer-Labor Party in the Twin Cities and iron-mining territory up north to the sprawling purple exurbs that sent conservative Republican Michele Bachmann to Congress in the 2006 election. Then, suddenly, in 2007, it all ended, as ownership changed yet again and a private equity company swept in. Albright was out—bought out and forced out—as corporate overseers in New York sought to impose a different editorial voice, as new owners often do. In this case, however, their vision was at once more narrowly focused and more conservative.

Looking back at 2006, Albright said she and her colleagues at the *Star Tribune* knew a devastating storm was brewing. In many ways, it was already an old story. Once a standout in the family-owned Cowles Media publishing empire, the paper had been bought by the McClatchy chain in 1998 and was on the block again. The internet had dismantled classified and display advertising revenue streams that once assured pensions and paychecks for journalists. Free, commoditized news—non-exclusive news easily available from many other sources—glutted the internet and upended decades-old reading habits, even among readers who had been highly engaged. McClatchy had been on an acquisition binge and needed an infusion of cash to pay down debt from its purchase of the Knight Ridder newspapers, which included the neighboring daily newspaper just down the Mississippi River in the state capital, the St. Paul *Pioneer Press*.[37]

The *Star Tribune*, then with a shrinking but still respectable circulation just over 360,000, was, like many newspapers across the nation, bleeding revenue and losing print readers.[38] Many Twin Cities journalists had hoped the great hollowing-out caused by the internet would spare them because of the region's high rate of literacy and civic engagement. For nine election cycles—both in presidential election years and midterm elections—Minnesota had the highest voter turnout record in the United States—a figure that is often seen as a proxy for engagement with news and civic affairs.[39]

Yet digital disruption was changing what engagement looked like. Rounds of layoffs and buyouts savaged the newsrooms of both the *Star Tribune* and the *Pioneer Press*. In December 2006, McClatchy sold the *Star Tribune* to Avista Capital Partners, a New York–based private equity group. The price: $530 million.[40] In hindsight, after the 2008 recession hit, even that half-billion-dollar price tag would seem like an artifact of a long-dead past. Laden with debt, the *Star Tribune* would file for Chapter 11 bankruptcy in 2009.[41] By some estimates, between 120 and 130 journalists lost their jobs at the *Star Tribune* and *Pioneer Press* newsrooms within a year.[42]

Albright's boss, Joel Kramer, who served as the *Star Tribune*'s editor from 1983 to 1992 and publisher and president from 1992 to 1998, left soon after the McClatchy deal for a brief foray into politics and a stint running Growth & Justice, a think tank. Albright hung on as editorial page editor throughout the McClatchy era and through the early days of Avista ownership. The arrangement was doomed from the start, however, given Albright's penchant for high-impact editorials with a progressive heart. "I lasted about six months after the Avista deal," she told us in an interview in *MinnPost*'s newsroom in 2019. "They fired me. Well, they bought me out. They wanted to go in a different direction: super-local and more conservative."[43]

Ultimately, though, Albright landed well and embarked on a new phase in an already illustrious career. She reunited with Kramer when she began writing for the digital upstart *MinnPost* and eventually joined the staff.

The drive to create a digital news site for the Twin Cities began when a number of prominent philanthropists and business executives, alarmed by the shrinking *Star Tribune*, contacted Joel Kramer in 2007 to suggest putting together a group of people to buy the paper. Their faith in Kramer was based on his experience in both sides of an industry traditionally divided by "church" (the newsroom) and "state" (the business office). But, as Kramer observed in an oral history on the tenth anniversary of the founding of *MinnPost*, the price was undoubtedly going to be too high. The global recession triggered by the subprime mortgage crisis had chilled the regional business climate.[44] Kramer also wanted to avoid the inevitable sticker shock that would attend any print acquisition and had spent enough time on the business office side of the house to know that the *Star Tribune*'s problems and pressures were likely "just the tip of the iceberg."[45] Kramer said, "I couldn't look anyone in the eye and say we'd make money [as a for-profit]." So Joel and Laurie Kramer founded *MinnPost* as a digital nonprofit news organization based on a revenue model that included philanthropic grants from foundations and high-wealth individuals, as well as smaller donations from reader-members.

This philanthropic model was nothing new for Minneapolis. "Corporate philanthropy has become a defining feature of Minnesota's public life," researchers Jon Pratt and Edson W. Spencer observed in a study at the turn of the millennium.[46] To start *MinnPost* in 2007, just four families contributed a total of $850,000, including the Kramers. The John S. and James L. Knight Foundation kicked in an additional $250,000, giving Kramer $1.1 million in seed money.

As money began to trickle in, the Kramers honed their business plan. Their first donation was from Joel's sister in Florida, for $50. In an analog moment, they rented a post office box downtown and mailed out letters. They signed up with PayPal to get online donations.[47] In their research of other nonprofit models, the Kramers found a compelling example in *Voice of San Diego* (*VOSD*), a digital news organization launched a few years prior by former *San Diego Union-Tribune* columnist Neil Morgan and Buzz Woolley, a retired venture capitalist, that booked revenue of slightly more than $2 million in 2020.[48] *VOSD*, a 501(c)(3), kept an eye on reader metrics and decided to pivot early on, bringing in new co–executive editors to focus squarely on politics and local investigative journalism, and diversifying sources of funding in order to remain sustainable.[49]

Kramer later explained his decision to form a nonprofit rather than a for-profit enterprise as an economic necessity because of the internet culture that had grown up around free news.[50] When *MinnPost* launched, few publications beyond *The Wall Street Journal* had put up metered paywalls to charge for digital content. *The New York Times* wouldn't roll out a metered paywall system until 2011.[51]

By fall 2007, *MinnPost* was cautiously staffing up. It would go live in November of that year with ten employees and a roster of nearly fifty freelancers.[52] Familiar local bylines populated the website, including Albright's. *MinnPost*'s founders initially updated the site regularly from Monday through Friday but gave the staff the weekend off. (They would later expand that schedule for populating the site with new stories.) They knew what they wanted to be: a serious journalism destination that would appeal to digital natives but also be navigable for curious Boomers and Gen Xers who might follow their favorite print beat writer to the new site. And, the founders determined, *MinnPost* would be a nexus of civic engagement and civil discourse; online comments were monitored from the very start to fence out destructive trolls.[53] Media observers gave the upstart site a stamp of approval. Ken Doctor, a former managing editor at the *Pioneer Press*, media analyst, and currently founder of the local news site *Lookout Santa Cruz*, told Minnesota Public Radio at the time that there was "no experiment around the country that has the pedigree of *MinnPost*."[54]

MinnPost briefly experimented with a free print version, distributed in the state capitol in St. Paul, coffee shops, and the ubiquitous elevated glass skyways that crisscross downtown Minneapolis. But the hoped-for crossover to bring in new online readers never materialized, and the print version of *MinnPost* was discontinued after a few months. A push to use more video was also ended when there wasn't enough traffic to justify the expense.[55]

At *MinnPost*, Albright plunged into the role of digital entrepreneur by necessity, working with then-editor Andrew Putz (pronounced "puts") and then CEO Andrew Wallmeyer to nurture a news outlet that needed to continually evolve in order to hold its own in the face of a suddenly resurgent *Star Tribune*.

That evolution is worth a deeper look, not just because *MinnPost* has survived but also because it holds lessons for digital sites that want to build a culture of experimentation in order to find a permanent foothold in a competitive local news environment. Albright, Joel Kramer, and other journalists who had been pushed out of traditional newsrooms formed a core that helped give credibility to *MinnPost* when it launched in 2007. But as the *Star Tribune* rekindled its flame under local ownership a few years later, it was time for the *MinnPost* newsroom to pivot again. When Putz arrived at *MinnPost* in 2014, his background in magazines and special projects helped the site double down on long-form narrative and analysis, with a sharp focus on politics, policy, and culture. The staff realized that the traditional bundle of newspaper sections—with news, features, sports, comics, and puzzles designed for mass appeal—did not necessarily translate into digital form.

This strategic flexibility is more important now than ever. Even the fizziest brands in digital publishing have not been immune to the decline in digital advertising The problem? A decidedly old-school revenue gap. The culprit? The advertising monopoly held by Facebook and Google, which used their massive scale to achieve market dominance. In 2018, Google vacuumed up 38.2 percent of all digital advertising, with Facebook close behind at 21.8 percent. Amazon claimed a 6.8 percent share.[56]

If it sounded familiarly depressing to print journalists hoping that transition to digital publishing could salvage an industry that is essential to democracy, it underscored the need to test new business models that draw from multiple revenue streams. And it seemed to validate the flexible, experimental thinking that has kept *MinnPost* in the mix of media options in the Twin Cities.[57]

"The *Star Tribune* has really bounced back," Albright said. "It never got back to the numbers of people in the newsroom, but they're doing serious journalism and winning awards." Albright was identifying one of the biggest challenges *MinnPost* faced since the site switched on in 2007: the resurgent *Star Tribune*. As welcome as the competition was—and no one wanted to see a major regional metro go under—it also led to some soul-searching and a shift at *MinnPost*.

"We have a whole different mindset now about what our niche is," Albright explained. "We used to try to chase a lot of stories happening right now and got something up within an hour. We've had to evolve to keep our niche and separate from all the other media. We've got more of a magazine personality, and Andy [Putz] was instrumental in that because of his background." Putz added: "*MinnPost* has had to change, because the media landscape here in the Twin Cities has changed pretty dramatically."

That shift to a magazine approach meant investing time and money in hiring and editing. Putz and Albright moved from managing a roster of freelancers to bringing journalists on staff, where writers could stretch out and work on developing voice and analytical depth. It also meant being more strategic about areas of coverage. "We're not going to be able to have boots on the ground, to mix my metaphors, to cover the waterfront, in ways that the *Star Tribune* or Minnesota Public Radio can," Putz said. He and Albright believed that "if we're just talking about what happened, we're failing." Albright added: "We ask how we got here, what it means, why it's happening, and where it might go."

THE RESURGENT *STAR TRIBUNE*

Just across town, in the gleaming Capella Tower, the *Star Tribune* is busy writing a new chapter in its 152-year history. It's a resurrection story, guided in part by a savvy coalition of interim owners who realized that journalism still mattered in the local media market, and in part by the return of local ownership.

In 2016, media analyst Rick Edmonds of the Poynter Institute wrote that he wondered whether the *Star Tribune* had a "secret formula for outperforming the rest of the newspaper industry." Two years later, in an update, Edmonds called the paper "a widely celebrated fast horse in the slow field of metropolitan newspapers."[58] After the paper's 2006 sale to Avista and the devastating staff cuts and bankruptcy that followed, an interim ownership group called Wayzata Investment Partners picked up the pieces. Under the leadership of Michael T. P. Sweeney, the *Star Tribune* began rebuilding.[59] Sweeney would later call his time at the *Strib*, as the paper is known, "the best business experience I've ever had."[60] Sweeney knew the challenges ahead and noted that the Cowles family had timed their billion-dollar sale of the paper just about perfectly: "If they missed the top [of the market for newspapers] they missed it by about a week."[61] Sweeney met with members of the editorial board and apologized for the way they had been treated during the ups and downs of ownership changes.[62]

Suddenly, community values were part of the corporate mission again. "We have a special role in the community," Sweeney said.[63]

Sweeney made a critical hire: Michael J. Klingensmith, a Minnesota native who'd had a distinguished career with Time Inc. Klingensmith became CEO and publisher of the *Star Tribune* in 2010, and the next year he was named publisher of the year by the trade magazine *Editor & Publisher*.[64] In 2013, the newsroom was awarded two Pulitzer Prizes, for local news and editorial cartoons.[65] And when the staff won the Pulitzer for breaking news reporting in 2021, the Pulitzer board praised the *Star Tribune* "for its urgent, authoritative and nuanced coverage of the death of George Floyd at the hands of police in Minneapolis and of the reverberations that followed."[66]

The *Star Tribune*'s return to local roots was cemented in 2014 when the paper was purchased for $100 million by Glen Taylor, a septuagenarian billionaire from Mankato, a city of about forty-four thousand people that is eighty miles south of Minneapolis.[67] Taylor, who has interests in scores of diverse businesses, told an interviewer he became interested in buying the paper in part because he was impressed that the managers under Wayzata had the business acumen to steer the company out of bankruptcy and begin chipping away at $660 million in debt.[68]

Perhaps Taylor's interest was not surprising given his longstanding passion for contributing to civic debate. He was a Republican state senator in Minnesota, serving as minority leader from 1984 to 1986.[69] "As good Minnesota business leaders have traditionally done, Glen Taylor made way for public service," said longtime *Star Tribune* columnist Lori Sturdevant. Sturdevant, who retired in December 2018 after a forty-year career in the newsroom and on the editorial page, had covered state politics since 1978.[70] Taylor, she said, was relatively nonpartisan—he had been president of a local chapter of the Jaycees, a civic organization, when a state senate seat opened up, and he was recruited to run not by the Republican Party but by the Jaycees.

Taylor found the economics of the newspaper industry to be a tantalizing puzzle—one he hoped to solve. He quickly got down to work. Taylor sold the outdated ninety-five-year-old *Strib* headquarters and adjacent property—which both happened to sit near the city's most prominent new landmark, US Bank Stadium, home of the Minnesota Vikings—for $38.5 million and moved the newsroom to a glass tower nearby.[71] Taylor's daughter Jean, now chair of the Star Tribune Media Company, sits on the editorial board, where she is an attentive but low-key presence who introduces herself as "Jean from ownership," Sturdevant said.[72] In 2015, the *Star Tribune* purchased the Twin Cities alternative weekly *City Pages* from Voice Media Group for an undisclosed sum and shuttered its own youth-oriented publication, *Vita.mn*.[73] *City Pages* was shut down in October 2020, and its thirty employees were offered severance and a chance to apply for jobs at the *Star Tribune*.[74] Several former *City Pages* staff members, including editor Em Cassel, started a digital alternative publication called *Racket*.[75]

"When Glen Taylor became the new owner, people like me who knew him breathed a huge sigh of relief," Sturdevant said. "We trust this guy to be a Minnesotan. He's not going to run us at a loss, but he's also not interested in it being a huge moneymaker. The whole episode that we went through with Avista has reinforced in the minds of other people of means in Minnesota that this community is well served by local ownership of its news organization. But the challenges are still there: this newspaper and every other newspaper in the country has to find ways to make more money online because that's where the future lies."[76]

The *Star Tribune* newsroom stood at 235 journalists when we interviewed editor Suki Dardarian in June 2022, serving Minneapolis, a city of nearly 430,000 people, and a larger metropolitan area of nearly three million.[77] That number represents a 37 percent decline from 2007, when the newsroom stood at 375.[78] Still, the *Strib* newsroom is comparable in size to that of *The Boston Globe*, which serves a city of 675,000 and a metropolitan area of more than four million people. Media observers note that the *Strib* remains more committed to print circulation than many regional dailies because there are still engaged readers to be found in many of the state's eighty-seven counties—even if far-flung. Print circulation stood at 216,788 copies on Sunday and 103,808 on average for Monday through Friday for the six-month period ending March 31, 2022. The *Star Tribune* online has 94,902 subscribers Monday through Friday, plus 19,710 who read a digital replica of the print paper.[79] Klingensmith, who has an MBA from the University of Chicago, said in 2018 that his goal was 100,000 digital subscribers. (The *Star Tribune* got its start in digital in 1994, said former editor Tim McGuire, now an emeritus professor at Arizona State University. "We wanted eyeballs, but in my view the newspaper industry made a fatal mistake because there was so much concern about keeping expenses in line with revenues. You didn't see Google and Facebook doing that; they built the hell out of it, and they came.")[80]

George Floyd's murder not only galvanized the *Star Tribune* newsroom; it also sped up a push for more diversity and a broader internal conversation about the experience of journalists of color. According to the 2018 Newspaper Diversity Survey conducted by the American Society of News Editors, now known as the News Leaders Association (NLA), the *Star Tribune* newsroom was 83 percent white, 6 percent Black, 6 percent Asian, and 36 percent women, a stark illustration of the task ahead.[81]

Dardarian, who was senior managing editor when Floyd was murdered but has since been named editor and senior vice president, said members of her staff—already coping with the stress of isolation during the early days of COVID—were injured by police projectiles during the protests.[82] Viewers of the PBS *Frontline* documentary film *Police on Trial*, which tracked police reporter Libor Janey and many others in the *Star Tribune* newsroom as they worked sources and fanned out to cover the city, got a sense of the danger on the streets and the tension in the mostly empty newsroom downtown.[83] In a scene that captures a Zoom call with members of her staff, the worry and strain on Dardarian's face are palpable. "It wasn't like we hadn't covered police shootings and protests before," she told us in a telephone interview, "but nothing—*nothing*—on this level. We got better at it every day and tried to be more strategic and have more support and supplies for people. Our in-house counsel was at the ready. We had to have numerous calls and conversations with the police, trying to get them to be careful around the journalists. We have a good-sized staff, a committed staff. They risked life and limb out there trying to get the story."

"I think a lot of people felt that this is where George Floyd was killed. We needed to be at the front of that," said Dardarian. The *Star Tribune* was one of the original newsrooms selected to be part of the Table Stakes program, an initiative underwritten by the Knight-Lenfest Local News Transformation Fund and the Knight Foundation that guides newsrooms in thinking strategically about digital transformation and audience engagement.[84] "That program has continued to serve us in all its iterations. We even have a few people who are doing another Table Stakes project now. It really helped unite us around the company—and in the industry—with others who were trying to innovate and change and find ways to move forward."

Working across news platforms collaboratively remains a crucial goal, Dardarian said, but so does adapting for a diverse readership and engaging with the audience, which will entail better hiring, diversity audits, and attention to hiring pipelines. In the end, she observed, "it's all audience-driven. It's where we have been headed, and where we are headed."

STEVEN WALDMAN

*The president of Rebuild Local News
outlines his vision for revitalizing
community journalism.*

Steven Waldman is president of the Rebuild Local News coalition, whose three-thousand-plus member news outlets, nonprofits, and other stakeholders are working on public policy initiatives to revive grassroots news reporting. He is also the cofounder and former president of Report for America (RFA), a national service program that places journalists, mostly young and relatively inexperienced, in local newsrooms and helps pay their salaries for two- or three-year stints to report on under-covered communities. He came up with the concept in 2014 and joined forces with the GroundTruth Project to launch RFA in 2017. During our reporting, we encountered a number of outlets that either had Report for America corps members or were in the process of recruiting them, including *The Colorado Sun, Sahan Journal, MLK50, The Mendocino Voice,* the *New Haven Independent,* and *NJ Spotlight News.* In a few short years, the program has become a crucial part of the local news ecosystem.

Waldman has a deep background in magazine journalism. He was national editor of *U.S. News & World Report* and national correspondent for *Newsweek.* He went on to cofound a multifaith religion website, *Beliefnet,* which won a National Magazine Award. He is also founder of the Rebuild Local News coalition, and he has crafted proposals for how government can help revitalize local journalism while preserving editorial independence—arguing that government intervention is needed on a large scale to sustain community news.

Our podcast interview with Waldman was posted on July 14, 2022. This transcript has been condensed and lightly edited for clarity.

DAN: You were one of the cofounders of a rather remarkable organization, Report for America, which is based right here in Boston. Can you tell us how RFA got started, how you honed the mission, how you fund it, and how many journalists you've placed in newsrooms?

STEVE: We describe Report for America as a national service program that places emerging journalists, talented journalists, into local newsrooms around the country to report on under-covered topics and communities. About a thousand reporters applied for 150 slots this last time. And the newsrooms also apply to us to get these great, talented, subsidized reporters. They have to prove to us that there's a really important need in the community and define what that is, and that they have good editing. It's not a fellowship or an internship. They're employees for a year or two, sometimes three. The financial model is that we pay half the salary in the first year and a third of the salary in the second year. We have three hundred corps members out in the field right now in fifty states, on a very wide range of beats. The corps is almost half journalists of color, so it's very diverse.

DAN: Given that it's going to be difficult for your corps members to find jobs once their Report for America terms are up, I'm wondering if you're involved in training or encouraging your young journalists to launch local news ventures of their own.

STEVE: I'll start by saying it looks as if something like three-quarters to 80 percent of the corps members do get jobs after they're in the corps. Some of them get hired by the newsroom that they're in, and others get hired by other newsrooms. But your basic point is right, that we're not going to be able to solve the local news crisis just on the basis of legacy news organizations. We need new players. So we have started a third-year track that we call a leadership track to help teach people about how you might start a news organization.

ELLEN: You also founded the Rebuild Local News coalition, and you've argued that government assistance is needed to support local news. Some would say that such government assistance is a threat to journalistic independence. Can you elaborate?

STEVE: We pulled together the Rebuild Local News coalition about two years ago when it became clear that there needed to be more focus on public policy and local news, that the crisis has gotten severe enough that we needed to really pay attention to this. Public policy doesn't necessarily mean government subsidies. It can mean other things, like antitrust law and how that affects consolidation in the news industry. I think we are in a new era where people understand that public policy has to be an important part of the discussion about how to save local news, along with business model improvements and digital subscriptions, nonprofit news, and a greater role for philanthropy. Those are all important elements. But I do think that public policy has to be one of the legs of the stool.

DAN: One of the proposals you've promoted is the Local Journalism Sustainability Act, which would provide tax credits for people who subscribe to a news outlet, for advertisers, and for publishers who hire and retain journalists. One of the challenges in moving ahead with such legislation is that the tax credits would help hedge fund owners and corporate chains as well as independent publishers. Do you think that's a worthwhile price to pay, or might there be some way of structuring the legislation to cut out owners like Gannett and Alden Global Capital?

STEVE: You could cut them out. The national legislation had a compromise in between, where it put a cap on the number of tax-credit slots that any given corporation could get. So even though Gannett has, I don't know, 7,500 reporters, they will be eligible for 1,500 slots. The same with Alden. There'd be a limit. But they still will get a lot. It's a judgment call. I certainly think in this case it's definitely worth it, because even though there are some folks that you might not want—and I'm really referring more to Alden in this case—you're still offering massive support for small publications, nonprofits, Black newspapers. This would be the biggest infusion of government support into local news, I believe, since President Washington signed the Post Office Act and the newspaper subsidy that commenced from there. But you certainly could, on a state level, further restrict who got the funds. The basic issue that we always struggle with here is that if you cut out some of these newspaper chains, you may ultimately be penalizing the people in those communities. We are on the side of supporting anyone that is providing local news.

DAN: In a similar vein, most of your Report for America corps members are working at independent news organizations, but not all. Are you concerned that when a corps member goes to work for a newspaper owned by a corporate chain that you may be helping the owners cut back elsewhere in the newsroom? Is there some way of preventing that from happening?

STEVE: Well, there's an explicit prohibition in our contracts with the newsrooms. They're not allowed to do that. Now, as you can imagine, it might be hard to prove that or hard to know that. So we just keep our ears to the ground to try to determine whether that's happening. We look at it from a few points of view. Are they doing an important beat that wasn't going to get covered otherwise? And are they treating the reporter well?

ELLEN: As we discuss nonprofits, the tax law states pretty clearly that nonprofit news organizations can't endorse political candidates. They arguably can't endorse specific pieces of legislation, ballot questions, that sort of thing. What if our news ecosystem becomes largely nonprofit and thus can't endorse candidates in elections? Should the nonprofit tax rules be amended to allow for more editorializing? Do we risk losing the editorial voice of the press?

STEVE: I change my mind on this every other month. On the one hand, I don't think it would necessarily be a good thing if the entirety of the local news system were nonprofit. It's going to need to be a mix of nonprofit and for-profit and hybrids. Having said that, I strongly believe that there need to be more nonprofit news organizations and a bigger role for philanthropy. Because no one covers local elections as a matter of news anymore, my only way of knowing is to look at who local news organizations have endorsed. It's a real service—editorial boards have close interactions with candidates. And it's a way of having impact.

On the other hand, we do have this issue where part of the erosion of trust in journalism is the confusion between opinion and news. For all the hard work we did in the newspaper world of having clear lines drawn between opinion and news, I think that's obliterated by what happens on TV for the most part. We have this problem in America now of trust in the media. And some of the erosion of trust comes from this perception that we're all biased, that there's no line between journalism and opinion. I wonder at this point whether it's worth the fight. Maybe we're at the point where the harm that's done by having opinion is so great that it's not worth the benefit. At a minimum, we should be just very, very heavy-handed about labeling things in a really, really clear way.

CHAPTER THREE

BEDFORD, MASSACHUSETTS

*A Homegrown News Site Comes
into Its Own*

M ike Rosenberg was walking along the Narrow Gauge Rail Trail,
a dirt path that takes its name from the type of train that used
to chug through the area. On this hot July morning in 2021, Rosenberg
was reporting on the new cultural district in Bedford, Massachusetts,
an affluent suburb about twenty miles northwest of Boston. Leading
the way were Alyssa Sandoval, the town's housing and economic development director, and Barbara Purchia, chair of the Bedford Cultural Council. The town's planning director, Tony Fields, joined the
group about halfway through the tour.[1]

A couple of cyclists rode by. "Hi, Mike," said one of them. Rosenberg returned the greeting and then said to no one in particular: "I
have no idea who that is."

It's the sort of thing that happens when you're among the most
recognizable people in town. For decades, Rosenberg worked as a
reporter and editor in his adopted community and then served as an
elected official. In 2020, he returned to journalism as the first paid
staff reporter at *The Bedford Citizen*, a nonprofit digital news site
launched in 2012. At seventy-two, an age when many people are retired, Rosenberg was taking notes, snapping photos, and swatting
mosquitoes.

Rosenberg pointed to his left, where a large new home—not quite
a McMansion—stood alongside a tiny greenish house. All across Bedford, he said, newcomers with money were demolishing older homes

and replacing them with oversized structures. "People are upset because it's destroying the sense of neighborhood," he said. "Every time there's a teardown, people lose their heads."

The new cultural district, Rosenberg's guides hoped, would help preserve a sense of history in a community that was rapidly changing. They inspected landmarks such as Bedford Depot, where a commuter rail line was in operation as recently as the 1970s and is now the terminus of the Minuteman Bikeway, a ten-mile paved path that connects with Greater Boston's subway system.[2] They also stopped by Fitch Tavern, where the minutemen of Bedford, as legend has it, gathered on April 19, 1775, for a breakfast of cold gruel and warm beer before marching off to fight in the Battles of Lexington and Concord, as well as visiting a 1966 sculpture, *Dance Rhythm*, by Chaim Gross, installed on a plaza near the town hall.[3]

Rosenberg probed, looking for some information he could use for the story he'd write. "What are the benefits of having a cultural district?" he asked.

"It puts a wrapper around our cultural institutions and a focus," Sandoval replied.

"Can the district be expanded?"

"Yes, with state approval."

"Will there be some sort of event to mark the unveiling of the district?"

"We're thinking about it, yeah," Sandoval said, explaining it couldn't be done earlier because of restrictions that were in place during the unvaccinated months of the COVID-19 pandemic.

Rosenberg's arrival at *The Bedford Citizen* in 2020 represented a significant step forward for the news organization. Founded by three members of the League of Women Voters to provide more comprehensive coverage of town government and community events than was being offered by the chain-owned weekly newspaper, the *Citizen* for most of its existence had been an unpaid operation. Then, with the help of a professional fundraiser who lived in the community and donated her services, the *Citizen* began to raise money from a variety of sources—voluntary memberships, foundation grants, and advertisements on the website and in a glossy town guide that was published once a year. Revenues rose from about $13,000 in 2016 to more than $135,000 in 2021, enabling the project to pay salaries to its full-time managing editor, cofounder Julie McCay Turner, and to Rosenberg, who worked part-time. Freelancers were paid to cover governmental meetings that Rosenberg couldn't get to, although the *Citizen* continued to employ volunteer labor as well.[4]

The Bedford Citizen is not widely known outside the town's 13.7 square miles.[5] Nearly a decade after its founding, it is sometimes confused with *The New Bedford Light*, a high-profile, well-funded nonprofit in a gritty working-class city some seventy miles to the south whose 2021 launch was the subject of flattering stories in *The New York Times* and *The Boston Globe*.[6] The *Light*'s forte is high-profile investigative reporting on issues such as the fishing industry and the homelessness crisis. The *Citizen*, by contrast, quietly goes about the task of covering the quotidian details of community life—what's going on at town hall, in the schools, and inside the police department, running features on community events and including odds and ends such as a regular column called "Ask Aunt Laura," with advice on matters such as how to make the perfect hard-boiled egg, complete with video.[7] Overall, the site published more than 1,800 articles in 2021 and hosted two virtual events, one on local governance and the other on how COVID had affected the public schools.[8]

The growth of *The Bedford Citizen* came at a fortuitous moment. After years of budget and staff cuts imposed by its corporate owner, GateHouse Media, which later morphed into Gannett, the *Bedford Minuteman* was shut down in May 2022, along with eighteen other Gannett weekly newspapers in the Boston suburbs.[9] By the time the *Minuteman* closed, its total paid circulation was just 445 in a community with a population of about 14,000.[10] The *Citizen*'s website, by contrast, was receiving about eighty thousand page views per month, a total that grew to more than one hundred thousand in the three months leading up to the March 2022 town election. The *Citizen*'s Sunday newsletter reached nearly 2,300 email subscribers, with an open rate of more than 60 percent. A separate daily newsletter generated automatically from the site's RSS feed was sent to about 1,350 subscribers and had an open rate of about 70 percent.[11]

A direct comparison with the *Minuteman* is not possible given that the *Citizen* is free; Gannett would not provide digital metrics. "We do not share site specific subscription data," the company said in response to our inquiry.[12] Nevertheless, the *Citizen* had clearly established itself as Bedford's leading news source. "The media outlet of record for Bedford is *The Bedford Citizen*," according to the town's state representative, Ken Gordon.[13] Katie Duval, who when we spoke was wrapping up her tenure as the director of Bedford TV, the local cable station, called the *Citizen* "the most important source of news for the Bedford community and really one of the most important parts of the fabric of the community."[14]

In announcing the end of the *Minuteman*'s print edition, Gannett said it would provide local coverage online and urged readers to purchase a digital subscription. "The *Bedford Minuteman* will continue to report on the news readers need and want. But it will no longer arrive at the end of your driveway or in your mailbox once a week," the announcement said in part.[15] In fact, though, the *Minuteman*, like most of Gannett's Massachusetts weeklies, was publishing very little in the way of Bedford news at the time that the print edition was discontinued, and there were no indications that was going to change once the paper converted to a digital-only format. For example, the *Citizen* published fifty-five articles about the March 2022 town election both before and after the ballots were cast. The *Minuteman* did not cover the election at all.[16] Moreover, several weeks before Gannett announced it was closing many of its weekly newspapers in the Boston suburbs, it was learned that the company would reassign most of its full-time staff reporters to regional beats such as racial justice, the environment, and education.[17] Those are worthy topics, but the shift was certain to leave communities that had no other news source without the day-to-day journalism they need to hold local government accountable and just to keep up with goings-on in town.

Still, though the presence of a thriving nonprofit news organization was a boon for the residents of Bedford, there were challenges both within and outside the community. Internally, the *Citizen* was faced with sustaining itself with a corps of paid and unpaid staff members who were nearly all of retirement age. Externally, the success of the

Citizen raised questions of equity. An affluent, well-educated community like Bedford was exactly the sort of place that a project like the *Citizen* could be expected to do well.[18] Studies have shown that wealthier suburbs are better served by local news startups than more diverse urban areas or rural communities since there is a corps of residents who have time to volunteer and money to donate.[19] Bedford may have solved its local news problem. It was unclear, though, whether that held any lessons for cities and towns that lack the social capital to muster support in terms of volunteer labor and fundraising that had been so crucial in building the *Citizen*.

Julie McCay Turner was looking for a place where she could publicize her church's plant fair. Born in Dubuque, Iowa, and raised in Hinsdale, Illinois, Turner had lived everywhere from Alaska to Antigua and points in between before moving to Bedford in 1968. There she established herself as an active member of her community. She co-chaired the Bedford Council for the Arts, for whom she produced a newsletter, and hosted a program on Bedford TV. And then, in the early 2010s, she wanted a one-stop venue to get the word out about a church plant fair without having to submit notices to multiple outlets. "There were so many places you had to go," she recalled, "and you could perhaps assure that you would get a tiny piece of penetration in each one of them. And I thought, 'Wouldn't it be wonderful to have something that everybody paid attention to?'"[20]

Turner began talking with two other women about the possibility of starting some sort of news outlet—Meredith McCulloch, the director of the public library, and Kim Siebert, who'd been covering local news part-time for the *Bedford Minuteman* and was unhappy with the tarted-up headlines she said the editor slapped on her stories. "They wanted to sell sizzle, and I wanted to sell content," Siebert said, adding that she had to remind her editor: "I live in this town." As Siebert recalled, the three of them had been attending local government meetings and reporting back to the League of Women Voters, to which they all belonged. They began to formulate the idea of doing it for public consumption rather than just for their fellow members.[21] "The *Citizen* grew out of a dissatisfaction with our local newspaper," said McCulloch. "They were having a lot of turnover in reporters, editors, and weren't really paying a lot of attention to Bedford-specific stories."[22]

Around the same time, *The Boston Globe* was inviting paid subscribers to attend its Friday-morning news meetings. Turner, McCulloch, and Siebert showed up one day and learned about an initiative the *Globe* was about to launch called *Your Town*. The new program would provide hyperlocal coverage of communities in the Boston area on the *Globe*'s free website, Boston.com (the *Globe*'s paid journalism had recently been moved to a different, subscription-only site, BostonGlobe.com). The *Globe* editor in charge of the project, David Dahl, was eager to connect with local bloggers who were interested in sharing their work. The three women told him of their plans. *The Bedford Citizen* debuted in the summer of 2012 with Turner as the managing editor, and before long the Bedford web page at *Your Town* was linking to stories in the *Citizen*. "We had cred; we had the *Globe*. We didn't have any money," Siebert said. "But we figured we would create content and the money would follow."[23]

Dahl, who's now retired from the *Globe* and serving as editor of the nonprofit *Maine Monitor*, said that Turner stood out among the local journalists he worked with. "She was sophisticated and remarkable and always seemed to have metrics and numbers, more so than other folks," he said. "And they were always growing the number of followers on their Facebook page or newsletter subscribers."[24] But after the Boston Red Sox' principal owner, John Henry, bought the *Globe* from the New York Times Company in 2013, *Your Town* began to wither away, and it was quietly shut down in 2014.[25]

The *Citizen*, however, kept growing. In 2014, the Internal Revenue Service approved its application for 501(c)(3) nonprofit status, which allowed the project to accept tax-deductible contributions.[26] Starting in 2016, Turner began to draw a modest salary for her work as the site's managing editor. And in the summer of 2020, following a COVID-induced delay, Rosenberg began work as the *Citizen*'s part-time community reporter—its first paid staff journalist other than Turner.

Rosenberg grew up in Rutland, Vermont, covering sports and politics for the *Rutland Herald* while he was in high school and then politics as a student at the University of Vermont. He moved to Bedford in 1973, taking a job as editor of the Tufts University alumni magazine in the hopes of being hired by one of the large city papers that served the area—which, in the 1970s, were *The Boston Globe* and the *Boston Herald American*. Instead, he was offered the chance to become the editor of the *Bedford Minuteman*, thus beginning a long career in community journalism. Rosenberg speaks with genuine passion about the years he spent covering his adopted hometown.

"Talk about divine intervention. The weekly was looking for somebody as a stringer," he said, using the newspaper term for freelancer, "and, so, they hired me to cover school committee meetings. And, almost immediately thereafter, the editor announced she was resigning to run for the legislature. Although we had different styles, we both had the same philosophy. This is a sacred trust, and we're responsible for it. This belongs to the community, and we have to tend it. We have to sustain and strengthen it."[27]

In those days the *Minuteman* was part of a small, independently owned chain of six weeklies, with the *Lexington Minuteman* serving as the flagship.[28] The Bedford paper didn't have its own office, so Rosenberg worked out of his home, pulling all-nighters at the Lexington headquarters once a week in order to lay out the paper and get it ready to be printed. "We did our own manual paste-up," he said, referring to the process of assembling the paper with strips of typeset articles and hot wax. "It was a labor of love." Rosenberg served a stint as editor of the Lexington paper—for "professional growth," he explained—but didn't particularly like it and returned to Bedford. A few years later, after the papers were sold to another local chain, Rosenberg left and took a job as an editor at *The Sun*, a daily based in nearby Lowell. He enjoyed the work, he said, but he quit the newspaper business in 1987 in order to spend more time with his family and to follow his growing passion for Jewish life.

After leaving *The Sun*, Rosenberg became involved in community affairs, serving as an elected member of the Bedford school committee and the board of selectmen, later renamed the select board. He continued to serve as the public address announcer at high school football games and was involved in Bedford in other ways as well, as co-president of the town's diversity committee and as a member of the tricentennial committee. ("It's not for another seven years," he said. "God knows some of us might not be around by then.") Those ties became something of an issue when his term on the select board expired in March 2020 and he began working at the *Citizen* five months later. Rosenberg said he sought guidance from the state ethics commission, which told him he should refrain from covering any issues in which he'd been directly involved until he'd been off the board for a year. Still, Rosenberg's entanglements speak to an ongoing issue at the *Citizen*: virtually everyone, paid and unpaid, is also deeply enmeshed in town affairs. "There's always going to be some overlap," he said. "And the question is, where are you going to draw the line?"

The many hats that Rosenberg wears speak to life in small-town independent community journalism. A chain newspaper company might assign to its weekly papers young reporters who would be bound by ethical rules forbidding involvement of the sort that Rosenberg engaged in. Those reporters, in turn, would invariably move on to better-paying jobs at larger news organizations before they could really get to know the community. Which is better? Reporters whose lives are rooted in the places that they cover or career-minded journalists who are just passing through?

Some years ago, the media scholar Howard Ziff wrote about that dilemma in describing what he called the "cosmopolitan" and "provincial" forms of journalism. Cosmopolitan journalism, according to Ziff, was based on traditional notions of objectivity such as maintaining a distance from the people you were reporting on and adhering to strict ethical standards. Provincial journalism, by contrast, harked back to an earlier time, when newspaper reporters were invariably people who grew up and lived in the places they were covering and had to balance truth-telling and independence with compassion and community involvement. Ziff quoted the editor of a group of small Connecticut weeklies as saying that big-city reporters "leave the bodies where they fall, we meet our victims face-to-face the next day in the local coffee shop." The most important point Ziff made was that neither model is superior—they are just different, with each suited to different circumstances.[29]

Certainly the provincial model can be taken too far. At the *Lexington Minuteman*, for instance, Alan Adams, who sold his papers several years before Rosenberg arrived, served as a selectman and in various other elected and appointed posts while also working as publisher and writing editorials.[30] Presumably he got good press. Overall, though, Rosenberg and his colleagues at the *Citizen* appeared to take their ethical obligations seriously while finding ways to be a part of the community in which they lived and worked.

The *Citizen*'s reliance on volunteers and people of retirement age is both a strength and a potential weakness. Julie Turner, who estimated she was working forty to sixty hours a week, was seventy-seven years old when we interviewed her in late 2021. The volunteer copy editor, Dorothy Bergin, was almost ninety-four and handling stories electronically from Vermont, where she was living with her daughter. "I want to hang in there as long as I can. Because I really love it, and it keeps my brain agile," said Bergin, who also wrote a column for the *Citizen* called "Dot's Reading Room," consisting of tidbits she'd encountered online, and contributed an occasional story as long as she could do the reporting by Zoom.[31] Meredith McCulloch, still on the *Citizen*'s board of directors, was residing in a retirement community.[32] (Kim Siebert, the third of the founders, had moved from Bedford several years earlier and was no longer involved.)

At a time when independent community news projects struggle to survive and thrive, retirees can help fill the need, whether they work as volunteers or at below-market salaries. There are indications that older people increasingly are turning to journalism as a way to serve their localities, with Report for America—which normally places younger reporters in understaffed newsrooms for two- and three-year stints—starting a new program called the Experienced Corps, enabling retired journalists to serve as mentors.[33] Lincoln Millstein, a retired executive who formerly worked at *The Boston Globe*, *The New York Times*, and the Hearst media company, is a strong advocate for retirees getting involved in covering their cities and towns. Millstein began a site called *The Quietside Journal* so that he could write about his community on Mount Desert Island in Maine. "I think there are now more retired journalists in the country than those actually working," Millstein told us on the *What Works* podcast. "That's a model I would really like to see emerge and enabled and exploited and encouraged."[34]

But younger retirees have a way of becoming older retirees. At some point, they may wish to hand the reins to a new group of people. This has been an ongoing challenge at the *Citizen*. By early 2022, its fundraising success had brought it to the brink of sustainability— provided that it continue its upward trajectory.

Consider the managing editor's job, the only full-time position at the *Citizen* and one that is crucial to the organization's success. After working for no pay for the first several years, Turner received a salary of a little less than $11,000 in 2016, a pittance that grew slowly for several years.[35] As fundraising increased, though, the *Citizen* was able to pay higher salaries. In 2021, Turner earned $44,000, and Rosenberg, who was slotted for twenty-four hours a week, was paid $35,000.[36] The *Citizen* was paying a part-time operations manager as well. Though those salaries were hardly in the range of what would be needed to live in a high-cost community such as Bedford, where the average per capita income was $68,000, they were not far off from the average in the notoriously low-paid newspaper business.[37] For instance, a study of fourteen unionized newsrooms at Gannett's daily newspapers in the fall of 2020 found that the median salary for journalists was just $52,000, and those with fewer than ten years of experience were making nearly $10,000 less than that.[38] Anecdotally, nonunion journalists at Gannett's weeklies were reportedly being paid even less than that.[39]

The *Citizen*'s fundraising success came just in time. In June 2022, Turner stepped aside as managing editor. "I'm humbled and grateful to have been part of the *Citizen*'s first decade," she wrote. "It's been an amazing run, and I look forward to helping set a course for the second decade."[40] Rather than replace Turner with a full-time editor, the board decided on a restructuring. By early August, the *Citizen* announced it was seeking a part-time managing editor and a part-time content manager, thus splitting work that Turner had done almost entirely on her own.[41] Turner would be hard to replace. But the publication's transition from a volunteer to a professional operation over the previous several years had turned what could have been a crisis into a surmountable challenge.

The person largely responsible for this growth is Teri Morrow, a top development official with the Appalachian Mountain Club by day and the executive director of the *Citizen* during her free time. As was the case with many others at the *Citizen*, Morrow donated her time. Her aim, though, was to help transform the organization into a professional, self-sustaining enterprise.

Morrow learned about the *Citizen* at Bedford Town Day, an annual fall event at which local businesses and organizations set up booths on the town common. It's an occasion that draws hundreds of people and includes plenty of food along with a parade and fireworks. Morrow said she was unhappy with the way the *Minuteman* was covering the town, so she decided to become a monthly donor to the *Citizen*. "A lot of the stories were inaccurate, and I didn't see that in the *Citizen*," she said. "And I wanted to support it." Soon thereafter, around 2014 or '15, Morrow joined the board, later serving as president and, after four years, moving over to the newly created volunteer position of executive director.[42]

It was under Morrow's guidance that the *Citizen* had been able to increase its budget so dramatically. The *Citizen* joined LION (Local Independent Online News) Publishers, an organization of more than three hundred digital news outlets, and the Institute for Nonprofit News (INN). Through INN, the *Citizen* began taking part in the NewsMatch program, under which INN raises grant money to match funds raised at the local level. In 2021, the *Citizen* received $31,000 in matching grants from NewsMatch and other organizations, including the Google News Initiative and the Knight Foundation. According to a breakdown of the *Citizen*'s revenues in 2021, nearly $77,000 came from donations (contributions from 525 readers), about $15,000 from grants, and nearly $9,000 from sponsorships—advertisements purchased by local businesses that appear on the website.[43]

Other than donations, though, the *Citizen*'s largest source of revenue is *The Bedford Guide*, the glossy magazine–style publication that began publishing in 2020 and consists of articles about community life, from town government to recreation to culture, chock-full of ads taken out by real-estate agents, banks, home contractors, restaurants, physicians, and—yes—the Cat Doctor of Bedford. The 2021 *Guide* brought in gross revenues of about $34,000 and netted about $20,000 after expenses.[44]

The *Guide* is the work of Gene Kalb, a volunteer board member at the *Citizen*. He said that the purpose of the *Guide*—in addition to raising money—is to answer questions that a new resident might have about the community. "If I moved to Bedford, what would I want to know? What does the parent of a sixth-grader need to know?" is how he explained it.

The debut issue, in the spring of 2020, went smoothly enough. But then the pandemic hit, and Kalb was worried that advertisers wouldn't come through. With smaller businesses forced to cut their spending, Kalb said he approached some of the larger corporations in town, as Bedford has a significant presence in the biotechnology industry. "They were very receptive," he said. "Basically, the idea for the big corporations is, this is a way to be a good corporate citizen in a visible way."

The *Guide* serves another purpose as well. Since the *Citizen* is digital-only, people don't see it when they stop at a grocery store or run into the library. Marketing is mainly by word-of-mouth. The *Guide*, though, is mailed to every household in Bedford, thus introducing the *Citizen* to residents who might not have heard of it.[45]

Kalb also writes features for the *Citizen*, including an occasional piece on local quirks called "Bedford Explained." In April 2022, he hosted the *Citizen*'s first podcast, an extension of "Bedford Explained," through the auspices of Bedford TV. His topic: pole-capping, a tradition that marks the revolutionary-era practice of adorning liberty poles with red caps as a protest against British rule.[46] Even though paid journalism was becoming more important to the *Citizen*'s business model, the role of volunteers such as Kalb remained crucial.

That is not unusual at local digital startups. According to Project Oasis, a study led by the University of North Carolina (UNC) that examined 704 such projects conducted in the spring of 2020, many were getting by with a mix of paid staff, part-time employees, freelancers, and volunteers. Among the 255 news organizations that provided detailed data to Project Oasis, half used volunteers, with unpaid labor accounting for about a third of the people working at those outlets. In many cases, such projects would not be able to get off the ground and continue to operate without unpaid help. But that creates problems of equity and exclusivity, according to Chloe Kizer, who wrote the report while based at UNC. She later became the data and projects manager at LION Publishers, which was also involved in the study.[47]

"I think the fact that so many independent local news organizations start out from a volunteer basis is an unfortunate part of the current reality," Kizer said. "Not everybody who has a voice that's worth sharing or whose perspective is worth being heard has the privilege to be able to start a volunteer organization. You have to live, you have to work, you have to be able to pull in a salary for your family, for yourself."[48]

Kizer added that it's not unusual for the founders of such sites to be former journalists squeezed out by legacy news organizations who begin their own projects with their savings without much in the way of a plan to move toward sustainability. That wasn't the case with *The Bedford Citizen*, which started as an explicitly volunteer project and only later embraced paid journalism. But that definitely describes the experience of Kara Meyberg Guzman, the chief executive officer and cofounder of *Santa Cruz Local*, a for-profit site launched in 2019 in California. Guzman, who'd quit her job as managing editor of the *Santa Cruz Sentinel* following drastic cuts by its corporate owner, Alden Global Capital's MediaNews Group, said she and her business partner, editor Stephen Baxter, bootstrapped the project with their own resources.

"I sold some of my retirement stock, sold my car, and used my savings to keep myself going for a year while getting zero dollars in salary," Guzman said in a Zoom interview.[49] Baxter kept his day job and worked at the *Local* as a side project. But with COVID-19 providing an unexpected boost to paid membership, as well as with grants from the Google News Initiative and Facebook, Baxter was able to come on full-time. By March 2022, Guzman and Baxter were paying themselves livable salaries and were employing a full-time community engagement and business development coordinator. Guzman is also a board member of the Tiny News Collective, which assists startups with funding, support, and technology, and was named LION Publishers' 2021 Member of the Year.[50]

Like Kizer, Guzman is troubled by the reliance on volunteers among many digital startups and the inequities that creates. "To really be sustainable, to really thrive as an industry, we need to get new people reading and listening to our work and bring more communities into the fold," she said. "And to do that, we really need to diversify media ownership and diversify the communities that local media serves. We need to pay living wages, make it a viable career for young people, women, people of color. I don't think you can really do that in a sustainable way with a volunteer-run organization."

By early 2022, Guzman said the *Local* had signed up 700 paying members and 6,200 newsletter subscribers. Internal measurements of open rates and clicks showed that 4,000 of those subscribers were highly engaged, she said. A central offering of the *Local* was its podcast, consisting of deeply reported audio stories on topics such as homelessness and mental illness that people can listen to while they're driving to their jobs in Silicon Valley—"over the hill," as she put it.

Since November 2020, *Santa Cruz Local* has had an additional challenge—*Lookout Santa Cruz*, a high-profile, well-funded startup. *Lookout* was begun by Ken Doctor, a respected news-industry analyst, as what was intended to be the first of a network. Another competing media outlet, the alternative weekly *Good Times*, greeted *Lookout* with a blast, claiming that Doctor was benefiting from the "false narrative" that Santa Cruz was a news desert.[51] Doctor responded by calling that "the greatest free publicity that we could ever get." In an appearance on the *What Works* podcast, he offered some praise for *Santa Cruz Local*, saying, "They cover city and county government in a thorough way, but they're covering government." The difference, he said, was that *Lookout* was attempting to offer something more comprehensive. "We intend to be the new primary news service," he told us. "That entails a lot more than what either of those are doing or, importantly, what either of those aims to do."[52]

Guzman's response: "We are the go-to source for deep, accurate news about what's happening in local government and how to get involved. But we are also the go-to source for deep reporting about the big issues facing our community. *Lookout* is a completely different product. It's much broader. They cover food and entertainment and have puzzles. We are very much more civic-oriented and community issues–oriented, I would say."

Guzman and Baxter have shown it's possible to build a sustainable news business even though they were not able to attract the sort of big-money funders who were available to a known quantity like Doctor. Volunteers can be essential, but long-term dependence on those who are able to donate their labor excludes too many people whose voices deserve to be heard.

On the surface, at least, Bedford's 2022 town election represented the ratification of the status quo. Those candidates for the select board (which runs the local government along with a professional town manager), the school committee, and the board of health who were regarded as liberal or progressive were elected (in some cases reelected) by comfortable margins.[53]

No surprise there. Bedford is the sort of town that is typical of Boston's left-leaning suburbs—more than three-quarters white and well-heeled, with an Asian population of about 18 percent and a Black population of just over 4 percent.[54] One of the few exceptions to the town's insular monoculture is Bedford High School. During the 2022–23 school year, 84 of the school's 848 students were from military families who lived at nearby Hanscom Air Force Base, and another 36 were students of color from Boston who were taking part in METCO, a voluntary program aimed at integrating suburban school systems.[55] A young Black woman from a military family who graduated from the high school in 2015 and who asked not to be identified said that though she and other Black students felt welcome, there was also a pervasive sense that they were outsiders. "I think people felt like it was an asset to have the base kids as well as METCO come to the high school," she said. "There were times when I definitely felt like I didn't fit in, certain classes where I felt like I didn't fit in. But I think, by and large, the administration and a lot of the teachers tried not to make it feel that way."[56]

Beneath the surface of this relatively accepting environment, though, there were signs that the polarization that has done such damage to national politics was beginning to affect the way people thought about local matters. There were no outbursts at school committee meetings about the teaching of critical race theory or gender identity. But a member of the board of health stirred a controversy by questioning how strict the town's COVID masking rules ought to be.[57] The trust that residents traditionally placed in their elected officials was beginning to fray as well. A much-needed new fire station barely cleared the two-thirds majority required to approve it at the annual town meeting, a New England ritual that is open to all registered voters in the community.[58] A proposal to extend the Minuteman Bikeway by paving and widening a dirt path called the Reformatory Branch Trail (at one time it was a rail line that extended to a prison in neighboring Concord) fell short of two-thirds and was thus defeated.[59] And, for the first time in anyone's memory, four candidates—two for the select board, one for the school committee, and one for the board of health—ran together as a slate, offering vaguely worded promises of change.

There was a sense among the Citizen's staff that the candidates' real agenda was to reverse the town's leftward drift, even though there was no clear evidence of exactly where the upstarts placed themselves on the political spectrum. Although members of the slate lost in 2022, there was no reason to think that would continue in future elections. "So much of what's happening this year is happening sub rosa, on social media and in private Facebook groups," Julie Turner said.[60] Joan Bowen, copresident of the board of directors, put it this way several weeks before the election: "It's more contentious than anything we have experienced in my fifty-plus years in Bedford. It's the first time that there's been any sense of a political divide, conservative versus more traditional or liberal."[61]

At a Zoom meeting of the editorial board following the election, members talked about how they could reach out to all segments of the community, left, right, and center. "I see a theme here of broader problems that are going to continue to be on the horizon," said Ginni Spencer, the other board copresident. "I don't want to be in a stand-off with a group that has a different opinion. How are we going to reflect that adequately in the *Citizen?*" She added that she'd been made aware of a post on one of the local Facebook groups that was "just an incredible thing about how the local election was a fraud and Bedford is dominated by new-money communists. On the one hand, I read that as 'This person is wacky.' But this person is part of our community."[62]

Earlier, Turner said that she saw some cleavages in the town be-tween old-timers who had moved to Bedford—or had grown up in the town—at a time when it was seen as a cheap place to live and newcomers who were driving up the prices of homes and were tear-ing down old structures so they could replace them with larger, more luxurious houses. It was the same issue that Mike Rosenberg had highlighted during the tour of the new cultural district. As Turner put it, "Bedford's become more stratified, I think, than we were when I came in. It felt much more like a little town when I got here. I think the fundamental piece that we're all grappling with is that we're turn-ing more into a suburb, a bedroom community."[63]

The divide that Turner talked about is reflected across Massa-chusetts. Although the state's reputation is that of a liberal outpost, that fails to reflect a deeper reality. There is a conservative streak in Massachusetts, especially in blue-collar areas, but many of the peo-ple who hold those views continue to register as independents or Democrats simply because the state's Republican Party is so mor-ibund, comprising fewer than 9 percent of all registered voters by late 2022.[64] That, along with the influence of right-wing media out-lets such as Fox News and the corrosive effects of social media, has brought the culture wars to the local level, even if they're still mainly bubbling beneath the surface in comparison to what's taking place in many other states.

S aturday, September 18, 2021, was a time for celebration as hundreds of people descended on the common for Bedford Town Day. Families strolled among dozens of booths set up by businesses and other organizations to celebrate the 292nd anniversary of Bedford's founding. The atmosphere was especially festive given that the event had been canceled the year before because of the pandemic. Julie Turner and Mike Rosenberg moved through the crowd, taking pictures and notes, while several of the *Citizen*'s volunteers hung out at a booth they had set up with copies of *The Bedford Guide* and signs with QR codes that would take people to the website. Jerry Wolf, the *Citizen*'s treasurer, said the purpose of the booth was to "publicize the *Citizen*," although he added, "Most people have heard of it by now." Gene Kalb said, "It's a community event, so we're here."[65]

A decidedly unscientific survey of attendees showed that most of those who were approached had heard of the *Citizen* and read it at least occasionally. "I get the *Citizen*. It's pretty good," said Sanjay Gupta. Dan and Alice Churella said they were *Citizen* readers as well. "The thing I like about the *Citizen*," said Alice Churella, "is that if there's anything with the school committee or the select board or any issues that come up, they report on both sides of the issue. It seems to me to be totally unbiased."

Nearly ten years after its founding, *The Bedford Citizen* has grown from a volunteer-driven upstart to the only local news outlet in town. Because of its success in fundraising, it was on the brink of sustainability, with more growth planned. A grant approved by the town's cultural council would pay for freelance coverage of the arts and related topics.[66] Teri Morrow told us that her eventual goal was to bring in enough money to pay for a full-time editor, two full-time reporters, and perhaps a part-time executive director.[67] Such a level of staffing would essentially replicate the coverage provided by the *Bedford Minuteman* before cutbacks under corporate chain ownership began to take a toll. It would also allow for some in-depth investigative reporting, which Ginni Spencer identified as a need when she spoke with us, saying, "We're very limited right now in what we can do."[68]

The challenge was to keep the momentum going and, perhaps equally important, to live up to the ideal expressed by Alice Churella by maintaining a reputation for fair, unbiased coverage and to act as a voice for everyone. In truth, the 2022 town election was not especially divisive, at least not openly, and there's certainly nothing wrong with opposing views. That's how a democracy is supposed to work. What robust local news coverage can do is explain those opposing views with the nuance and complexity they deserve, allowing members of the community to debate and resolve their differences in a civil manner. So far, at least, the *Citizen* appears to have been successful in doing that.

CHAPTER FOUR

DENVER, COLORADO

The Sun *Rises over a
Complex Media Landscape*

Toward the end of the documentary *News Matters*, Jennifer Brown, a longtime reporter for *The Denver Post*, is greeting soon-to-be-former colleagues at her 2018 going-away party. The *Post* had been under siege following its acquisition by the hedge fund Alden Global Capital in the early 2010s. Now Brown was leaving the paper, where she had worked for thirteen years. Her departure would have come earlier, she said, but she had wanted to finish a reporting project on the fate of children who were aging out of foster care. "I couldn't leave," she explained, "until I got these kids' stories out of my notebook."

Her next stop: *The Colorado Sun*, a startup digital news organization where she would be one of the founders and co-owners as well as a staff reporter. As she told the filmmakers, it was a prospect she found both exhilarating and daunting, pointing out that something like 80 percent of new business ventures fail. "It's terrifying," she said.[1]

Three years later, in late 2021, Brown was firmly ensconced in her new job. She had continued to write about kids in crisis, including a series about children who run away from residential treatment centers, produced in collaboration with the local NBC affiliate. She also reported on a wide range of other topics, such as a series about a homeless couple known as Cyxx and Jay, whom she followed for months as they moved from place to place, and the federal Bureau of Land Management's efforts to round up wild horses in the drought-stricken Sand Wash Basin in northwestern Colorado.[2]

It was a transition she had never expected to make. Brown grew up in rural Montana, in the proverbial cabin in the woods, raised by parents who did not finish high school and who were divorced when she was twelve. For a while, they got by on food stamps. But she was able to graduate from the University of Montana in Missoula, where she fell in love with journalism, and then landed jobs at small papers in Montana and Texas as well as the Associated Press. When she was hired by *The Denver Post*, she thought she had finally arrived. "I really thought that was my dream job, like where I wanted to stay maybe even for the rest of my career," she told us. The competition with the city's other daily, the *Rocky Mountain News*, was fierce. Both papers fielded newsrooms of about three hundred full-time journalists. "It was the kind of environment where it was adrenaline all the time," Brown recalled. "You'd wake up and open the *Rocky* and flip through to see if you got scooped."[3]

That, however, turned out to be the apex of daily newspaper journalism in Denver. The *Rocky*, beset by declining circulation and advertising revenues, was shut down by the Scripps chain in 2009, just shy of its 150th anniversary. The following year, the *Post*'s parent company, MediaNews Group, declared bankruptcy, opening the door to Alden, and the cutting soon began. By late 2021, the newsroom count was down to around sixty.[4]

Toward the end of her years at the *Post*, Brown said, the situation became intolerable, with no time to produce the deeply reported journalism that was her forte. "They'd want to know, charts and graphs, how many stories each person bylined a month," she said. "I was a projects reporter, right? So sometimes it took me a month to come out with a really good, hard-hitting investigative piece. And that obviously wasn't going to work, because I'd be shown the door. What I write about—homelessness and child welfare and these things—you wouldn't get that many reads, but it would still be important work. You could write some silly thing that took you an hour, and it could get two hundred thousand page views."[5]

The pressures on journalists at *The Colorado Sun* are different. Rather than having to produce quick-hit stories that will attract clicks and page views, the folks at the *Sun* are trying to figure out how to build a financially sustainable news organization based on deep engagement with its readers. Launched by former *Post* editors and reporters in September 2018, the website is among the most closely watched local news ventures in the country.

The *Sun* had its origins in a newsroom rebellion so unusual that it garnered national headlines. In April 2018, faced with yet another round of cuts, the *Post* published an editorial castigating Alden as "vulture capitalists" and calling on the hedge fund to get out of town: "Denver deserves a newspaper owner who supports its newsroom. If Alden isn't willing to do good journalism here, it should sell the *Post* to owners who will." The editorial was accompanied by a number of essays on the importance of local journalism.[6]

Several years later, Chuck Plunkett, who was the editorial page editor at the time, talked about why he decided to deliver such a pointed message to his corporate overlords. "One of the great desires to publish that series and that editorial was to let our readers know that this was going on," he said in an interview. "Because any time over the years leading up to the Denver rebellion, you'd have these cuts of fifteen, eighteen, twenty people at a time. And it may get written about in the business section, a tight little story that references market conditions and the changing advertising structure, those kinds of things. But it never mentioned our hedge-fund ownership. Our readers didn't know. And when we published the editorial and made it clear that we were dealing with a hedge fund that was avaricious, they were like, 'Oh, something else is going on here.'"[7]

Plunkett did not get his wish. Alden wasn't selling. He left, becoming a journalism professor at the University of Colorado in Boulder. Ten other journalists, including some of the *Post*'s top editors and reporters, resigned in the following months and began planning what would ultimately become the *Sun*. By mid–2022, the *Sun* had grown to twenty-five full-time journalists covering news in Denver and across the state;[8] significantly, the new hires were more racially diverse than the original mostly white group, which the editor, Larry Ryckman, frankly acknowledged was needed. The *Sun* could be regarded as a full-service news site. Though it was lacking coverage in areas such as sports and the arts (areas that Ryckman hasn't ruled out adding in the future), it offered a wide array of reports on politics, climate change, development, education, and health; opinion pieces; and Jennifer Brown's specialties: child welfare, homelessness, and other issues that might be regarded as not click-friendly. The *Sun* also published stories from the Associated Press—a relationship that was fostered by Ryckman, a longtime AP editor—and from other news outlets such as *Chalkbeat*, a national nonprofit that covers education.

O n a September afternoon in 2021 at the Buell Public Media Center, home to Rocky Mountain PBS as well as the *Sun* and several smaller media organizations, Ryckman reflected on what the *Sun* had accomplished and where it was going. Ryckman's office looked out on a shared newsroom that was mostly empty, a consequence of the COVID pandemic. Of his decision to leave the *Post*, he said, "It was a gut check. Here we are three years later. We've learned a hell of a lot."[9]

There are three aspects to the *Sun*'s business model that are worth noting. The first is that the original plan was to build it on a foundation of cryptocurrency—a foundation that proved, not surprisingly, to be made of sand. Or virtual sand. The *Sun* was one of a number of news organizations that partnered with the Civil Foundation, which received most of its funding from ConsenSys, a for-profit blockchain company. Fourteen of those media outlets, including the *Sun*, got some crucial startup money. But Civil's attempt in the fall of 2018 to raise $8 million from the sale of tokens fell short, bringing in just $1.4 million. Journalists in some Civil newsrooms talked about having to borrow money to pay their rent. The failure ultimately led to Civil's shutting down in mid–2020.[10] "It was a sobering result for the prospects of a new ownership technology to somehow 'save the media' in any easy or automatic fashion," wrote Nathan Schneider, a media studies professor at the University of Colorado in Boulder.[11]

Even though the *Sun* was left scrambling to raise money from other sources, Ryckman has nothing but good words for Civil. "I'm forever grateful that they gave us the seed money to get started," he said. "I said on day one, 'This isn't about blockchain or cryptocurrency or any of those things. This is about us demonstrating our value to Colorado.' What Civil gave us was the opportunity to make our case to the people of Colorado."

Civil gave the *Sun* something else as well. Most *Sun* stories are accompanied by a "credibility bar" that explains to readers whether any original reporting was involved (a pop-up explainer defines original reporting as "new, firsthand information"), if sources were cited, if the reporter visited the scene, and if the reporter is a subject-matter expert. It's a way to provide transparency and explain to the audience why it should take a particular story seriously. "That was a Civil innovation that we loved and our readers love," Ryckman said. "That was one of the few holdovers from Civil that we kept. We just thought that was brilliant."

The second notable aspect of the *Sun*'s business model is what could be called a reverse paywall. Many news organizations publish free newsletters aimed at enticing readers into purchasing digital subscriptions. The *Sun* does the opposite: the website, certain newsletters, and a daily podcast are free, but readers are asked to become paid members in order to access the premium newsletters, which offer exclusive coverage not available on the website. It's based on the model of the classic customer-engagement funnel. At the top of the funnel are readers who are checking out the website or who might have gotten a link to an article through Facebook or Twitter. The goal is to pull them down through the funnel so they become paying customers. The first stage is to get them to sign up for one or more of the free newsletters—a guide to the day's news called "The Sunriser," which consists of a curated selection of stories from the *Sun* and other Colorado media; "The Headlines," an RSS scrape of the *Sun*'s site; or "What's Working?," a weekly newsletter about jobs and the economy that's produced by another of the founding journalists who came over from the *Post*, Tamara Chuang. After that, become a Basic member for $5 a month, which includes invitations to members-only events, or sign up for Basic Plus at $10 a month, which brings with it Colorado Sunday, a magazine-style recap of the week's news. Premium members, who pay $20 a month, can sign up for newsletters that offer deep coverage of politics ("The Unaffiliated"), the outdoor recreation business ("The Outsider"), climate change and health ("The Temperature"), and early access to opinion writer Mike Littwin's columns.[12] It's not a revolutionary model; in fact, it's similar to *Politico*, which offers a free website while selling specialized newsletters to lobbyists, think tanks, and the like for many hundreds of dollars a year. But the *Sun* is unusual in adapting that model to a general readership.

How well has it worked? As of June 2022, Ryckman said, the *Sun*'s website was drawing between 1.2 million and 1.3 million unique visitors a month. That's a pure top-of-the-funnel measurement of casual traffic that represents the pool from which paying readers can be recruited. More telling was the number of newsletter subscribers—about two hundred thousand, of whom seventeen thousand had been enticed into becoming paying members. Most of those members were at the $5-a-month level, but about two thousand were paying $10 a month, the cost of the Sunday newsletter, and another two thousand were paying $20, giving them access to all of the *Sun*'s products.[13]

The third unusual part of the *Sun*'s business model may be the most significant: its corporate structure. Unlike many local news startups, the *Sun* is not a nonprofit. Rather, the *Sun* is a for-profit, but not in the traditional sense: it's a public benefit corporation, or PBC, a legal designation that is essentially a statement of values. A PBC's charter, for example, must state that the purpose of the enterprise is to serve society in some way. There is no fiduciary obligation to enrich the owners, which means that profits, if any, can be reinvested in the journalism. Designation as a PBC also serves as something of a "poison pill," as Ryckman put it, making the *Sun* an unattractive acquisition target.

In a sense, a public benefit corporation is a for-profit company with the soul of a nonprofit, and it is gradually becoming a popular structure for journalism. Perhaps the largest such example is *The Philadelphia Inquirer*, which, after years of tumultuous ownership, was donated to the nonprofit Philadelphia Foundation in early 2016 by H. F. "Gerry" Lenfest, a billionaire who had acquired the *Inquirer* and endowed it with $20 million. The nonprofit that was set up to manage the *Inquirer* was named the Lenfest Institute for Journalism the following year; Lenfest himself died in 2018.[14] Other journalism PBCs include *The Provincetown Independent*, a Massachusetts digital and print community news project founded in 2019, and *Lookout Santa Cruz* of California, a digital-only outlet launched in 2020 whose chief executive officer and founder, media business analyst Ken Doctor, intends to build a chain of such sites and who has been among the *Sun*'s advisers.

For a news organization, the advantages of PBC status are perhaps more perceptual than specific. There are, for instance, no tax benefits, unlike nonprofits, which do not pay taxes and whose funders are able to write off donations on their own taxes. Holly Ensign-Barstow, who is the stakeholder governance manager for B Lab, which tracks PBCs, told us one advantage for news outlets is that a PBC designation shows that an organization is mission- rather than profit-driven, which can help attract grants. PBCs also are required to publish annual reports on how they are fulfilling that mission, an exercise in transparency that may counteract public distrust in the media. "I think that the benefit corporation," Ensign-Barstow said, "potentially because it removes companies from this focus on profit generation at all costs, is a way to reposition some media companies to focus more on providing accurate, quality journalism for the benefit of their stakeholders rather than on sensational, partially untrue stories that drive profit."[15]

As Ensign-Barstow pointed out, potential donors may be attracted to the sense of mission that comes with PBC designation. Still, their inability to make tax-exempt gifts would seem to be a significant obstacle. There is, however, a workaround, and it's one that the *Sun* is pursuing along with a number of other news organizations: donors may make a tax-exempt gift to an affiliated nonprofit to pay for reporting at the *Sun*. The nonprofit takes a cut and passes on the rest of the money to the *Sun*. The *Sun* works with the Colorado Freedom of Information Coalition, but some for-profits have established their own nonprofit arms.

Despite all this, Ryckman isn't entirely sold on the PBC model and said that he and his fellow co-owners might consider taking the *Sun* nonprofit at some point. A disadvantage to pursuing that route is that nonprofit news organizations may not endorse political candidates or specific pieces of legislation, but Ryckman said that's already off the table.[16] (The *Sun* is nonpartisan, though it does publish signed opinion pieces.) One dilemma that becoming a nonprofit would solve, though, is what to do about disparities between the nine founding staff members who are still at the *Sun*, all of whom are co-owners, and the newer employees, who have no ownership stake. "We would like there to be a path to ownership for them," Ryckman said. Carol Wood, the *Sun*'s chief operating officer, told us that one of her roles is to integrate newly hired reporters into a newsroom culture that's dominated by the veteran journalists who launched the site. "The new people on staff outnumber the founders," she said. "We have to make sure that the new staff members understand our mission."[17] Surely one way to ease that divide is to eliminate the two classes of employees, one with ownership shares and the other without, whether by reorganizing the existing structure or by taking the nonprofit route.

As of late 2021, the *Sun* appeared to be on its way to becoming financially sustainable. Ryckman was wary about sharing numbers, but he said the project was making progress toward breaking even. He declined to provide compensation data except to say that the *Sun*'s journalists are paid "adult salaries" with health care, competitive with *The Denver Post* and Colorado Public Radio—an assertion we were able to confirm independently. His goal was to emulate *The Texas Tribune* (at one point *Tribune* founder Evan Smith came to Denver to speak at the *Sun*) with a four-legged stool built on paid membership, sponsors (advertising), grants, and events. The COVID pandemic set back the events business, and, well into 2022, the *Sun* had been most successful with membership. "We're out of balance," Ryckman said, but he added: "We have a strong plan. We have the money to make it happen—to operate at a loss long enough for the revenue part to catch up. I have enough money in the bank that we could have forty people on the staff today right now if we wanted to. But money equals time, and that gives me less runway. Our plan is to be patient."

David Gilbert, a reporter with Colorado Community Media (CCM), was summoned into publisher and co-owner Jerry Healey's office one day in the spring of 2021. "I've got news for you," Healey told him. "I've sold the papers." Healey wanted Gilbert to write the story about the transaction. CCM published twenty-four weekly and monthly newspapers in Denver's suburbs. Gilbert, who'd been on staff for four years, imagined the worst—namely, a corporate chain owner was coming in that would slash costs and eliminate jobs. His first thought, he said, was "Oh, crap, time to pack up my things. I wonder if I can get my job back driving a truck."[18]

Gilbert needn't have worried. Jerry Healey, along with his wife and business partner, Ann Healey, had decided to retire, and they'd been looking for a way since the previous fall to sell to someone who would preserve their papers. A complicated transaction came together quickly. Their company was purchased by the nonprofit National Trust for Local News in collaboration with locally based media organizations. A new public benefit corporation, the Colorado News Conservancy, was set up to run CCM, to be owned jointly by the National Trust and *The Colorado Sun*; the *Sun* assists with operations as well. The *Sun*'s minority stake could grow to majority ownership over time. "We had basically three weeks between the time that the funding commitments were made and we had to close the transaction," said Elizabeth Hansen Shapiro, chief executive officer of the National Trust. "So it was a lot of work, and we had to get bare-bones agreements just so we could move forward to close."[19]

The sale was heartening because it showed that the owners of independent newspapers don't always have to sell out to cost-cutting corporations. The question, though, is how many owners are willing to make the financial sacrifice that might be necessary to sell to a community-based organization rather than to a national chain that would be willing to pay top dollar and then earn it back by cutting coverage and staffing. The price of the CCM deal was not made public, and Jerry Healey explained that the two sides had signed a nondisclosure agreement; the transaction was financed with a loan for $1.5 million from FJC, a philanthropic investment foundation.[20] But Healey did say that he and his wife "potentially" left some money on the table by not selling to a for-profit chain, and he said they also agreed to help with financing. "This was outside our comfort level," he said. "But we believe in the importance of this that much where we are willing to take some of that risk." Added Ann Healey, who was CCM's executive editor off and on as well as a high school journalism and Spanish teacher: "We left our papers in a good place and, with good leadership, which it looks like they've got, they will be successful."[21]

The merger has provided the *Sun* with an opportunity to recruit talented CCM journalists to its own staff. For example, David Gilbert, the CCM reporter whom Jerry Healey asked to report on the sale, was later hired by the *Sun*; we met him in the *Sun* newsroom on the first day of his new job. Larry Ryckman described CCM as profitable and said, "Our job is not to break it." Nor did CCM present any financial challenges to the *Sun*, Ryckman said, since the *Sun*'s contribution was not cash but, rather, "sweat equity and know-how, boots on the ground, operational muscle."

Among the first orders of business after the CCM acquisition had been completed was to hire a publisher. That turned out to be Linda Shapley, a veteran Colorado journalist and executive with experience in news and business operations at *The Denver Post* and elsewhere. In an interview at the CCM offices in suburban Englewood, Shapley said she was recruited by Ryckman and Dana Coffield, another *Post* veteran, who is the *Sun*'s senior editor. "I thought about it really hard," Shapley said. "But I've been a lieutenant for a lot of really great generals. And this is my opportunity to be a general."[22]

The combined newsroom at CCM comprises about twenty-two journalists, Shapley said, although she hoped to be able to add to that total over time. Total circulation was somewhere in the neighborhood of 120,000 to 130,000; some of the papers are paid and some are free. Her goal, she said, was to improve the papers' digital presence while not alienating customers who prefer print. That might require a culture shift, especially on the part of advertisers. Jerry Healey, for example, said that he sometimes offered deals to advertisers combining print, digital, and email only to be told they weren't interested, informing him: "We called you for print." Shapley's response: "I totally get that there are advertisers out there who don't necessarily see digital as a way forward. But they recognize the fact that this is going to be how people find you. So I don't see them as playing against each other but as something that can work in tandem."

In a business whose upper ranks remain dominated by white men, Shapley also said she hoped to use her position as a visible Latina leader to encourage more diversity in journalism. "I'm very cognizant of the fact that there aren't enough journalists of color and that there are communities that aren't getting heard," she said. "Obviously that conversation has really started to grow in volume. And I've really tried to be somebody who's listening to that and trying to figure out what I can do."

If you relied solely on national headlines about what has happened to the media in Denver in recent years, you might come away with a simplistic and wrong view: Hedge fund destroys daily newspaper. Digital startup tries to fill some of the gap. In fact, the picture is more complicated than that. What we found was that Denver, a city of about 711,000 in the center of a metro area with a population of nearly 2.9 million, was served by an array of media—including *The Denver Post*, which, even with a staff of just sixty full-time journalists, remained one of the largest news organizations in Colorado. The *Post*'s combined paid print and digital circulation in 2021 was about 208,000 on weekdays and 256,000 on Sundays, making it by far the state's largest newspaper.[23]

Although the media universe in Colorado no longer revolves around *The Denver Post*, the paper still looms large in the civic imagination. Founded in 1892, it was known during its early decades for its populism and sensationalism. One example of its rollicking brand of journalism dates back to 1900, when the co-owners, Harry Tammen and Frederick Bonfils, were both shot by a lawyer they had accused of cheating a man who'd been convicted of cannibalism. The *Post*, you see, was crusading to free the cannibal from prison, one of many publicity stunts the paper engaged in during its disreputable early decades. Later, Bonfils resigned from the board of the American Society of Newspaper Editors to escape censure over his role in the Teapot Dome scandal, which brought down associates of President Warren Harding. By mid-century, though, the paper had upgraded its standards. Under editor Palmer Hoyt, the *Post* was one of the very few newspapers in the country to stand up to Senator Joseph McCarthy and his anticommunist witch hunt.[24]

Independent ownership ended in 1980, when the heirs of Frederick Bonfils, after years of infighting, sold the *Post* to the Times Mirror chain. Seven years later the paper was acquired by Dean Singleton, at that time a thirty-six-year-old newspaper entrepreneur from Texas. Singleton was building a national chain known as MediaNews Group. He moved his company to Denver, thus establishing the *Post* as his flagship. Those were heady days for Singleton, who made a name for himself as a cost-cutter but who, by the standards of today's chain owners, seems benevolent. By 2010, though, the deteriorating newspaper economy caught up with Singleton, with his holding company for MediaNews Group, then up to fifty-four daily newspapers, filing for bankruptcy.[25]

Singleton stuck around after Alden gained control of MediaNews Group over the next several years, serving as non-executive chair of the *Post*, a largely ceremonial position, and on its editorial board. But he quit in 2018, not long after the rebellion begun by Chuck Plunkett's editorial led to a stampede of high-level departures. "They've killed a great newspaper," Singleton said of Alden at the time.[26] Several years later, he offered a somewhat more nuanced view, conceding that he would have had to keep cutting if he had still been in charge. "I'm glad I'm not doing it today because I wouldn't have the stomach to do what has to be done," he told us. "But I don't necessarily disagree with it." He added: "As a reader of the newspaper, I still admire a lot of the good journalism they do. It's just not nearly as broad as it used to be."[27]

The editor of the *Post* for much of the Singleton era and the early Alden years was Gregory Moore, who was recruited in 2002 from *The Boston Globe*, where he was managing editor. Greg Moore was perhaps the most prominent African American editor of a major US

newspaper until 2014, when Dean Baquet was named executive editor of *The New York Times*. Denver doesn't have an especially large
Black population; 9 percent of city residents are Black, compared to
nearly 30 percent Latino and 69 percent white (those numbers add
up to more than 100 percent because a portion of the Latino population identifies as being part of other groups as well).[28] Still, Moore
was attuned to issues of diversity in the *Post*'s coverage. He recalled
telling his staff, "If I see another white kid licking an ice cream cone
or running through a fountain on a 100-degree day down here on
the mall, which is like right outside our door, I'm killing somebody.
You've got to go out to the equivalent of Roxbury," referring to a
mostly Black neighborhood in Boston. "They actually lick ice cream
cones over there."

The way Moore told it, Singleton was a tough-minded owner
when it came to spending decisions but nevertheless supported the
Post's journalistic mission. That began to change once Alden moved
in. Moore was particularly enraged by a demand to cut costs right
after his staff had been working nonstop for several weeks following the Aurora theater shootings in 2012. "It got harder because they
wanted more," he said. "They started sending in these really young
number-crunchers. They would be sitting in meetings and they'd say
stuff like 'So, why do you still have photographers? Why can't you
use freelance photographers?' I said, 'Well, you see that wildfire we're
having out there that's burned four hundred homes? You see that flood
out there that's washed away roads? There's no freelance photographer that knows how to get around that terrain. There's no freelance
photographer who's going to risk their life to cover that story. That's
why we have photographers.'" Finally, in 2016, he resigned. "Look,
it was really a great run, but by then I'd just run out of patience with
them," said Moore, who later took the top editing job at a business
communications company in suburban Denver. "They didn't really
want to get in a fight with me, and I really didn't want to get in a
fight with them. But I knew it was time for me to go."

Like Singleton, Moore praised the downsized *Post* but lamented
the constraints on what it was able to do. "They still hit high notes,
but there's so much wire copy and *The New York Times* and AP and

stuff like that," he said. "It's a shell of itself. They're committed, but it's really hard to do what they need to for a community of this size with the resources that they have. And that's really the shame here."

Both the current editor of the *Post*, Lee Ann Colacioppo, and the managing editor, Matt Sebastian, declined to be interviewed.[29] But John Wenzel, the *Post*'s arts reporter, spoke of a newsroom that was pulling together despite having been decimated. Several years earlier, at the time of the rebellion, Wenzel wrote a rather pessimistic assessment for *The Atlantic* in which he described being moved out of the *Post*'s downtown offices to a windowless printing plant in the suburbs.[30] Three years later, he told us, staffing had stabilized, and, despite the paper's diminished reporting capacity, he expressed pride in the work that he and his fellow journalists were able to carry out. "I'm still at the paper because I still believe in it," he told us. "I think it's bigger and better than its ownership. There's still a lot of value in what we offer."[31]

In addition to the *Post* and the *Sun*, the most significant news organization in the state is Colorado Public Radio. With a newsroom of sixty-five, based just a short distance from the state capitol, it may also be the largest in Colorado, though executive editor Kevin Dale—yet another alumnus of the *Post*—said that one or two of the city's television stations might be bigger. CPR includes a website called *Denverite*, a digital startup it acquired in 2019, giving the operation both statewide and local coverage.[32] "Our goal was to become a primary news source," Dale said, explaining that his operation tried to offer important contextual stories rather than breaking news. "I've been very careful all along to use the article 'a' instead of 'the,' because I think 'the' has connotations that end up in practices that we're not interested in," he said. "We're not going to be out covering a major house fire or a major traffic jam unless it has implications beyond that."[33]

In many cities, alternative weeklies were a major presence until the past decade or two, when a good number of them failed. That created a void, as alt-weeklies covered local arts and politics, published deep investigative pieces, and, crucially, kept a close eye on established media outlets. In Denver, fortunately, the venerable *Westword* persists. Patty Calhoun, the editor and founder of the paper, told us that *Westword* had survived in part because of marijuana ads (Colorado was a leader in legalization). Circulation of the free weekly was about thirty thousand, Calhoun said in an interview in her memorabilia-strewn office, a number that had fallen by about half since the beginning of the COVID-19 pandemic. "People will still come to us for the sheer pleasure of holding something in their hands and reading," she said, although she added: "That's a small part of our mission now, because we're digital-first."[34]

There's also a new daily newspaper of sorts—*The Denver Gazette*, launched in 2020 by the Colorado billionaire Philip Anschutz. Unlike his other Colorado paper, *The Gazette* of Colorado Springs, the Denver edition is strictly digital, but it's formatted to look like a print publication. A year after its debut, the *Gazette* was winning plaudits for its investigative reporting, and its conservative opinion section appealed to readers who might feel left out of Denver's blue mainstream. The editor, Vince Bzdek, who had previously worked at both *The Denver Post* and *The Washington Post*, wouldn't share with us much in the way of metrics, though he did say that the combined newsroom of the two *Gazette* papers and the Anschutz-owned *Colorado Politics*, a website with a weekly print edition, was around ninety full-timers. "We're one of the few places that are really expanding, and we're trying to take advantage of local ownership," he said. "Our owner is invested in Denver." The owner is also in his eighties, and Bzdek said he didn't know what succession plans might be in place, but he noted that Anschutz's son, Christian, was on the editorial board.[35]

Smaller media outlets were reporting on the region as well, including *Axios Denver*, a daily email newsletter that's part of a nationwide network aimed at young professionals looking for a quick gloss on the day's news. The editor, John Frank, is a *Post* alumnus who was also one of the original *Colorado Sun* founders. "Each of the local media here in Denver has a niche—and we work to bring it all together," Frank said of his project, a quick read designed for mobile that combines a bit of original reporting with aggregation from other news sources.[36] Less locally focused but still based in Denver is *Colorado Newsline*, a website that's part of the nonprofit States Newsroom national network, which specializes in politics and public policy.[37]

B ut if the Denver area is reasonably well covered, the same cannot be said about the rest of the state. Colorado has a population of almost 5.7 million, which means that about half of its residents live outside of Denver and its suburbs—many of them in news deserts.[38] Consider Pueblo, a city of about 112,000 that's nearly two hours south of Denver.[39] About a decade ago, John Rodriguez, a local resident, bought a monthly publication called the *Pueblo Pulp* so that he could offer an alternative to the *Pueblo Chieftain*, the oldest daily in the state. Rodriguez thought the *Chieftain* was too cozy with the local establishment, and that situation did not improve when GateHouse Media bought it in 2018. (GateHouse later merged with Gannett and took its name.) The *Pulp*, meanwhile, could not survive the COVID pandemic and ceased publication. At a panel discussion about the possibility of public funding for local news, Rodriguez gave voice to his lament. "Get down to southern Colorado," he said, according to an account in the *Columbia Journalism Review*. "We need you to get out of Denver. We are in a crisis that is beyond what Denver can even imagine."[40]

Yet Colorado is also home to a number of media activists and organizations that are trying to address the shortage of news coverage described by Rodriguez. The need may be greater than the capacity, but an unusual amount of experimentation is taking place there. Corey Hutchins, a journalism professor at Colorado College in Colorado Springs and the author of a well-read weekly newsletter on the state's media scene called *Inside the News in Colorado*, was moderating the panel at which Rodriguez spoke out, so he's far from naive about the state of journalism outside of Metro Denver. But he told us that Colorado is unique in its efforts to address the decline of news at the local level. "I don't know of any other state where there's such a focus and attention from folks here who want to support a thriving local news ecosystem matched with attention from funders, smart media thinkers from around the country," he said in an interview at the college's new media center—itself the outgrowth of a collaboration with Colorado Public Radio.[41]

The Colorado Sun is among the organizations that are trying to bring news to under-served areas. We asked Larry Ryckman why the *Sun*'s small staff put so much effort into reporting on stories in the rural parts of the state rather than doubling down on accountability journalism in Denver. He replied that calling the site *The Colorado Sun* rather than *The Denver Sun* was a deliberate choice. "The need was so great elsewhere around the state," he said. "We've got some counties that have one newspaper. I actually think Denver's fairly lucky." Dana Coffield, who, as the *Sun*'s number-two editor, directs much of the paper's day-to-day coverage, grew up in the hinterlands of Colorado. Both her family and her husband's family owned small newspapers, and she and her husband owned a paper at one time too. She told us she was proud of the coverage the *Sun* had been able to provide outside of the Denver area, which can be republished for free by other news outlets. "We've been able to provide quality journalism to some of the smallest outlets in the state," she said. "I like being able to contribute to a healthy ecosystem for smaller newspapers, since I came from that heritage."[42]

Then there are the Colorado Media Project and the Colorado News Collaborative (better known as COLab), both of which were involved in connecting Jerry and Ann Healey with the National Trust for Local News. Melissa Milios Davis is the director of the Media Project and vice president for informed communities at the Gates Family Foundation (not to be confused with the foundation run by Bill and Melinda Gates). The project was launched, she said, to see if a buyer could be found for *The Denver Post* after Chuck Plunkett issued his call for Alden to sell. Though that effort went nowhere, Davis went on to lead a survey of the media landscape in Colorado, to connect the *Sun*'s founders with business strategists, and to help foster cooperation among news organizations. "The purpose of it was really around the idea that the solution is not one outlet," she said. "The Media Project tries to keep pushing forward the idea of collaboration, and that with fewer reporters on the beat, there's just power in numbers."[43]

Laura Frank wears many hats. Among other things, she is the executive director of COLab, a past board president of the Institute for Nonprofit News, and the founder of I-News, a nonprofit investigative news organization that became part of Rocky Mountain PBS in 2013. Like Melissa Davis, Frank devotes much of her work to fostering a collaborative environment. "We help news organizations from the *Sun* to places like the weekly newspaper in Eads, Colorado, where a single person is the editor and the publisher and the reporter," she said. "All platforms, television, radio, newspaper, digital—we help them do stories they couldn't do alone."[44]

On a warm, sunny day in late September 2021, the *Sun*'s education reporter, Erica Breunlin, and the *Sun*'s Report for America corps member, photographer Olivia Sun ("no nepotism involved," she quipped), were standing outside Denver North High School, where hundreds of students had gathered to demand the resignation of a school board member who'd been censured for inappropriate behavior with an underage student and for social-media posts that could have intimidated witnesses. After gathering on the steps of the school, they headed off for Denver Public Schools headquarters, some two and a half miles away, the air punctuated with angry, profane chants from more than a thousand students across the city.[45]

Breunlin, who'd worked for several GateHouse and Gannett papers before coming to the *Sun* in 2019, live-tweeted the action on her phone. Before long, the *Sun* had posted a full story, pieced together by her editor, Lance Benzel, from her tweets and from phone calls. "He was great, because he was telling me to really just focus on the scenery and talking to people and tweeting and really capturing that color," she said. "And then he was embedding my tweets into the story. It really was a good team effort."[46]

Report for America mainly recruits young journalists with a few years of experience; typically, it's a second or third job. Sun had been a staff photographer for the *Des Moines Register* before she applied to Report for America. She was turned down the first time but was chosen when she reapplied, and she had been at the *Sun* for about three months. Like all Report for America journalists, her stint would last for two or three years. She said that at the *Register*, a Gannett paper, her job consisted of shooting an endless stream of breaking news, crime, and high school football games. "The institutional knowledge I gained from working somewhere like that is really irreplaceable," she said. "I really got to learn from old-guard veteran journalists. But essentially I wanted to see what else was out there and how I could personally put my skills to a more streamlined use in just illustrating local issues."[47]

Ironically, both Breunlin and Sun said what had attracted them to *The Colorado Sun* was the chance to work on in-depth stories—and here they were covering a breaking-news story. It was not the typical fare for a news organization whose strength, as Dana Coffield put it, is to "articulate broader issues in the state." On an early summer day in 2022, for instance, the *Sun*'s home page featured stories about Colorado's real-estate market, a surge in renewable energy projects, and steps the recreation industry was taking to appeal to a more diverse clientele.

Though the Colorado media scene may be richer and more complex than outsiders might appreciate, *The Colorado Sun* remains the state's shining example of how journalists can fight back against corporate downsizing while serving the public interest. In just a few years, the *Sun* had established itself as a crucial part of the journalistic landscape in Colorado. At a moment when the idea that every city and every region needs a dominant news source of record has given way to a more complex reality, the *Sun* was a key player amid a host of players in keeping Coloradans informed.

KARA MEYBERG GUZMAN

*A former Alden editor talks about her
reinvention as a publisher and her
work as a local news advocate.*

Kara Meyberg Guzman is CEO and cofounder of *Santa Cruz Local* in California, a private, for-profit news organization that runs a website, a podcast, and a free newsletter. Before the *Local*, she was managing editor of the *Santa Cruz Sentinel*. She left her job at the *Sentinel*, which is owned by Alden Global Capital's MediaNews Group, in 2018, citing differences with the company's management. Guzman connected with another former *Sentinel* reporter, Stephen Baxter, and the two of them launched the *Local* in 2019.

Santa Cruz Local's revenue model is a mix of memberships, business sponsorships, grants, and advertising. Santa Cruz isn't exactly a news desert. Media analyst Ken Doctor founded *Lookout Santa Cruz* in 2020 as a public benefit corporation, and there's an alternative weekly called *Good Times* (founded in 1975), an independent nonprofit launched in 2017 called *Voices of Monterey Bay*, and local television and public radio stations.

But Guzman wanted to focus on public policy on a county-wide level. By all accounts, Santa Cruz is a beautiful and largely affluent coastal community where the median household income in the city is $86,000 a year. But 20 percent of the population lives at or below the poverty level, according to the US Census. The *Local* focuses on issues that lie beneath the surface, like homelessness and public health.

Our podcast interview with Guzman was posted on May 25, 2022. This transcript has been condensed and lightly edited for clarity.

DAN: Kara, here at *What Works* we love to hear about origin stories, about what prompts founders to do the hard work that it takes to launch an independent newsroom. Why did you decide to leave the *Santa Cruz Sentinel*, and what was it about that experience that made you want to do things differently?

KARA: When I was promoted to the top editor position at the *Sentinel* in 2017, I thought I was set for life and thought that this was going to be the last job I'd ever have. A couple months into the position, it became clear that was not going to be the case. I resigned in 2018. Stephen randomly reached out to me on Twitter and said, "Let's start a competitor." I jumped in with both feet. I was working full-time on the idea. I just knew I wanted to be in local journalism serving Santa Cruz County, and the only option was to start our own project. We both felt strongly that Santa Cruz and Santa Cruz County deserved a stronger, fair, accurate, and sustainable local news source.

DAN: What it was like to launch and then later to have a well-funded, high-profile competitor arrive in the form of Ken Doctor's *Lookout Santa Cruz*? How would you differentiate between what he's doing and what you're doing? And do you think there's room for both of you?

KARA: *Lookout* is starting off with, comparatively speaking, an enormous amount of seed money that comes from institutional funders across the country—and starting out big. Our approach, in contrast, is starting out small. We started out with the money that we had in our pockets. And we're really taking it slow, trying to build the products and approach along with the communities that we're trying to serve, asking people at every step of the way: What kind of news do you want? How do you want it delivered? And fine-tuning our product as we grow in cooperation with our audience, which is constantly growing and changing. We're iterating, testing, researching, just doing that over and over, running experiments to see what works. I think there needs to be a transformational change in how philanthropy works in local journalism and how funding of new startups works. It's working, but I think it could be a lot better.

ELLEN: Dan and I love to hear about the nuts and bolts of how things work in newsrooms, and I think our listeners do too. Could you expand a little on how everything comes together? What size is your newsroom? How do you manage coverage, investigations, a podcast, and a newsletter with a relatively small staff?

KARA: Right now we have a staff of four. Our newest hire started last week, and her role is to interview Latinos and Spanish speakers in our county to understand what kind of news they want and how they want it delivered. We're developing a new product to serve Spanish speakers, and we want to base it off what we're hearing from the community. Our staffing is structured so that community listening and community engagement are core to what we do. We rely on freelancers for a lot of our stories, we assign out a lot of local government coverage.

DAN: I'm going to ask you a two-part question. I should note that you have said you have more than six thousand newsletter subscribers and about seven hundred paid members. I'd like to know, first of all, what's your revenue mix? What's the balance between membership, business sponsorship, grant funding, and advertising? And the second part of the question is this: So many smaller local news startups are nonprofit. Why did you and Stephen decide to go the for-profit route?

KARA: We started with a for-profit limited liability corporation (LLC) framework because it was the easiest thing to launch. It took me two days to set up the LLC in California. But as we're growing, we are thinking about a possible nonprofit approach. In the last maybe fifteen months, we have had a

fiscal sponsor, the Lenfest Institute, which allows us to get
tax-exempt gifts that are generally $5,000 or more. And it
has allowed us to test to see if this revenue stream works
for us. Membership right now is about 30 percent of our
revenue, grants are about 15 percent, and fiscal sponsorship—that is, nonprofit funding coming through the *Local*'s
arrangement with the Lenfest Institute—is about 40 percent.
Over 2021, we've raised about $125,000 in revenue from the
fiscal sponsorship, which is a huge chunk of our operating
budget of about $200,000.

ELLEN: You've made this concerted effort to hear from readers
to identify issues. Can you talk a little about exactly how
that works?

KARA: It dovetails so neatly with our revenue model of memberships and philanthropic gifts. What we're trying to do with
our approach is to build a relationship with our community. This is really important for our industry as a whole: to
make an intentional effort to build trust with the community
that you're trying to serve. We have running surveys that are
automated through Zapier [a software tool that automates
routine online operations]. When people join our newsletter,
they get a welcome series. And in one of the emails we ask
them, what's at the top of your mind right now? What local
issue is pressing on you? What kind of news are you looking for? The other big part of our community engagement is
in-person listening. Our election reporting started with an intense listening tour, going around to twelve places around the
county and doing quick five-minute interviews. We're trying
to include voices that we wouldn't hear in an online survey—
people who might not have access to a computer.

DAN: You've also given back through your work with the Tiny
News Collective. Could you tell our listeners about that?

KARA: The Tiny News Collective is a new nonprofit that helps
communities start newsrooms. It provides the tools like a
ready-made website, a newsletter process that's ready to go,
and training. It will also help you get set up with a fiscal

sponsor. That just makes it a lot easier for news entrepreneurs to get their projects off the ground. There are about sixteen founders that are part of the collective so far, and the Tiny News Collective is looking to ramp up very quickly, with a goal of reaching a thousand new entrepreneurs in the next three years. Independent online news startups are the future of local media, and we need to make it a lot easier for news entrepreneurs from communities of color, from historically underrepresented backgrounds, to launch these companies.

CHAPTER FIVE

MEMPHIS, TENNESSEE

*A Digital Newsroom Holds
Power to Account*

To understand how far Wendi Thomas has come, it's instructive to look at where she started. On April 4, 2022, Thomas celebrated the fifth anniversary of the launch of *MLK50: Justice Through Journalism*. The newsroom team linked arms in front of the vibrant "I Am A Man" mural on South Main Street in Memphis. They were sending an unmistakable signal: this is what success looks like. Founding editor and publisher Wendi C. Thomas and her staff, including executive editor Adrienne Johnson Martin, visuals editor Andrea Morales, digital editor Stephanie Wilson, and reporters Carrington J. Tatum and Jacob Steimer, were not merely marking an anniversary. They were also marking their success in carving out a place in the media ecosystem of Memphis—and making an impact with "unapologetically progressive"[1] watchdog coverage in a newsroom led by three women of color that focuses on the intersection of power, poverty, and justice.

But about that beginning: Thomas launched *MLK50* on April 4, 2017, using $3,000 borrowed from friends and family and living off credit cards for the first year and a half so she could use what revenue was coming in to pay freelancers. The site was originally intended as a one-year project amplifying the purpose of Dr. Martin Luther King Jr.'s last trip to Memphis, on April 3, 1968—he was there to support striking sanitation workers in their fight for a living wage. By many accounts, King was tired and troubled, concerned about the future of his movement. History records how it ended. But King's focus on the deep racial and economic disparities in Memphis during his last visit was an inspiration for Thomas as she built out her digital news site some fifty years later. As she put it in the *MLK50* mission statement, she intended to "examine the systems that make it hard for workers to make ends meet and interrogate those who profit from the status quo."[2]

Thomas, who grew up in Memphis, chose her launch date for its historical resonance. In retrospect, King's preaching that night seems prophetic: "Like anybody, I would like to live a long life—longevity has its place. But I'm not concerned about that now. . . . I've seen the Promised Land. I may not get there with you. But I want you to know tonight that we, as a people, will get to the Promised Land."[3] He was assassinated the next night, on April 4, at the Lorraine Motel—now the site of the National Civil Rights Museum. A white wreath hangs on the railing in front of the motel's second-floor balcony, devastatingly familiar from news footage. A tour through the museum ends in a stunned silence—a silence that just might be called worshipful— for a group of ticket holders peering into the motel room where King spent his last night.

Thomas nurtured her idea as a Nieman Fellow in the class of 2015 in Cambridge, Massachusetts. Thomas was one of twenty-four journalists selected for the program, which offers a paid fellowship and the opportunity to attend classes at Harvard University. A cum laude graduate of the journalism program at Butler University in Indianapolis, Thomas planned to research and test her theories on how to deepen public conversations about economic justice.

She brought experience as an editor and manager, columnist, and investigative reporter, having worked for metro papers in the Midwest, South, and Southeast, including the *Indianapolis Star*, *The Tennessean* in Nashville, *The Charlotte Observer* in North Carolina, and *The Commercial Appeal* in Memphis. At *The Commercial Appeal*, she won a number of awards and was inducted into the Scripps Howard Hall of Fame for commentary in 2008. She left that paper in 2014, becoming a visiting scholar at the University of Memphis.

From the outset, Thomas planned a website with no paywall. "I think *MLK50* fills a very specific niche in Memphis, where we're really centering the people that Dr. King would be centering if he were still alive," Thomas told us.[4] Reasoning that paid subscriptions would pose a barrier for residents in a city where the overall poverty rate is slightly more than 21 percent and median income for Black households is about $35,000,[5] Thomas decided to pursue a diverse revenue model funded by donations, grants, and sponsorships from individuals, organizations, and foundations. She said she is committed to making "content accessible to the general public regardless of ability to pay."[6]

Despite starting on a shoestring, Thomas would soon make an enduring impact. She won the prestigious 2020 Selden Ring Award for Investigative Reporting for a 2019 series that exposed aggressive debt collection practices by a large Memphis hospital affiliated with the Methodist Church.[7] The *MLK50* series, titled "Profiting from the Poor," was produced in partnership with the Local Reporting Network at *ProPublica*—a nonprofit that provides additional resources for local journalists working on investigative projects—and led to significant reforms.[8] The hospital erased millions in medical debt for its poorest patients and raised the salaries of its low-wage workers.

As Thomas planned her newsroom, she knew what she didn't want. "When I worked at the daily paper in Memphis, if you made a list of people who were quoted on the front page, maybe 95 percent would be white. Maybe 85 percent were men. And this is in a city that is 66 percent Black," she told an audience at the International Journalism Festival in Perugia, Italy, in 2022.[9] At *MLK50*, she would not only hire a staff that matched the racial makeup of the community it served; she would also conduct audits to ensure that stories quoted a diverse array of sources.

"I was at *The Commercial Appeal* for eleven years," she told us.[10] "Just by way of context: When I left the paper in 2014, there were two Black women in the city's history that had written reported commentary. That was me and Ida B. Wells." Wells, a Black editor and co-owner of *The Free Speech and Headlight* newspaper in Memphis, investigated the lynching of Black men by white mobs. On May 27, 1892, while Wells was visiting Philadelphia, a white mob destroyed her newspaper's office in Memphis and threatened her life if she returned to the city.[11] Wells relocated and is buried in Chicago.

"Objectivity, as a lot of journalists have said, just meant cis, het-ero, American-born, able-bodied, likely Protestant white men. That's all it meant," Thomas said. "That demographic is not the majority of Memphis. So, if we were to reflect that position, we would be a niche publication."

Back in Memphis, she began building. She moved from relying on freelancers to hiring staff and moved into an office at the non-profit Memphis Music Initiative, which donated space. She received national grants from the Surdna Foundation, the Jonathan Logan Family Foundation, Borealis Philanthropy, the Emerson Collective, and the American Journalism Project, among other philanthropic or-ganizations. A member of the Institute for Nonprofit News, *MLK50* abides by INN's standards for fiscal transparency.[12]

The Selden Ring award prompted additional interest from fund-raisers. Other awards have followed. The eighty-eighth annual Head-liner Award from the Press Club of Atlantic City, a venerable group that honors journalistic merit nationwide, recognized a series of stories about the fight against the Byhalia Connection Pipeline written by twenty-three-year-old staffer and Report for America corps member Carrington J. Tatum, a graduate of Texas State University who joined *MLK50* in the fall of 2020.[13]

Tatum broke the story about the use of the power of eminent do-main to seize land from Black homeowners for the pipeline and wrote nearly forty stories that "gave Black residents the fortitude to fight," the judges wrote. "The issue got so big that even former Vice President Al Gore weighed in on the controversy."[14] Tatum's series recounted the successful effort by Memphians to fight plans by Plains All America Pipeline and Valero Energy Corporation to build the Byhalia Connec-tion Pipeline through Southwest Memphis, a majority Black neighbor-hood. Residents, who saw the pipeline as a threat to the city's water supply, led months of protests. In July 2021, the developers canceled the project, citing a drop in oil production during the pandemic. But Gore attributed the cancellation to community activism, tweeting: "Byhalia Pipeline canceled! Congrats to @MemphisCAP_org & the community of SW Memphis who made their voices heard to stop this reckless, racist ripoff! No more oil in our soil!"[15]

He made some headlines of his own in June 2022 when he wrote a guest essay about leaving *MLK50* and moving back home to Texas because his rent had increased and he couldn't maintain payments on his student loans, which amounted to $90,000 after he graduated. "I realized that if I'm going to stay ahead of student loans and survive, I need to make a lot more money," Tatum wrote, adding that "the best money I can make in journalism isn't paid for the stories I want to do: justice reporting from the ground up."[16] Thomas wrote a companion essay about Tatum's dilemma, rising rents, and her responsibility as a founder. Her take was well-researched, painstakingly honest—and pulled no punches: "That I wasn't aware until it was too late is a reflection of my shortcomings. I knew student loans are a millstone around too many necks and I knew rents were rising, but I didn't know how much it was cratering a colleague's career plans."[17]

Thomas's research showed that salaries at *MLK50* were better than average "in a city where historically, living expenses have been low." Tatum's total compensation when he resigned was just under $50,000. Thomas, whose overall budget for *MLK50* in 2022 was just over $1 million, concluded: "We're talking to other newsrooms and trying to figure out what we could do now, what we want to be able to do soon, and how to get from here to there. If you've got ideas, let me know."

When it comes to keeping her newsroom funded and functioning, Thomas speaks openly about the difficulty journalists of color face in raising philanthropic dollars. "The evidence-based rigor we demand in other sectors doesn't seem to apply here," she told us. "The threshold to become a newsroom founder is too high and the sacrifices required of some (women, people of color, those who aren't well-connected) are obscene."[18]

She added that she is increasingly uncomfortable being held up as a model and ticks off some of her advantages: "Single, no kids, no partner, and I'm not a caregiver, which means I could work eighteen-hour days for weeks on end. All of that also made it easy to uproot myself and do a Nieman Fellowship, which gave me access to an incredible network of well-connected alums. I got my start at a union paper, so I've always been paid well in the business—which means I had some savings to tap into while launching *MLK50*. I've had wonderful mentors at several papers and the opportunity to gain the solid reporting/editing skills that make me good at my job. But when I look across the industry for other Black journalists who have had the same mix of experience, there aren't many, not because they're not talented, but because they didn't have rainmakers to create the opportunity."[19]

One such person she did find was Evan Smith, the cofounder and CEO of *The Texas Tribune*, the digital nonprofit launched in 2009 that is considered a model by many entrepreneurial journalists we have interviewed on our *What Works* podcast. Smith announced in January 2022 that he intended to step down at the end of the year, prompting an outpouring of memories and praise on social media.[20] Thomas took to Twitter to recount her experience listening to Smith on a webinar about nurturing digital newsrooms.

In the webinar's chat room, Thomas said, she asked about strategies that might work for a newsroom like hers. The moderator invited Thomas to unmute and ask her question live, and she said that Smith also unmuted and said he intended to help her solve that problem. "AND THEN HE DID," Thomas tweeted. "Evan has been generous with his time, advice, and connections. I can count well over six figures that came directly from his leads. . . . Evan has been a mentor, but more importantly, he's been a rainmaker. The startup life can be incredibly lonely, but it gets easier when someone of Evan's caliber supports you."[21]

That lonely feeling reflects a challenging reality. According to Borealis Philanthropy, which focuses on social justice and transformation, between 2009 and 2015 a scant 6 percent of the $1.2 billion in grants invested in journalism, news, and information in the United States went to organizations serving specific racial and ethnic groups. Only 7 percent went toward projects that served economically disadvantaged populations.[22]

"After our story about Methodist Hospital published, funders that had told me 'no' called me," Thomas said. "Now nothing had changed—they knew I was working with *ProPublica* when they told me we were risky, we weren't big enough. This is part of why I'm so explicit and vocal about it, because people should not have to clear the bars that I've had to clear."[23]

She has built a diverse team led by three women of color. "People sometimes ask me, 'Are you a Black publication?' And I say, 'Well, 66 percent of Memphis is Black, so by virtue of reflecting our community accurately, most of the faces you are going to see are going to be Black. If you go up to people of color, it's about 75 percent," Thomas said. "If we look like our community, it's going to be mostly people of color. I don't think that makes us a Black publication."

In addition to her editing and fundraising duties, Thomas has continued to partner with *ProPublica*, including a 2020 examination of workplace safety at FedEx, Memphis's main employer, after Duntate Young, a twenty-three-year-old temporary worker, died in an accident on the job.[24] (The investigation was published on both the *MLK50* and *ProPublica* websites.) And while covering a trial for *MLK50* about police surveillance, Thomas found out that she herself was part of the story. She wrote about her experience for *ProPublica*: "On Aug. 20, 2018, the first day of a federal police surveillance trial, I discovered that the Memphis Police Department was spying on me."[25]

The ACLU of Tennessee had sued the Memphis Police Department (MPD), alleging that the department had violated a 1978 consent decree that barred police from conducting surveillance of residents for political purposes. Thomas reported that she had her head down and was writing in her reporter's notebook when she heard her name intoned by a police officer on the witness stand. The officer, who was white, said he had posed as a "man of color" on a fake "undercover" Facebook account to monitor activism and protests around the Black Lives Matter movement. The officer testified that he was following Thomas's account. Thomas was shocked, and she never received an answer about why she was being tracked. "My sin, as best I can figure, was having good sources who were local organizers and activists, including some of the original plaintiffs in the ACLU's lawsuit against the city," she wrote.[26]

Thomas filed a public records request with the city of Memphis, asking for "all joint intelligence briefings, emails or other documents that referenced me or any of the three other journalists that the MPD was following on social media."

She wrote that she was puzzled by the results that came back more than a year later: some screenshots of seemingly benign social media posts sharing information about grassroots coalition meetings or public demonstrations. "I still don't understand what would make police see me as a threat worthy of surveillance in the name of public safety," she wrote.

Thomas would challenge the establishment again when the Reporters Committee for Freedom of the Press and the Memphis law firm Adams and Reese filed a public records lawsuit. Thomas and The Marshall Project, a nonprofit that covers criminal justice issues, were the named plaintiffs in the suit against the Memphis Shelby Crime Commission, which sought to make public a donor list for corporations that contributed to the commission, a nonprofit that raised millions of dollars in private funds to aid the Memphis Police Department.[27] She reasoned that because the commission was helping steer criminal justice policy in the city, the donor list should be open to public scrutiny.

The suit contended that the commission—whose fifty-member board includes Memphis mayor Jim Strickland and other public officials—was the "functional equivalent" of a government agency and thus subject to public disclosure laws. A list of names was eventually released.

"We won, not in court but in a settlement," Thomas told us. "Now this nonprofit that sets criminal justice policy hand-in-hand with the police department has to say who is giving them money. It was a lot of big corporate folks, institutions with a vested interest in protecting their investment but not necessarily the people of the city. And, so, that was a win. My lawyer said there's more information available now about this nonprofit than there ever has been available before because of the lawsuit. I'm sure that doesn't win me a lot of friends."

As a columnist writing about race, class, and justice for *The Commercial Appeal*, Thomas realizes, she amplified issues that challenged the status quo in Memphis. "Getting local funding has been really challenging," she said. "That's why national foundations have been so critical to our success and will remain so. But again, nobody owes us any money, right? I've got to be able to make the case for support. Like any nonprofit newsroom, we want to diversify our revenue streams. We do get a decent bit of money from local small donors. But we also want to think about—what does a membership program look like?"[28]

Her first national funder came from a philanthropic organization that wasn't known for backing journalism: the Surdna Foundation, which supports nonprofits devoted to solving "many of the long-term and embedded social, environmental, economic and cultural challenges that communities across the United States face."[29] As Thomas put it: "They believed in the mission and believed in the dream well before I could get any journalism funder to believe in the mission and the dream. Maybe a path forward for other nonprofit newsrooms is to look outside to supporters that believe in the underlying values of the organization. And see journalism as a tool to achieve that."

As revenue from philanthropic donations grew, she not only paid off that initial credit card debt, she also set a path for growth. In December 2019, *MLK50* received a grant in the first round awarded by the then-new American Journalism Project (AJP), a nonprofit dedicated to supporting local civic news organizations—a total of $178,000 over two years to be used for business and revenue development.[30] Ann Marie Lipinski, curator of the Nieman Foundation, tweeted her support with a "special hurrah" and noted: "So much to do; this is a start."[31] As *Nieman Lab* reported, AJP—cofounded by Elizabeth Green of *Chalkbeat* and John Thornton of *Texas Tribune* fame—raised $46 million to form a venture philanthropy fund to support civic-minded local news outlets. AJP funders include the Knight Foundation, Emerson Collective, Craig Newmark Philanthropies, Democracy Fund, and the Facebook Journalism Project.[32]

MLK50 lists donors who give $5,000 or more per year and prominently posts its commitment to transparency and an independent newsroom: "Our news judgments are made independently—not based on or influenced by donors. We do not give supporters the rights to assign, review or edit content."[33] One supporter listed, Kathleen

Kingsbury, is opinion editor of *The New York Times*. Kingsbury and her husband, Brian Hindo, donated in the $5,000–$9,999 category. Asked why she became a donor, Kingsbury told us: "*MLK50* shows what happens when you marry a deep knowledge of a community and the challenges it faces with strong investigative muscle and journalistic instinct. The medical claims investigative work Wendi and her team accomplished and the impact it had for the people affected is, to my mind, the best version of local journalism we have today, and that is something worth investing in."[34]

Thomas is still building readership and a newsletter subscriber base. She'd like to reach people who are not on social media and has experimented with distributing printouts of stories. She noted that the pandemic curtailed the all-important in-person reporting her staff does: walking door-to-door and riding buses to talk with residents about their lives.

"I know we have a lot of work to do in terms of becoming recognized among just regular workers who aren't part of social justice networks," she said. "We already have a really solid following, but it's a work in progress." Founding a digital newsroom means more than just finding freelancers and hiring reporters, she noted: it means devoting resources to the business side of publishing. In September 2022, *MLK50* advertised for its first full-time development director, with a goal of ensuring long-term sustainability. She has never lost sight of her goal: "To make a measurable, tangible difference in the lives of people in Memphis."[35]

Otis Sanford, a columnist and longtime editor and reporter in Memphis who now teaches journalism at the University of Memphis, observed, "[*MLK50*] fills a niche that nobody else is filling. They're covering underserved populations. They are dealing with the issues that affect people who are marginalized or overlooked or taken advantage of in the community. I don't know that they intended to go more than a year or so, but it's an outstanding digital site." He told us that Thomas was already a noteworthy columnist and added: "She's not only an in-your-face journalist, she's also just very thoughtful. The Methodist Hospital story got picked up by all the news organizations, and it forced the hospital to make those changes. It was an outstanding piece of journalism."[36]

Richard Thompson, a former *Commercial Appeal* business writer who now runs the Mediaverse website, mediaversememphis.com, which tracks developments in Memphis news organizations, told us that *MLK50* "is on the leading edge of what I would call counter-journalism, journalism that goes against the narrative and clarifies what's really going on in the city." In a city with a Black majority, Thompson noted, "I'm very proud of the fact that it's predominantly run by women and led by Black women. That's a significant shift and a significant moment for our city."[37]

As Thomas told a panel at the International Journalism Festival in April 2022, "I think what makes us different than other news outlets is that we do start with some foundational truths. Workers deserve enough to live on. Health care is a human right. LGBTQ+ rights are human rights. And that's just the side that we're on. We want to disrupt the status quo where it has not been in service of vulnerable people. And that really means challenging power and authority. We believe that supports democracy. We want to give residents the information that they need to then persuade policymakers to be more fair and more just. Because if it's not journalism who's going to save democracy or be part of saving democracy, who's going to do that?"[38]

By the summer of 2022, COVID-19 had lifted a bit, and we traveled to Memphis to tour the airy *MLK50* newsroom on the first floor of the Memphis Music Initiative (MMI). Thomas recalled the early days, when she was the sole employee working on the Methodist Hospital investigation in a compact first-floor office at MMI. She's still there. Posters are still taped to her office wall, covered with a rainbow of Post-It Notes from strategy and visioning sessions. One note reads: "Scare the people who need to be scared."

MLK50's core principles were much in evidence as we went around the conference table and talked during the briefing session and afterward. Visuals director Andrea Morales, who said she is Peruvian by birth, Miami-bred, and Memphis-based, talked passionately about the need to "do no harm" by seeking consent for photos in an era of law enforcement surveillance in public spaces, adding: "We want to re-enfranchise people's relationship to us as media makers."[39] The executive editor, Adrienne Johnson Martin, explained how she frames stories and works with reporters who are eager to gain experience. "We start stories with *MLK50* values in mind: power, poverty, policy. We ask questions as we are starting to think about stories: Who's being harmed, how many are being harmed, who's doing the harming?"[40] She also provides coaching and training for young reporters, promising them, "This is a place where you can get better," and she sits down with them and works through the chapters of *Wordcraft: The Complete Guide to Clear, Powerful Writing*, by journalist and writing coach Jack Hart.

A writer with a flowing and elegant style, Johnson Martin brings her own experience as a Black journalist to bear. She has worked at *Duke Magazine*, *The News & Observer* in Raleigh, North Carolina, and the *Los Angeles Times*, where she was part of the 1994 Pulitzer Prize–winning spot news team that covered the Northridge earthquake. Her attention to editing and storytelling is apparent on the website. "I talk about clarity and rhythm," Johnson Martin said. "And we listen to their own vision for their work."

In five years, Thomas noted, *MLK50* had moved from an annual budget of $150,000 to $1 million. She hoped to have a $2.3 million budget by fiscal 2024 and ticked off more goals: beef up the revenue side, hire someone full-time who is committed to revenue, and shore up engagement with the community. The night after the newsroom briefing, *MLK50* threw a fifth-birthday party at Brickwood Hall, an event space in a former cotton-sorting warehouse. Strings of twinkling lights and scattered rose petals contrasted with the funky industrial space. An exhibit of Morales's vivid photos adorned the walls. There were food and drink stations, a dance floor, and a DJ.

The anniversary party was also a chance to let loose with an outburst of joy, for the staff of *MLK50* and for its champions and sponsors in the room. Speakers noted that Thomas had just been awarded the 2022 "Local Champion" Freedom of the Press Award by the Reporters Committee for Freedom of the Press.[41]

Torrey Harris, a member of the Tennessee House of Representatives, surprised Thomas with a proclamation signed by House Speaker Cameron Sexton that expressed "gratitude for her effective journalism and leadership." A few tears flowed, and Thomas took to a microphone onstage and quoted Ida B. Wells: "The people must know before they can act, and there is no educator to compare with the press." Then she added her own coda: "The press is also a learner." The audience, which included her parents, Merle and Russell Thomas, stood and applauded, and the staff stepped off the stage to take a well-deserved turn on the dance floor as the music began to thump.

Make no mistake: Memphis doesn't meet the definition of a news desert. The city of 635,000 people is served by *The Commercial Appeal*, *MLK50*, *The Daily Memphian*, a *Chalkbeat* site, business publications, a public television station, public radio, and broadcast television newsrooms. Indeed, it would seem like there's much to cover in this metropolitan area of some 1.2 million people, which has a storied place in music history—from Elvis Presley to "Father of the Blues" bandleader W.C. Handy—and is home to companies and nonprofits like FedEx, International Paper, AutoZone, and St. Jude Children's Research Hospital.[42] Yet the metro newspaper, *The Commercial Appeal*, has endured rounds of downsizing through three changes of ownership in the last decade. The newspaper, once known for its robust regional coverage of and influence in Tennessee, Arkansas, Mississippi, and parts of Missouri, had been owned by the E.W. Scripps Company since 1936.[43] The paper won a Pulitzer Prize for Public Service in 1923 for its "courageous attitude" in publishing critical editorial cartoons and news coverage about the Ku Klux Klan.[44] (Scripps shut down the afternoon paper, the *Memphis Press-Scimitar*, in 1983.)[45] It was once a paper with an ambitious newsroom of more than two hundred journalists, a place to make a career.

In 2015, Scripps merged with Milwaukee-based Journal Communications Corporation, and the newspapers were rolled into a new company, Journal Media Group. But that didn't last long in a period of consolidation and closures that prompted writer James Fallows to warn of "the Great Extinction of local and regional papers."[46] In 2016, the Journal Media Group, which also included the *Knoxville News Sentinel*, was sold to Gannett for $280 million, effectively giving the chain a lock on Tennessee; it already owned *The Tennessean*, in the capital city of Nashville. Mark Russell became the first African American executive editor of *The Commercial Appeal* in 2017 after serving as interim executive editor.[47]

Unfortunately, Gannett soon deployed cost-cutting strategies. The newsroom continued to shrink; as of mid-2022, *The Commercial Appeal* website listed twenty-seven staff members.[48] The company moved *The Commercial Appeal*'s printing operations from Memphis to Jackson, Mississippi, in 2017, and sold the longtime headquarters in 2019, moving to a smaller office downtown.[49] The vacant old *Commercial Appeal* building was turned into a COVID-19 overflow hospital in 2020.[50] That hospital facility was closed in July 2021 without having treated any patients.[51] In January 2022, the newspaper announced it was dropping its Saturday print edition—both home-delivery and newsstand sales.[52] The total combined average paid circulation for *The Commercial Appeal* for the six-month period ending March 31, 2022, was slightly more than 29,000 for Sunday and about 21,000 for weekdays, with more than 10,000 digital subscriptions.[53] But those numbers show a significant drop. Just six years earlier, in 2016, paid circulation was 103,300 on Sunday and 67,000 daily.[54]

Gannett's Tennessee network echoes other statewide content-sharing networks, such as those set up by NJ Advance Media in New Jersey and Hearst's Connecticut Media Group, which are described elsewhere in this book. Although Memphis, Knoxville, and Nashville have distinct identities, *The Commercial Appeal* benefits from publishing news about the state legislature and state budget from *The Tennessean* without having to field a statehouse bureau. But hyperlocal stories didn't always resonate when published beyond their home region. Sanford, the *Commercial Appeal* columnist, said there have been fewer of those of late. "I think it depends on what the stories are," he told us in June 2022 on our *What Works* podcast. "If they are broad statewide stories like what's going on in the legislature or what the governor is doing or economic development issues that would apply statewide, then it's fine. But everything else is not well-received, especially here in Memphis."[55]

Sanford is something of a journalistic legend in Memphis. He covered the death of Elvis Presley as a young general assignment reporter for *The Commercial Appeal* in 1977. He told us that while *The Commercial Appeal* is "still a force in this community, it has nowhere near the level of influence and reach that it historically has had."

Confronted with a metro newspaper that seemed diminished in staff and scope, in 2014 a group of civic-minded Memphians began discussing making a bid to buy *The Commercial Appeal* or launch a competitor. That competitor turned out to be *The Daily Memphian*, a digital startup. "There was a widespread feeling [the *Appeal*] wasn't our paper anymore," Eric Barnes, CEO and interim executive editor of the *Memphian*, told us in an interview in June 2022 at a sun-splashed coffee shop in the city's South Main Arts District.[56]

"We tried to buy *The Commercial Appeal* about seven or eight years ago," Memphis businessman Andy Cates told us in a Zoom interview in April 2022. "I've always been a believer in the critical role of the Fourth Estate, and I think any healthy city must have a newspaper of record. But I'm deeply grateful I failed [to buy the *Appeal*], partly because I've been humbled by how hard the business is."[57]

Cates said he is a "deep believer" in a nonprofit model for local newsrooms in mid-sized and smaller cities, in part because such models turn on "a clear mission that you're doing it for community service and for social good." Yet, he makes clear, he believes a nonprofit should be run like a business, with a diverse revenue stream, sustainable for the long run. Cates, the CEO of RVC Outdoor Destinations, was part of a successful effort to bring the Grizzlies NBA team to Memphis from Vancouver, among other projects, and began pulling together a fundraising campaign for what would become *The*

Daily Memphian. His partner on the publishing and newsroom side: Barnes, a PBS host, novelist, and publisher of a group of community newspapers in Tennessee as well as the former president of the Tennessee Press Association. Originally from the Pacific Northwest, Barnes holds a graduate degree from Columbia University in fine arts and worked in a small newsroom in Connecticut early in his career as well as for business magazines.[58]

Fielding a team of reporters, editors, and others who are veterans of *The Commercial Appeal* or other local publications, *The Daily Memphian* launched in 2018. The site draws revenue from paid subscriptions, advertising, sponsored events, and philanthropic donations to Memphis Fourth Estate, Inc., an umbrella nonprofit that owns and operates the *Memphian*. Cates, a University of Texas at Austin graduate in business who is also a partner in Value Acquisition Fund, an asset management company he founded, serves as president and chair of the *Memphian*'s nine-person board of directors.

As media-business analyst Ken Doctor wrote in 2020, "First and foremost, *The Daily Memphian* aims to be a *replacement* news company—the primary supplier of local news and information for its area."[59] By many accounts, a replacement paper, even one transported into the digital era, aims to deliver a bundle of coverage—local news, politics, events, sports, and business developments—that generations of readers came to expect from their print metro daily. And like that metro daily, which might once have cost a quarter a copy in a news box, then eventually much more, *The Daily Memphian* charges for subscriptions.

In 2021, the site reported revenue of $7 million from a mix of subscriptions, donations, and philanthropic grants, as well as events and podcasts. In May 2022, when we interviewed Cates, he reported that the *Memphian* had 16,500 subscribers who pay an average of $100 a year; there is sometimes a "light discount," he said, but not the deep "Gannett 99 cents." The site uses Piano as its paywall platform, and, like many digital newsrooms, continues to analyze metrics and tweak the number of stories readers can sample for free without subscribing. "We have about 60,000 emails with a high open rate," Cates told us. Without disclosing specific numbers, Cates said, "We're seeing growing traffic, and we are having a bigger impact than even that 16,500 would tell you."

Barnes holds the title of CEO but added the job of acting executive editor when newsroom leader Ronnie Ramos departed for another job in 2022. (Barnes is still listed as CEO of the Daily News Publishing Company, a group of smaller Tennessee papers.) "Memphis is a weird anomaly. We're not a news desert," Barnes told us on a Zoom interview in 2021, "because the Scripps-Media General-GateHouse-Gannett paper has a newsroom of twenty-seven but has the resources, although diminished, of Gannett. But even as a midsized city, Memphis could support the launch of *The Daily Memphian* because there was a desire to have quality local news."[60]

As they prepared to launch in 2018, Cates and Barnes lined up an initial $6.7 million in philanthropic donations. Because the original $6.7 million was donated anonymously, *The Daily Memphian's* fundraising strategy has been called "unorthodox and opaque" by Doctor.[61] The *Memphian* is not a member of INN because it doesn't meet INN's stated standards for transparency in fundraising.[62]

Cates is open about his disagreements with INN and the American Journalism Project, which do not allow members that receive anonymous donations. "I've been involved with nonprofits in Memphis and raised money in Memphis for more than twenty years. It's not sustainable, if you're asking me to raise three million in philanthropic dollars every year. And by the way, if you're not charging for subscriptions, you're saying journalism isn't valuable," Cates said, adding that free subscriptions are provided to schools and libraries, and in underserved neighborhoods.

Cates explained his rationale for allowing anonymous funding. "I know who it comes from. It's local money; there's no clawback. This is a small town, so our journalists would be affected. I mean, positively or not, either trying to overcorrect and prove they're not going to give them a break or going overboard and giving them a break. I think anonymity is a huge advantage, but I understand the trepidation and the concern about it. We can agree to disagree with some people."[63] Doctor was clearly one who disagreed, writing, "Transparency in funding has become a mantra in the nonprofit news movement, and there *The Memphian* is lacking. . . . Keeping the high-rollers anonymous doesn't typically help with conflict-of-interest worries."[64] Listed *Daily Memphian* funders include the Community Foundation of Greater Memphis, the Lenfest Institute, and the Google News Initiative, among others. The Knight Foundation announced a $250,000 grant to the *Memphian* on August 16, 2022.[65]

Barnes describes himself as a paywall evangelist. "We've never devalued the product, and we are a fair price," he told us. His budget is a little over $5 million a year. "We think we can get to three million in subscriptions and two million in advertising, sponsorships, et cetera," he said. Barnes and Cates were hoping to break even by 2023. To offset the subscription fee in a city with a significant population of residents at or below the poverty line, Barnes said, "We're pretty aggressive with free access programs. That will get more aggressive over time." Barnes said *The Daily Memphian* is free in every school—public, private or charter—that wants it and free in every library.

In terms of coverage, *The Daily Memphian* signed marquee sports columnist Geoff Calkins from *The Commercial Appeal*, who drives significant traffic, according to Cates and Barnes. A mix of freelancers and staff serve up news from city hall, the Shelby County Commission, and other government agencies. *The Daily Memphian* runs opinion columns and letters to the editor but does not publish unsigned editorials. (Nonprofit organizations, including news outlets, may not take a stand as an institution in terms of endorsing a political candidate or a specific piece of legislation. They are perfectly free to publish signed opinion pieces. Many nonprofit news outlets choose not to publish unsigned editorials at all.)

In 2018, *The Daily Memphian* partnered with the Institute for Public Service Reporting, an independent corps of reporters led by Marc Perrusquia at the University of Memphis. Under a business arrangement, *The Daily Memphian* has first crack at publishing the institute's investigative reporting in return for providing some funding.[66] Perrusquia won numerous awards for his watchdog reporting during a twenty-nine-year career at *The Commercial Appeal*. At the institute, Perrusquia has reported on secrecy at the Tennessee Valley Authority, and, with the Reporters Committee for Freedom of the

Press, sued the Memphis Police Department under the Tennessee Public Records Act to obtain the records of police officers who were subject to disciplinary proceedings.[67]

Although affiliated with the University of Memphis, Perrusquia emphasized that the institute retains editorial independence: "We're here to be real journalists and do real independent investigative and enterprise reporting without being controlled or influenced by the state or the university. I consider that to be a very important firewall."[68] Perrusquia also told us that he embarks on Freedom of Information Act "crusades" because "there's a whole culture that's grown up where it's so hard to get information these days. It's all over the country, but it's especially intense here in Memphis."

When we met Barnes at a coffeeshop in Memphis in June 2022, he thoughtfully took stock of his goals.[69] The cafe was suffused with a cosmopolitan bustle—the night before marked the Memphis premiere of the Baz Luhrmann biopic *Elvis* at Graceland, and the film attracted movie stars, fans, influencers, and Elvis scholars (yes, it's a thing).[70] Amid all that Elvis energy, Barnes talked business. He said his search was still under way for a new executive editor for his thirty-eight-person newsroom—he had a budget for forty and hoped to add more. He had nine additional staff working in sales, marketing, tech, and audience development. Like many newsrooms, the *Memphian* dropped its paywall for COVID-19 coverage for a time, although when we talked the wall was back up. Barnes said, "We're trying to strike a balance of getting people to pay for our journalism, along with our civic responsibility."

CHAPTER SIX

MENDOCINO COUNTY, CALIFORNIA

A Rural Startup Seeks to Find Its Footing

About fifteen people had gathered on the second floor of the Ukiah Brewing Company, a craft beer and burger place near the court-house in downtown Ukiah, California. It was Super Tuesday, March 3, 2020, and these locals, mostly supporters of Bernie Sanders, were hanging out and watching the returns on a television set in the corner that was tuned to CNN. Their optimism would soon turn to disappointment. Though Sanders, an independent socialist seeking the Democratic nomination, would take California easily, the big winner of the night was Joe Biden—a victory that ultimately would propel him to the presidency.[1]

The sponsor of the event was *The Mendocino Voice*, at that time a three-and-a-half-year-old, two-person digital news operation covering Mendocino County. The cofounders, publisher Kate Maxwell and managing editor Adrian Fernandez Baumann, were planning a series of such events to generate excitement and support for an idea that they envisioned would put their project on a more viable, democratic path: to reorganize the *Voice* as a cooperatively managed enterprise under the control of what they also envisioned would be a growing roster of employees as well as members of the public. "We are going to be owned by our readers and our staff," Maxwell told the crowd. "We think that's the best way to be sustainable and locally owned."

As it happened, that would be the last in-person event the *Voice* would hold for at least the next two years. That Thursday, at a news conference at the county offices just outside downtown Ukiah, officials gave their first briefing on what was then still being referred to as "the novel coronavirus." The interim public health officer, Dr. Noemi Doohan, assured everyone there were no cases in Mendocino County at that moment. A poster was unveiled showing a fist bump with the caption "Safer Than a Handshake—Cooler Than a Wave," a piece of advice that would soon seem woefully inadequate as the nation, and much of the world, entered lockdown mode. Baumann broadcast the video to the *Voice*'s Facebook page, his iPhone mounted to a tripod, while Maxwell took notes. There was concern in the crowded, windowless room, but there was no sense that the world was on the brink of the most devastating pandemic in a century.[2]

COVID-19 did not put the *Voice* out of business. More than a hundred local news outlets shut down from the start of the pandemic through the end of 2021.[3] But many startups survived and even thrived because their business models depend more on reader revenue than on advertising—and those readers were hungry for news about how COVID was affecting their community. The *Voice* too experienced modest growth during that period. But the pandemic took a toll in other ways. Baumann departed, taking a personal leave that eventually became permanent. And Maxwell put the co-op initiative on hold, citing the pressure of day-to-day coverage and the impossibility of holding community meetings to explain and refine the idea. "I think we basically had a year's worth of events that we were planning," she lamented in mid–2022.[4]

For years, cooperative ownership has been held out as a promising business model for local news. Similar to a credit union or a food co-op, a news co-op could, at least in theory, foster deep public participation, leading to a new type of news coverage. Depending on how the co-op was organized, employees and the community could take part in setting coverage priorities and even elect the editor. Readers could become members of the co-op by paying a fee or, under some models, by contributing labor, similar to a grocery co-op whose members work at the store once or twice a month.

To date, this idealistic vision for a cooperatively owned community journalism project has largely gone unfulfilled. There are a variety of reasons for that, but a lot of it comes down to sheer complexity.

W. Jeffrey Brown, the founder and chair of the Fourth Estate, a public benefit co-op with an international focus whose activities range from advocacy to operating a wire service with content provided by journalist members, is a strong supporter of cooperative ownership models, but he has no illusions about the degree of difficulty needed to maintain them. "Startups are hard. Journalism startups are harder still. Co-ops are a unique kind of hell for a variety of reasons," said Brown, who's based in Wellington, Florida. "You've got a million things that need to come together in order to make a co-op work." The payoff, he added, is that co-ops are more resilient than other forms of ownership because they are governed through distributed decision-making. "Co-ops last a long time when they have begun to gain traction and reach their critical mass," he told us.[5]

All that may be more than a local news startup can manage. One or two people trying to keep up with the news, with bills, with technical issues, and with everything else that goes into operating a media venture may not have the bandwidth to deal with the added complications of cooperative ownership, whether it's something they pursue at the outset or—as in the case of *The Mendocino Voice*—after several years of operation. Over the course of its existence, the *Voice* has established itself as a crucial part of a regional media environment that has been decimated by hedge-fund ownership. That's a significant accomplishment regardless of its business model.

As with so many similar projects, the *Voice* was begun in response to the depredations of corporate chain ownership. In March 2020, in the cramped second-floor studio at KMEC, a low-power community radio station whose Ukiah offices they sometimes used, Maxwell and Baumann talked about their careers, the origins of the *Voice*, and their hopes for future growth.

In 2016, Maxwell was reporting for *The Willits News*, a twice-weekly paper in Mendocino County that was part of MediaNews Group, which was then also known as Digital First Media. The owner: Alden Global Capital. As she described it, she was making $11 an hour and was fed up with the working conditions. She'd talked with some local residents who wanted more and better news coverage and who encouraged her to do something about it. She left her job and contacted Baumann, who'd preceded her at the *News* and was in the Los Angeles area, where he was trying to find work but kept bumping up against staff cuts at the Alden papers in that region. He'd just had an interview at the *Orange County Register*. It hadn't gone well. He recalled that one person asked him, "How would you feel if we hired you and then laid you off immediately?" It was while he was driving home that he decided to go into business with Maxwell. "I called up Kate and said, 'Yeah, the newspaper is dying,'" he recalled. "'Let's start a newspaper.'"[6]

What Maxwell and Baumann decided to launch wasn't a newspaper. Rather, it was a website, which would save them the cost of printing and distribution but would make it harder to become known in their large, hardscrabble coverage area. A two-hour drive north of San Francisco, Mendocino County is about two-thirds the size of Connecticut. The population, though, is a fraction of that, just a bit more than ninety-one thousand; nearly two-thirds of residents are non-Hispanic white, with Latinos making up around 27 percent of the total. The median household income, about $53,000, is $26,000 below the state average. The largest community is Ukiah, the county seat, with a population of just under seventeen thousand.[7] Ukiah is in the southern portion of the county, toward the eastern border, just west of the rugged Mendocino National Forest. It can take an hour and a half to drive west through the redwood forest out to the Pacific, where towns like Fort Bragg and Mendocino hug the coastline. It is a dauntingly difficult area for just two journalists to cover, but Maxwell and Baumann—with the help of a few freelance contributors—were not deterred. They started publishing that September, their timetable moved up when the prototype of their website accidently became public.

The two cofounders are a study in contrasts. Both in their midthirties at the time of our conversation, Maxwell is angular and softspoken but with a firm, no-nonsense edge when she talks. Baumann is large and garrulous, ever ready to share his philosophy of journalism and of life. Their backgrounds are different as well. Maxwell's father worked on telecommunications policy for the Clinton administration. She lived in San Francisco when she was younger, graduated from Brown University, moved to Portland, Oregon, for a while, and then returned to San Francisco, where she helped run a bookstore for several years. She relocated to Mendocino County temporarily to help a friend and wound up staying, taking a job with the independent *Willits Weekly* before jumping to *The Willits News*. The bookstore, not coincidentally, was cooperatively owned, and would serve in part as the inspiration some years later for attempting to convert the *Voice* to co-op ownership.

Baumann is bicultural—his father is white and from Los Angeles; his mother is from Mexico—and bilingual. Among his tasks at the *Voice* was translating some of its articles into Spanish, especially those with a public-safety dimension, such as coverage of the region's numerous wildfires. Born in Santa Monica, he spent most of his childhood in Whittier, then earned a degree from the University of California at Berkeley. After graduation, he worked in plumbing and carpentry, as a substitute teacher, and in retail. He drifted around Central America and taught English in Mexico City, where he still has family. When the Great Recession hit, he applied to the Columbia School of Journalism but said he flunked out before earning his master's degree. "I have the debt and some of the knowledge," he said, "and none of the credentials." His parents had moved to Mendocino County to retire, and Baumann traveled north to work on their house. His switch to journalism came about after he shot himself through the hand with a nail gun. He took a job at *The Willits News* and left after a year.

The economy of the region that Maxwell and Baumann set out to cover is based, you might say, on weed, wine, and tourism. The recreational use of marijuana has been legal in California since 2016, but the economy of Mendocino County had a significant cannabis component long before then.[8] Early on, the *Voice* had to contend with the perception that the project was being sponsored by marijuana growers. Maxwell and Baumann don't deny that they were approached by people who were looking for a more progressive brand of cannabis coverage, but they insist that the *Voice* has been independent since its debut. "Those rumors have been around," Maxwell said. "The people who were really encouraging us to start something were people in the cannabis industry, and that is in part because they were dissatisfied with coverage in the papers that was very biased toward the sheriff's department. I have been told that a number of prominent people in the cannabis industry are supposedly funding us, but that's not the case."[9]

The *Voice*'s website promises "useful news" for its readers, offering a mix of serious reporting and lighter fare. On an early July day in 2022, for instance, the home page featured stories on a salmon barbecue in Fort Bragg, an update on a nearby wildfire, and a rally in favor of reproductive rights following the US Supreme Court's decision to overturn *Roe v. Wade*. Prominently displayed on the home page was an article on how the public could participate in governmental meetings—a classic example of service journalism that provides information readers can act on.[10] The *Voice* garnered some attention early in its existence from a series of articles Maxwell wrote about Khadijah Britton, a young Indigenous woman who disappeared in 2018.[11] The outlet also carries a lot of political news, including live video coverage of debates. Weeks before the COVID pandemic hit, for instance, the *Voice* hosted a debate among candidates for county supervisor at a bar in Potter Valley. Pulled-pork sandwiches were sold at the event, with the proceeds going to the Ukiah Farmers' Market. It was an ideal way for the *Voice* to raise its profile in a way that underlined its involvement in the community.[12]

Much of the journalism, though, is devoted to breaking news, especially wildfires, which have hit Mendo County with increasing frequency and intensity in recent years. The *Voice* has developed such a reputation for its fire reporting that Maxwell and Baumann were asked to help with a national story published in August 2020 by the Center for Public Integrity on how climate disasters have affected mental health.[13] "We liked working with them, because they had this local knowledge that we don't have. And neither do national investigative reporters," said Kristen Lombardi, who oversaw the project as head of Columbia Journalism Investigations, the Columbia Journalism School's postgraduate reporting program.[14]

The *Voice* depends heavily on Facebook distribution—perhaps more so than on its own website. Although the *Voice* has only rarely paid Facebook to promote certain posts, as of July 2022 its Facebook page had more than twenty thousand followers.[15] Because of that, Maxwell and Baumann have used Facebook as a primary news outlet, especially in emergency situations. That can have unexpected consequences, as they learned in the midst of a particularly serious fire. The sheriff's department asked the *Voice* to get the word out that people living in the national forest would run into danger if they tried to evacuate through the nearby community of Covelo. It was potentially lifesaving information, but Facebook took it down. "It had like a thousand shares in an hour," said Maxwell. "Facebook flagged that post and deleted it." The article was restored about a half-hour later following an uproar from the community. Maxwell said she never got a good explanation of what happened, even after talking with someone from Facebook at a conference. Maybe it was because the algorithms identified it as fake news. Maybe, as Baumann speculated, it was because the article included a reference to "Indian Dick Road." In any case, the experience illustrates the dangers of news organizations that depend on third-party platforms they can't control. Fortunately, Maxwell said, no one was injured as a result of Facebook's arbitrary censorship.

Despite its small population, the region has a rich newspaper history. According to research by Alyssa Ballard, the historian and archivist at the Mendocino County Historical Society, many of the smaller communities had their own sources of news in the late nineteenth and early twentieth century. Ukiah generally had two newspapers, one aligned with the Democratic Party and one with the Republicans. The county's leading paper today, *The Ukiah Daily Journal*, can be traced back under different names to 1860. The county was also home to a significant countercultural back-to-the-land movement in the 1970s, leading to the rise of a free monthly alternative newspaper, *The Mendocino Grapevine*, which published from 1973 to 1986 and whose debut issue featured poetry and recipes as well as reprinted "Mr. Natural" cartoons by the legendary artist R. Crumb.[16]

The Ukiah Daily Journal was acquired by MediaNews Group in 1999, which in turn was absorbed by the hedge fund Alden Global Capital in the early 2010s.[17] By 2020, Alden controlled most of the newspapers in Mendo County: the Journal, the twice-weekly Willits News, and two weeklies, the Fort Bragg Advocate-News and The Mendocino Beacon. In charge of all this was an unprepossessing woman named K. C. Meadows, who was the editor of the Ukiah and Willits papers, the general manager of the two weeklies, and the supervising editor of the Lake County Record-Bee. We met in early 2020 at the Advocate-News's oceanside offices in Fort Bragg, where she was orienting a new editor for the weeklies she'd just brought in from Alden's Enterprise-Record newspaper in nearby Chico. Meadows, a native of New York City, had been at the Journal since 1991 and over the years had seen the newsroom shrink from a dozen or more people to five full-timers spread across the four papers. The Journal's paid circulation had shrunk too, she said, from about ten thousand to five thousand on Sundays and less than that on Tuesday through Saturday; the Journal had stopped printing a paper on Mondays some years earlier.[18] The downsizing had taken a toll. "We hardly do any enterprise work anymore," she said. "Every year, we did one major project—marijuana, prescription drugs, water supply, things like that, just big issues that were affecting the community in one way or another. We won awards for those almost every year. And we just don't have the resources to do that anymore."[19]

Two and a half years later, Alden's footprint in the county was even smaller, as the print edition of The Willits News had been eliminated and the Fort Bragg office had been closed. The Ukiah operations were moved to a small office housing clerical staff while journalists were working from their homes. The news staff had shrunk to three as well.[20]

Meadows blamed much of the news business's woes on the practice of giving away journalism for free on the internet, but she did not spare Alden in her critique. Her papers, she said, were making a profit, but she expressed resignation rather than anger at the reality that those profits weren't being reinvested in journalism. "We make money," she said. "But their budget is their budget. Everybody knows, when you have a corporation that's running things, they're going to take some money out of the property." Even so, she said her staff was still able to do a respectable job of covering day-to-day developments such as city council meetings and police news. "Yes, resources are short, and, God, we wish we had more money, and I wish I had more people, but it's still a darn good job," she said. "I mean, people love these jobs, and there's nothing like being a reporter in a small town. There's just nothing more fun than that."

The Mendocino Voice and the Alden papers represent two legs of the county's media tripod. The third leg is KZYX, a public radio station whose ramshackle headquarters are located in a wooded section of Philo, in the south-central part of the county. We interviewed the program director, Alicia Bales, outdoors on the patio between the main building and a trailer that served as an auxiliary outpost, accompanied by a black and white cat named Pepe. At the time of our interview, the station was carrying news from both NPR and the independent progressive newscast Democracy Now!, and it was in the process of trying to bolster its local coverage. The station had booster signals in Willits and Fort Bragg, which gave it county-wide coverage, and was staffed by nearly a hundred volunteers. "We're a big part of the local media ecosystem here in Mendocino County," Bales said.[21]

Bales's connection to the Voice goes back almost to the beginning. In 2017, she offered to sublet space at KMEC, the tiny community radio station and environmental center where she was volunteering at the time and where we interviewed Maxwell and Baumann. By 2020, she was partnering with the Voice on stories, putting Maxwell and Baumann on the air and making plans to share a Report for America journalist with them. "Anything that's going on, they're covering it," Bales said. "I have no idea how they do it."

The county is served by several smaller news outlets as well. One of those, Willits Weekly, where Kate Maxwell got her start, is a free paper supported by donations and advertising. The Weekly was cofounded in the early 2010s by Jennifer Poole, the publisher and editor, and Maureen Jennison, the art director and photographer. Poole, who got her start in journalism working for the alternative press in the Bay Area (including a stint at the legendary San Francisco Bay

Guardian), had been at *The Willits News*; she left just as Alden was moving in. When we met at a Mexican restaurant in downtown Willits, Poole was worked up about a new California law that put a cap of thirty-five on the number of pieces a freelance writer could submit to any one publisher over the course of a year. The law was aimed at cracking down on the abuse of freelancers who were essentially functioning as employees. It failed to work as intended, though, and it was substantially amended within a few months.[22] Poole described her paper as a shoestring operation that could not stay alive without its freelance contributors. "We make enough money to pay the bills," she said. "Pay the print bill and pay the freelancers."[23]

In mid-2020, yet another news outlet cropped up: *MendoFever*, begun by a local resident named Matt LaFever. Within two years, the site was offering a fairly robust mix of news about government, crime, and cannabis. *MendoFever* and *The Mendocino Voice* look a lot alike, and there's a reason: Maxwell, Baumann, and LaFever all received guidance from Kym Kemp, the founder of a site in four of California's northern counties called *Redheaded Blackbelt*. Kemp said she believes in mentoring and getting people "excited" about local news. Despite helping to foster a competitor, she said of the *Voice*: "I have a lot of respect for the work they do."[24]

Essentially, then, the media environment in Mendocino County as of 2020 consisted of a few chain-owned newspapers that were unable to provide the sort of coverage they once had; a public radio station working to build up its modest local news presence; a handful of small independent outlets like *Willits Weekly* and *MendoFever*; and *The Mendocino Voice*, with two full-time staff members and ambitions to do much more. Central to that ambition was a plan to convert what had been a for-profit enterprise into a cooperatively owned news organization governed by readers and what the founders hoped would be a growing staff. It's a hope that may yet be realized, but it's been delayed, perhaps indefinitely. Nationally, there are essentially no examples of a community news project that has gone fully co-op. But there are lessons that can be drawn from previous attempts. And nowhere did the co-op idea get a longer look than in

Haverhill, Massachusetts, a post-industrial city of about sixty-seven thousand north of Boston.[25]

Haverhill is not exactly a news desert. The community is covered by the daily *Eagle-Tribune* and the weekly *Haverhill Gazette*, both owned by CNHI, a newspaper chain based in Montgomery, Alabama. But news coverage had been on the decline for years. Neither paper had an office in the city, a far cry from when the *Gazette* had been an independently owned daily. So it's a place that made sense for Tom Stites, a veteran journalist who lived in nearby Newburyport, to try out his idea for a news co-op. Stites's long résumé included working as an editor at *The New York Times* and *Chicago Tribune*. Starting in the late 2000s, he began promoting what he called the Banyan Project, intended as an off-the-shelf co-op plan that local groups could adopt. Using software that eased the technical challenge of engaging effectively with readers, Stites aimed to foster a string of cooperatively owned news ventures across the country. The pilot project would be known as *Haverhill Matters*.

A board of community activists was formed with the goal of raising money and launching the site. Under Stites's plan, the board would hire an editor as well as a general manager whose duties would include reporting and engaging with the public. Readers could join the co-op and have a say in its governance by paying a membership fee or by contributing labor, such as writing a neighborhood blog that would be published on the site. The board hoped to launch in the second half of 2013,[26] but that date kept getting pushed further and further into the future. Stites was unable to raise grant money he'd been hoping for. Community support for the fundraising campaign was minimal. At one point an events calendar was unveiled, but *Haverhill Matters* never came close to raising enough money to begin covering news. Finally, in early 2020, the project was shut down. "We worked hard seeking various routes to build a new cooperative news business model for a local news and information service," wrote John Cuneo, the board chair, adding: "Let no one mistake the demise of our efforts to signal that the application of a coop business model to local journalism isn't feasible."[27]

Ironically, during the years that Stites, Cuneo, and others were attempting to start a news co-op in Haverhill, an independent outlet began operating in the city—WHAV, a low-power FM station with a newsy website. The station was acquired in 2004 by the owner of a local advertising agency, Tim Coco, and reorganized as a non-profit with a stronger news presence in 2014. Coco, who took part in a few early *Haverhill Matters* meetings before striking out on his own, once described WHAV's mission as "hyperlocal: local people, local stories, lots of local names. Subjects that some would consider boring—school committee and city council and the Haverhill police log. But, nevertheless, that's exactly the kind of news that's missing these days."[28] Although WHAV has struggled financially, as of late 2022 it was still on the air, hosting conversations with newsmakers and posting updates on its website. WHAV's relative success was perhaps an indication of how much simpler it is to start a news outlet under a more traditional form of ownership than it is to get a co-op off the ground.[29]

Not long after *Haverhill Matters* ceased operations, Stites reflected on what went wrong and what might have led to a better outcome. Some of it, he said, was unavoidable—illnesses among key people at the national level who were providing advice and assistance, the lack of model bylaws, difficulties in finding pro bono legal help. Some of it was a strategic decision, grounded in financial constraints, to raise the needed funding before actually starting to publish.[30] "There was no way to effectively describe by speaking, writing, waving hands, whatever, what this would be," he said later on. "Starting the first one required something we didn't have, which was 'Here it is. This is what you'll get.' Because the heart of it, and what sets it apart from other online news efforts, is the engagement part. The Banyan model connects the engagement to the very heart of the enterprise."[31]

Two and a half years after the end of the Haverhill experiment, Stites said he was beginning to doubt that any local news organization would convert to cooperative ownership. He said he was tracking about a half-dozen outlets that had expressed interest—including *The*

Mendocino Voice, to which he had provided some early advice—and none seemed ready to take the next step. Still, he said he hadn't given up hope, adding that the *Voice* struck him as especially well positioned to make that move. "They're starting from a strong place," he said. "They have paid subscribers. They have not-insignificant distribution in their community digitally. And I think they have community respect. I think it could just really strengthen an already pretty thriving news organization, and the county would be deeply served by that."

If Haverhill offers one set of lessons, Akron, Ohio, offers quite another. That city was the home of what appeared to be a successful cooperative news venture called *The Devil Strip*—a digital magazine whose ownership model was being studied closely by local news observers. Indeed, it was a project that the *Voice* was looking to for guidance. Unfortunately, it flamed out in rather spectacular fashion. The magazine took its name from local lingo for the strip of grass between a sidewalk and a street; its specialty was reporting on arts and culture in Akron. *The Devil Strip* seemed to be doing well until suddenly, in October 2021, it ceased operations, citing a lack of funds. The staff was laid off. Chris Horne, who founded the project in 2014 and transferred it to co-op ownership in 2019, had already left on a sabbatical. Three board members tried to revive the site but ended their efforts the following January, reporting that the project was $186,000 in debt. Essentially they found that Horne had been using grant money to cover operating costs and that there was no way for *The Devil Strip* to sustain itself once the grants ran out. They also reported that the co-op's bylaws were too cumbersome to provide for needed oversight. "We certainly wish our conclusion was different," they wrote, "because Akron deserves high-quality, independent local journalism."[32] As with Haverhill, *The Devil Strip*'s woes would appear to be specific to that project rather than an indictment of the co-op idea in general. Even so, once again an attempt to build a community-based news co-op had failed.

Olivia Henry, who studied cooperative ownership as a graduate student at the University of California at Davis, worked on co-op membership for *The Mendocino Voice* as a summer intern in 2020. She believes that certain organizational barriers need to be cleared out of the way before news co-ops can become truly successful. "The legal and financial obstacles to broad-based stakeholder ownership are significant," she said. "We need more infrastructure for this work."[33] That's not to say that media co-ops are nonexistent. At the national level, *The Defector*, a sports website begun by former *Deadspin* employees, is owned by its workers in a cooperative arrangement. At the state level, *Bloc By Block News*, which provides coverage of Maryland, is owned by readers and producers.[34] But the idea of a true bottom-up local news co-op, owned and governed by members of the community, has not been fully realized.

I n March 2020, *The Mendocino Voice* was getting by as a for-profit operation; the business was marginal, though growing. Maxwell and Baumann were writing most of the stories, introducing the *Voice* to people at farmers markets and other events, and making plans to convert the project to cooperative ownership. Both of them were working part-time to bring in extra money as well, although Maxwell said the need for that had diminished as the site's revenues had increased. "We are financially sustainable at our current level, effectively," she said. "We reached that point late last year. It's not necessarily a middle-class job, but it's more than I was making at *The Willits News*." They were hoping to keep on growing regardless of whether they ultimately moved to co-op ownership. Baumann talked in terms of replacing the reporting capacity that had existed in the county a generation earlier. Maxwell said her goal was to have an editorial staff of seven full-time employees plus ad salespeople and tech support. And she did not necessarily see seven as the ceiling if growth allowed for more than that.[35]

Then COVID hit. The *Voice* continued publishing, but the pandemic upended the plans that Maxwell and Baumann were making. An events coordinator they had brought in had little to do, given that there were no in-person gatherings. And Maxwell and Baumann's long-standing professional partnership started to unwind. Baumann was on an extended leave in late 2020 and early 2021. At some point, Maxwell said, it became clear that Baumann was not coming back.

She described his decision to step away as mainly personal but added that he was unlikely to stay much beyond the conversion to cooperative ownership—and that had been pushed indefinitely into the future. Baumann confirmed that he left the *Voice* for personal and family reasons.[36]

By late 2022, the *Voice* was in flux. A well-known local writer who'd been hired to replace Baumann as managing editor, s. e. smith, left after fewer than two months on the job. Lucy Peterson, one of two Report for America corps members who were working full-time at the *Voice*, quit after just a few months, leaving Maxwell with just one full-time reporter—Kate Fishman, also from RFA. Both smith and Peterson told us they quit because of differences with Maxwell over her management practices.[37] Maxwell declined to comment on the reason for their departures, citing legal constraints.

Still, Maxwell said the *Voice* was poised for growth. Freelancers were picking up the managing editor's duties as well as the governmental coverage that was Peterson's beat. The site had added a regular freelance farm column, which Maxwell said was an important part of the mix, given the county's reliance on agriculture. The *Voice* had a full-time membership coordinator as well. Maxwell was trying to set up a board of advisers to help find a permanent replacement for Baumann, a hire she hoped to make in early 2023, and to chart the project's future. Although the *Voice* was still organized as a for-profit, it had joined the Institute for Nonprofit News and obtained fiscal sponsorship through a San Francisco–based nonprofit called Independent Arts & Media, which made it possible for the *Voice* to receive tax-exempt contributions—an arrangement similar to that at for-profits like *The Colorado Sun* and *The Provincetown Independent*.[38] Given the county's sparse population, the *Voice* had attained impressive reach as well, according to Maxwell. As of mid–2022, the website was drawing about sixty-five thousand unique visitors a month, and about six thousand readers had signed up for the *Voice*'s weekly newsletter, with an open rate of about 40 percent. Most important, the site had signed up about seven hundred members who were paying anywhere from $3 to $100 a month. Businesses could sign up for $250 a year. Paying members received an enhanced version of the newsletter.[39] Some readers also made one-time contributions, Maxwell said. And there were all those Facebook users, providing the *Voice* with an ongoing opportunity to convert them into paying members.

Maxwell and Baumann's idea of cooperative ownership was grounded in idealism, as a way to engage more deeply with the community. "I am a firm believer in workplace democracy," Baumann told us. "I'm a firm believer in democracy generally, and specifically the realm of American society that is completely antidemocratic is your work, your job. Your job is a dictatorship. I don't think that should be the case." Maxwell's vision was based on her experience at the cooperatively owned bookstore in San Francisco. When we spoke in March 2020, she said she took away lessons that she hoped to apply to the *Voice*. At the bookstore, she recalled, "there wasn't a good way for someone to leave. So you'd have employees quit, but then they'd still have this piece of stock that would have to be bought back. It was very complicated. We want to avoid those problems."

Two and a half years later, Maxwell had not given up on the co-op. As of late 2022, the *Voice*'s home page described the project as "worker-owned," an artifact of plans that may or may not come to pass.[40] At the same time, though, she was pondering other ways to engage with the community, such as reorganizing the *Voice* as a nonprofit with the help of the board she was trying to put together. "We have examples of nonprofit bylaws that are structured in a way that facilitates democratic decision-making," she said. "You can be a formal 501(c)(3) but really have your board structured in such a way that members are reflective of your employees and readers. You could have a union of your employees that then participates in the board."

Governance matters. Community involvement matters. Day to day, though, a news organization's primarily role is to provide members of the public with the news and information that they need. Cooperative ownership could be a way to build something sustainable that is responsive to the community in ways that aren't possible with other forms of control—certainly not with a corporate chain or hedge fund that places cost-cutting above all else. But committed local stewardship, whether in the form of a for-profit, a nonprofit, or some other type of organization, is the most important factor in operating a journalistic enterprise. More than six years after the *Voice*'s founding, Maxwell was struggling to overcome setbacks she had endured as a result of the pandemic as well as ongoing challenges with replacing her cofounder and building up her staff. Nevertheless, she had succeeded in establishing a worthwhile source of "useful news" in a mostly meager media environment. It was a significant accomplishment she hoped to build on in the years to come.

MEREDITH CLARK, PHD

What does the future of local news look like? More diverse, with an emphasis on social change.

Meredith Clark is an associate professor at Northeastern University's School of Journalism and the Department of Communication Studies. Before arriving at Northeastern in 2021, she was a faculty fellow at Data & Society, an independent nonprofit research organization based in New York that brings together researchers, policymakers, technologists, journalists, entrepreneurs, and artists to "challenge the power and purpose of technology in society." In 2015, *The Root* included her on its list of 100 Most Influential Black Americans.

She is also the founding director of Northeastern's Center for Communication, Media Innovation, and Social Change. The new center is intended as a "hub for the advanced study of race, ethnicity, and activism, with an emphasis on media impact and the empowerment of marginalized communities," according to the university. Dr. Clark said she hopes that in addition to traditional research projects, the center can become a place where people in communities surrounding Northeastern can work with teachers and students to pursue their own projects. Her own research focuses on the intersection of race, media, and power, and covers everything from diversity in newsroom hiring to social media communities.

Clark, who holds a doctorate in mass communication from the University of North Carolina at Chapel Hill, has worked in a number of newsrooms, including the *Tallahassee Democrat*, the *Austin American-Statesman*, and *The News & Observer* of Raleigh, North Carolina. She also has contributed to *Poynter Online*'s diversity column and has written for *USA Today*.

Our podcast interview with Dr. Clark was posted on June 15, 2022. This transcript has been condensed and lightly edited for clarity.

DAN: Meredith, a project that you were working on made headlines recently, so I'd like to start with that. The News Leaders Association, formerly known as the American Society of Newspaper Editors, partnered with you in 2018 to lead its annual survey of diversity in newsrooms. Your goal was to get at least 1,500 responses, but only 303 organizations responded, and you've stepped away. Can you tell us more about what happened and what that means for journalism?

MEREDITH: The Newsroom Diversity Survey is now forty-four years old. It was created by a group of editors who were reflecting on the state of diversity in the news industry in the 1970s, about ten years after the Kerner Commission Report that indicted journalism and, more specifically, newsrooms for their failure to accurately reflect what it was like to be Black in this country. This is something that we had worked on for three years. We advertised this in NLA's newsletter. We did some social media blasts around it. We asked partners and affinity groups to join us and convince or persuade news organizations to participate. And, ultimately, we fell far short of that 1,500 number. And to further clarify, the bulk of those responses came from corporate giants like Gannett and McClatchy. So you're really talking about one or two corporations that are really driving the response to this query.

DAN: Gannett, regardless of what other problems they have, and they are many, does have a reputation for being pretty good on diversity issues, so that ends up skewing the sample even further. Let me follow up by asking you this: I understand you got some nasty responses as well. The rounds of layoffs that have battered newsrooms really can't excuse that.

MEREDITH: No, they absolutely can't. I think that this is something that folks who work in journalism know happens. But we don't talk about it very openly. We don't acknowledge it. We consider this almost an occupational hazard. And I want to say that this wasn't anything different than what I would receive when I was working as a columnist in a newsroom. This was along the same tenor. If you talk to journalists, specifically women, nonbinary folks, journalists of color, when they write, and specifically when they write about issues that are connected to disadvantaged, structurally marginalized communities, they will tell you about the folks who come out of the woodwork who say some of the ugliest things. They're things that you generally cannot print or say in a family publication. We wouldn't want to see these above the fold. We wouldn't want to hear them in the 8 a.m. broadcast. But we receive them.

ELLEN: I'd love to find out more about this new Center for Communication, Media Innovation, and Social Change at Northeastern, which you are founding director of. I'll start with a broad question: What's your vision for the center?

MEREDITH: My vision for this center is really to serve specifically the local community because, I think, while Northeastern has international aims in terms of lifting its profile and being influential in academia, there's something to be said about the displacement that is done when we begin these sorts of campaigns of conquest in places like Roxbury [a predominantly Black and Latino Boston neighborhood that surrounds the university]. As we expand physically, as we're buying up blocks within the neighborhood, we're displacing people. One of the things that I want to see us do is work on projects that help improve communication within the communities that we are having an effect on. We are looking to put together a grant program where folks can come and work with some of the researchers and the teachers and the students at Northeastern on a project that they're already working on. The other thing that I'm looking forward to doing with this center is to engage in a program of micro reparations.

DAN: Some of the local news organizations we're looking at are really small, with maybe two or three people. How do you see the challenge of diversity in journalism at some of these smaller media outlets?

MEREDITH: The key challenge I see is sustainability. In order for startups to last and to have the sort of impact that their founders want them to have, we have to think about financial sustainability, and that may not mean forever. It may mean that these startups are a twenty-year project, a thirty-year project, a fifty-year project—or maybe five. We live in a time where the economic cycle of news and of business as a whole is much, much shorter and much, much faster than it used to be. The other thing that I think about with sustainability is creating legacy beyond the founders and the initial participants in some of these projects. I think about the talent pipeline or, as I say, the irrigating of the talent within an area in order to make these startups sustainable long term.

ELLEN: I'm curious about the social-change aspect of your research. A number of smaller newsrooms are using traditional tools of journalism—investigative reporting, community feedback—to bring visibility to issues that haven't always been covered by larger metros. Is this a means to change?

MEREDITH: In order to build the kind of future news that we're looking for, we have to examine the tools that we're using. Investigative reporting isn't just a matter of going in and extracting information from a community, from a database, from centers of knowledge, whether they are human or paper or electronic records. It means partnering with people who live, work, are invested in that community and were there before you got there—and sharing power with them. That means elevating people who didn't come through the same channels that you came through but are essential parts of your reporting to credit as part of the team putting together this story. That means paying people for their work. That means employing them. We don't pay sources, but there is not a problem with paying someone to be a researcher on your project or paying them to be a fact-checker on your project, especially if they have access to knowledge that you don't. That to me shifts us towards social change in media.

CHAPTER SEVEN

NEW HAVEN, CONNECTICUT

*A Longtime Digital News Project
Takes to the Airwaves*

Babz Rawls Ivy, the morning host on WNHH Community Radio in New Haven, Connecticut, was mixing it up with her sparring partner, station manager Harry Droz.

"CNN is reporting that Biden and Kamala are at war," said Droz.

"I don't believe it," Rawls Ivy responded. "How could he not like her? He's not like McCain, who picked that stupid Sarah Palin. She was as cuckoo as a Cocoa Puff. I think they like each other fine. She's not his wife. She's his coworker."

Over the course of an hour on this day in November 2021, Rawls Ivy, Black and progressive, and Droz, a Donald Trump supporter whose background is Puerto Rican, ping-ponged from one topic to another—public education, anti-vaxxers, Christmas movies on the Hallmark Channel, Black Lives Matter, even a quick detour to the Book of Revelation.[1]

Rawls Ivy's show, *LoveBabz LoveTalk*, is carried on multiple platforms. In addition to its low-power signal at 103.5 FM, which reaches most of New Haven as well as neighboring Hamden, WNHH streams online and on Facebook Live.[2] Those watching the video version get the full effect. On this particular morning, Rawls Ivy, with chunky glasses, oversized earrings, and close-cropped blue hair, was sitting in her cluttered apartment in Newhallville, a mostly Black neighborhood in New Haven, in front of a poster of Paris, her favorite city. Back in the downtown studio, the bespectacled Droz, his head shaved and his salt-and-pepper beard grown long, appeared on the screen alongside her.

WNHH was launched in 2015 by the *New Haven Independent*, a nonprofit digital news outlet that's been publishing since 2005. At the time, the Federal Communications Commission (FCC) was granting low-power FM licenses across the country in an effort to provide more local programming. *Independent* founder and editor Paul Bass's application, submitted in collaboration with several partners, was approved, and he installed a small transmitter in a hilly area in Hamden near the New Haven line.[3] Rawls Ivy has been part of WNHH from the beginning, and within a few years she was holding down the weekday 9–to–11 a.m. slot. For the first hour, she and Droz shoot the breeze. During the second hour, she talks with guests ranging from political figures to community organizers, from authors to artists. She laughs easily but can turn serious when the situation warrants. Rawls Ivy is smart, widely read, and of eclectic tastes. Listening to *LoveBabz LoveTalk* is like tuning into the heartbeat of New Haven, a racially diverse city of about 134,000[4] where poverty exists in the shadow of Yale University, and where a burgeoning medical industry thrives alongside middle-class and working-class neighborhoods.

In an interview at her home, Rawls Ivy explained that her approach to broadcasting is to keep things simple. "I don't do a whole lot of preparation," she said. "I don't consider myself a reporter or a journalist or any of that. I'm just a conversationalist. I love a good conversation. And I'm very probing. Sometimes it makes people uneasy, but I think my personality is a little disarming."[5]

Bass, the driving force behind WNHH, was so certain he wanted Rawls Ivy on the air that he made her his first recruit, starting her off weekly. She has emerged as the voice and face of the station, serving on various community boards, turning up at events around town, and taking part in special programs like WNHH's election night coverage—a raucous roundtable with voting results, wine, and laughter.[6] "More than anyone in New Haven, she can speak in a fun, intelligent, raw, and meaningful way about everything that matters in town," Bass said. "What food is like at a restaurant, what music is like, why kids are going to prison, what's happening in neighborhood streets, how we should police. She's had ninety-five lives."[7]

Indeed she has. Rawls Ivy, fifty-eight at the time of our conversation, is as open about her own life as she expects her guests to be. While growing up in New Haven, she was beaten and subjected to horrendous sexual abuse by her father, who, among other things, prostituted her to other men. Despite that difficult beginning, she overcame, graduating from Barber-Scotia College, a historically Black institution in Concord, North Carolina. Coming home, she worked at a variety of jobs. She was a respected member of the community, serving, among other things, as an appointed member of the police commission and as an elected member of the board of aldermen— now the board of alders. She and her then husband adopted four kids who'd been in foster care.

All that, though, didn't prevent her life from going off the rails. In 2007, she was sentenced to thirty days in federal prison after she pleaded guilty to stealing about $49,000 from a federally funded social-service agency that she headed.[8] Afterward, rather than going into hiding, she slowly rebuilt her life in a very public manner. She began blogging. She also started hosting a show on Blog Talk Radio, which is what led to her job at WNHH. "I embezzled money from a non-profit," she said matter-of-factly. "I couldn't hide from that. I don't want to give anybody the chance to be, like, gotcha. No, no. I'm going to tell you it myself. And it frees me and it liberates me, because I don't have to worry about anybody."[9]

Her transparency led to a riveting forty minutes of radio one morning when she told listeners that FBI agents had showed up on her doorstep a few hours earlier with her son, who had been arrested and charged with a crime that she did not disclose. Her conversation with Droz that day was by turns heartbreaking and sober, punctuated with unexpected moments of humor. "You know I don't run from anything, Harry," she said. "But this is a journey he's got to take on himself. Because this is a lesson he should've learned the first time he did this mess. This is not the first time, it's the second time. But the second time has a higher consequence, because what he did was a larger stake. I love my son. But I'll tell you what, this is where Mommy cuts the umbilical cord, right here."[10]

It was not the sort of topic that many people would talk about openly, let alone for the benefit of several thousand listeners. Later, Rawls Ivy told us why she did it. "I'm not ashamed of my son," she said. "I mean, I'm ashamed in the sense that I wish he could have gotten his act together. But I'm not ashamed of him as a person. And I know that other people out there are dealing with similar things. I never want to suffer in silence about anything. It is the silence that allowed me to be trafficked; it is the silence that allowed my mother to be abused; it's the silence that cripples you."[11]

W NHH is part of what's grown into a community media network. The *Independent* is the hub, providing comprehensive coverage of New Haven and, to a lesser extent, Hamden. The spokes comprise WNHH; *La Voz Hispana de Connecticut*, a for-profit Spanish-language newspaper whose cramped third-floor offices down the street from New Haven Green are also home to the *Independent* and the radio station; and *The Inner-City News*, a Black-focused print weekly. There is a considerable amount of overlap among the outlets. *La Voz* publishes some of the *Independent*'s journalism in translation, and the two organizations share the radio station along with another unrelated outlet, offering English- and Spanish-language programming. *The Inner-City News*, edited by Rawls Ivy, republishes *Independent* stories along with articles from national wire services geared toward an African American audience and from *CT News Junkie*, a for-profit website covering state politics and policy whose work is also sometimes picked up by the *Independent*.

For a small digital start-up, the *Independent* has been remarkably stable. By 2010, five years after its debut, the site was attracting about 70,000 unique visitors a month, according to its internal Google Analytics data.[12] In late 2021, that number had increased to about 200,000 to 250,000—down from as much as 500,000 to 600,000 during the peak of the pandemic and Black Lives Matter protests, but still an indication that readership had grown steadily over the years.

Web metrics can be deceptive; Bass said he believed the *Independent* probably had between 35,000 and 50,000 regular readers. The site also had 32,000 followers on Facebook and more than 14,000 on Twitter. In addition, nearly 3,900 had signed up for the *Independent*'s free newsletters—a five-days-a-week update on what was new on the site plus a Sunday arts newsletter sent to the same list. The open rate was about 46 percent.[13]

Readers engage with the *Independent* mainly through its lively comments section. The often-toxic nature of online comments has led many publishers to abandon them or to steer them to social media. From the *Independent*'s earliest days, though, Bass has taken comments seriously; he and other staff members prescreen each submission to keep out racist language and hate speech. "People believe it's the best part of the site," Bass said. "The way I see comments is as a greatly enhanced and better op-ed section. Sometimes it kind of wears me down. But mostly it excites me. Because I feel like it's the last place in America where even Trumpies can have a conversation."[14]

The *Independent*'s annual budget runs about $600,000 to $700,000. That's enough to pay for the main site, for a satellite site begun in 2010 in the nearby Naugatuck Valley called the *Valley Independent Sentinel*, and for WNHH. Although Bass has had to scale back his ambitions for the *Valley Indy* (at one time it employed three staff members, but by late 2021 it was down to one), the rest of the operation has held steady, with some slow growth. Bass is always scrambling for money, but he tries to secure funding a year ahead, which allows him to plan coverage and staffing. About half of his budget comes from a few large local foundations. The rest comes from wealthy individuals, small donations, sponsorships, advertising, and miscellaneous items such as $400 to $600 a month from NewsBreak, an aggregation service that pays to republish articles. The *Independent* also solicits voluntary memberships for $10 or $18 a month; Bass was unable to provide a number when asked how many members had signed up.[15]

Those revenues pay for salaries that are in line with or slightly higher than what is typical in community journalism. As of late 2021, Bass was earning about $80,000. Managing editor Thomas Breen and *Valley Indy* editor Eugene Driscoll each made $60,000. Harry

Droz was paid about $51,000. The three staff reporters, all young and relatively inexperienced, were paid $36,000 each. Babz Rawls Ivy earned $24,000 as a part-time host.[16]

Measuring the size of WNHH's audience is difficult. No one really knows how many people listen over the air. In the spring of 2021, the livestream on the *Independent*'s website was attracting nearly 1,900 visitors a day, but Bass and Droz said they were not closely tracking how many additional listeners (and viewers) they were getting through other platforms such as Facebook Live, SoundCloud, YouTube, and Apple Podcasts.[17] It's probably fair to say that WNHH has established itself as a small but visible presence. The *Independent*'s share of WNHH's programming is live from 9 a.m. to 2 p.m. each weekday, with programs repeating online. The rest of the time is taken up by *La Voz* and by another organization that shares the broadcasting license with the *Independent* and *La Voz*.

Although *LoveBabz LoveTalk* is the *Independent*'s signature program on WNHH, the *Indy*'s share of the station also features a diverse and eclectic line-up ranging from *The Tom Ficklin Show*, whose cerebral host interviews local guests on matters such as public health and community news, to *Cannibis Corner with Joe the Weed Guy*. (Recreational cannabis has been legal in Connecticut since mid-2021.)[18] Bass is on twice a week and helms a weekly roundtable of local pundits. For a time, board of alders member Shafiq Abdussabur, a retired New Haven police officer, cohosted a program called *Urban Talk Radio*. That raised an ethical question since it helped him boost his profile as an elected official. Bass, though, said he didn't see a problem since Abdussabur was an important part of the community. (Abdussabur later resigned as an alder because his cleaning company was competing for a contract in the public school system.[19]) The station also features programs on the arts, music, and the local business community. It's a lot, but from Bass's perspective the station has not realized its potential. "We're not there yet," he said. "We built up the body of people involved and the quality. But we haven't done a lot with it yet to let people know it exists."[20]

Presiding over all of this from a tiny studio at *La Voz*—and, during much of the pandemic, from his home in Waterbury, Connecticut—is

Harry Droz, who runs the *Independent*'s share of WNHH. When we visited him at *La Voz* one afternoon, he was perched with three computers arrayed in front of him so he could switch among tasks such as editing audio, promoting shows on social media, and moving them over into podcasts. A native of Brooklyn, Droz came to Bass's attention because he had a contract to maintain *La Voz*'s computer system. "Paul and I used to have back and forth on politics," he said. "I was a Trump supporter. Of course, Paul isn't. So right after Trump won—I don't know what got into Paul's head, but he told me, 'Would you be interested in being the radio station manager?' I was like, 'Sure. What does it entail? But let's go for it.'"[21]

At a moment when political polarization makes it nearly impossible for people with different views to have a civil conversation, it's significant that Droz has thrived in a work environment dominated by liberals and progressives. Not to overstate matters, but it speaks to Bass's goal of reaching the entire community, not just its progressive elements. During the Trump presidency, Droz hosted a WNHH show called *Breaking the News*, which he described as "pointing out the hypocrisy of the media." As for his role on *LoveBabz LoveTalk*, he said he and Rawls Ivy will sometimes debate politics, but he'll back off if it makes her uncomfortable. "The thing is, politically we're so far apart, and those are the times you'll hear me and her argue on the air when it comes to politics," he said. "But if there's ever a topic she doesn't want to speak about, she cuts me off. And I'm fine with being cut off, because it's her show."

The emergence of the *Independent* and WNHH has played out against the backdrop of a legacy daily newspaper, the *New Haven Register*, whose fortunes have fallen and risen several times over the past several decades, including two bankruptcies and a stint under the ownership of the notorious hedge fund Alden Global Capital. In recent years, the paper has been on a better path. In 2017, the *Register* and several related properties were acquired by the privately held Hearst chain, a national media company that also owns broadcast outlets and magazines and whose twenty-four daily newspapers stretch from San Francisco (where the legendary William Randolph Hearst got his start) to Houston to Albany, New York.[22] Since then,

Hearst has taken a regional approach, putting together what is essentially one newsroom encompassing all of its Connecticut outlets. The Hearst Connecticut Media Group comprises eight print dailies and fourteen weeklies as well as a statewide website, *CTInsider*, that was unveiled in 2021. The two largest of the dailies are the *Register*, with a circulation of 19,982 on weekdays and 25,331 on weekends, and the *Connecticut Post* (18,494 on weekdays, 22,460 on weekends), based in Bridgeport.[23]

This regional strategy, similar to the approach Advance is taking in New Jersey, discussed in chapter 1, appears to be working. In 2022, the staff of Hearst CT was about 160 and growing. Combined print and digital circulation was close to 100,000, with about 39,000 of that in the form of digital subscriptions—up from just 21,000 in a little more than a year. Hearst's embrace of digital was so thorough that the company closed its Connecticut printing plant, transferring operations to its *Times Union* newspaper in Albany. Wendy Metcalfe, Hearst Connecticut's senior vice president of content and editor in chief, said the approach did not come at the expense of local news, telling us, "We are very focused on all levels of reporting, from local and regional to statewide reporting. This can involve everything from town meeting coverage and local high school sports games to enterprise work and extensive months-long investigations."[24]

Hearst's expansion in Connecticut was particularly well-timed given that what had traditionally been the statewide daily of record, the *Hartford Courant*, was absorbed by Alden when the hedge fund purchased the Tribune Publishing chain in the spring of 2021.[25] "We believe our expansion will serve everyone and lead to better journalistic products across Connecticut and in areas including Greater Hartford," said Metcalfe. At the same time, though, it wasn't possible for Hearst to provide New Haven with the sort of granular local coverage that it had several decades earlier, when the city was served by two daily newspapers.

Flemming "Nick" Norcott Jr., a prominent member of New Haven's large and politically active Black community, recalled growing up in the city and reading the *New Haven Journal-Courier* in the morning and the *Register* in the evening. The papers were under the same ownership, but they competed fiercely. "I'm seventy-eight," said Norcott, a retired justice on the state supreme court. "I remember as a young man, as a teenager even, when you got the *Journal-Courier* you felt like you were getting real, nitty-gritty news, stuff you and your friends were talking about. Things that were going on at the football game on Friday night or Saturday, what was going on in the schools, what was going on in city hall, and things like that. And the *Register* would give you more of a broader perspective—what I call the AP perspective, the worldwide, global perspective. Of course, that dwindled down and dwindled down to now."[26]

Unlike most readers, though, Norcott was in a position to do something about that decline. At the time we spoke with him, he was the outgoing chair of the Community Foundation for Greater New Haven, which provides significant grants each year to the *New Haven Independent* and the *Valley Independent Sentinel*.

"We feel that our continuing support fills that void that's left between what traditional journalism should have been doing and what needs to be done in terms of connecting the community with one another, and with the broader landscape of what's going on in the world," Norcott said. "With all due respect to the people who are covering the community from the *Register*'s perspective, I would say that the *Independent* people have their ear closer to the ground."

Perhaps no one in New Haven has his ear closer to the ground than Paul Bass, who arrived in New Haven in the late 1970s and has been reporting on the people, institutions, and culture of his adopted hometown ever since.

The roots of the *New Haven Independent* were planted during Bass's years as an undergraduate at Yale. Like many students, he was an outsider to New Haven, having grown up in White Plains, New York. Unlike many, he stayed. He gravitated to journalism from the start, meeting his future wife, Carole Smith—now Carole Bass—at the *Yale Daily News* and turning to freelancing after he graduated in 1982. Among the places he and Carole worked was the *New Haven Advocate*, an alternative weekly that they worried was becoming too mainstream and less immersed in the progressive politics they embraced. They left, and with two friends they launched a weekly newspaper to provide the kind of in-depth local coverage they thought was missing from other outlets in the city. The name of the paper: the *New Haven Independent*.

The original *Independent* was published from 1986 to 1990, and it folded amid a shortage of cash and a surplus of acrimony. After that, Bass returned to the *Advocate*, where he established a reputation for dogged investigative reporting. Eventually, though, working at the *Advocate* became tiresome for Bass, especially after 1999, when the weekly was purchased by the Times Mirror chain, whose holdings included the *Hartford Courant*. Bass left in 2004 to write a book, *Murder in the Model City*, coauthored with Yale political scientist Douglas W. Rae, about the redemption of a New Haven member of the Black Panthers who had been convicted of killing a fellow member on orders from the Panther leadership. The following year, rather than return to the *Advocate*, Bass decided to revive the *New Haven Independent*—this time as an online-only nonprofit. He raised some grant money and started publishing in September 2005, figuring he'd run it as a one-person shop and add content aggregated from other New Haven news sources. The *Advocate* struggled along under corporate ownership until it finally closed in 2013.[27]

Bass proved as talented at raising money as he was at journalism. Before long, he was hiring staff, cutting back on aggregation, and establishing the *Independent* as the city's leading source of news. Whereas the *Register* tended to focus on Yale and crime, the topics that presumably held the most appeal for its mostly suburban readership, the *Independent* portrayed a different side of New Haven—the Black neighborhoods and the lives of its residents; the school system, with frequent visits inside the classroom; the foreclosure crisis that followed the Great Recession; and, always, local politics. By 2009, the *Independent* had (depending on how you counted) five full-time journalists and a stable of freelancers.[28]

But this second incarnation of the *Independent* had some shortcomings. Most significant, the full-time staff was entirely white, covering a city where people of color are a majority; according to the most recent census data available, about 44 percent of New Haven's residents are white, nearly 34 percent are black, and about 31 percent are Hispanic or Latino.[29] The *Independent* earned praise from Black residents for its diligent reporting on their neighborhoods and issues, but the lack of diversity meant that their stories were being told by outsiders who weren't attuned to the nuances and complexities of life in Black America. "They reported from the white gaze," said Babz Rawls Ivy. "I tell Paul that. He knows. Anytime white people come into our community, they don't see the things that we see. They see it from a different place. It's not bad in that your whiteness makes you bad. Your whiteness blinds you to the reality of other people and other people's plight."[30]

Within a few years, as some of the original staff members moved on, Bass worked to diversify the *Independent*. By 2015, the site had two full-time Black reporters. As of early 2022, though, only one of its five staffers was Black. More significant, however, is that nearly all of the twenty or so people who host programs on WNHH are people of color—though only two, Harry Droz and Rawls Ivy, are paid staff employees, and Rawls Ivy is part-time. Still, if you regard the *Independent* and WNHH as two different arms of the same entity, then what's being offered today comes from a considerably more diverse range of journalists, commentators, and personalities than was the case during the *Independent*'s early years. "It's part and parcel of what we do," Bass said. "It's not a separate radio station versus the news site. It's definitely made us more diverse." Still, Bass conceded that more progress needed to be made in diversifying the staff of the *Independent* itself. "We're not that diverse yet," he said. "But we're getting there."[31]

One of the first Black reporters Bass hired was Markeshia Ricks. Bass tends to bring on young, inexperienced journalists and mentor them while they learn on the job. Ricks, though, was an exception: an Alabama native who earned her master's degree from the University of Alabama and who'd reported for newspapers in her home state, in Florida, and in Georgia. She was in the Washington, DC, area, working for the *Air Force Times*, when she contacted Bass about a job opening in 2014. At that point, she already had fifteen years of experience, so she thought it was odd when Bass asked her to come up for a trial run. "I'm glad he did," she said, "because it was definitely very different from my reporting experience in terms of being in a traditional newsroom. We just clicked, and I had a good time."[32]

Not long after she started working at the *Independent*, Ricks began to understand the importance of having a Black reporter covering the African American community. It wasn't that the white reporters weren't doing a good job, she said; it's that there was a different level of trust when she interviewed Black residents. "It meant so much to people," she said. "People just really felt at home talking to me in certain ways. People would call me. They would be like, 'Markeshia, this thing is going on.' And I'd be like, 'Absolutely. I'll come.' It mattered to them that I was the one covering it. Older Black women were obviously way more comfortable talking to me because they could talk to me. Not like they were my auntie, but like they felt protective of me." Ricks left in 2019 to run a youth journalism program in New Haven (she's now a market-access analyst at a health-care company[33]), but she remains in the *Independent*'s orbit, popping up on programs such as the radio station's election night coverage and on a weekly pundit roundtable hosted by Bass.

Ricks was an experienced journalist when she came to the *Independent*. Maya McFadden, the *Independent*'s lone full-time Black staff member as of 2022, was anything but. Twenty-three years old when we met, McFadden joined the staff in February 2020—"just before COVID," as she pointed out. The daughter of a New Haven police officer, she'd done some work at the *Independent* the previous summer, paid through a scholarship she'd received from the Massachusetts College of Liberal Arts while she was a senior there. She'd done some freelancing. Suddenly, though, she found herself—like millions of others—locked down, trying to report and write from her bedroom during the worst, unvaccinated months of the pandemic.

Reporters at the *Independent* are not assigned on the basis of race—that is, Black reporters aren't specifically asked to cover stories perceived as being of particular interest to the African American community. As with Ricks's experience, though, McFadden found that her identity as a young Black woman helped ease the way in certain situations. For example, one evening we drove to the Farnham

Neighborhood House so she could report a story about RespeCT Hoops, a youth basketball program. She met the head of the program, Victor Joshua. Unfortunately, there weren't any kids in the gym, so she called Bass and asked if she could come back on Saturday. She then interviewed Joshua, talking with him about everything from what it's like to start a program to how basketball has changed over the years. Could a white reporter have covered the same story? Of course. But as McFadden put it, "When you send a reporter out who's a person of color into whatever community, whether they like them or not, it sends a message, and it says, 'I'm dedicated to this.'"[34]

Perhaps the best way to describe the *Independent*'s efforts to include more Black voices is that the organization has made progress but still has more to do. The same can be said about its connections to the Latino community. The *Independent* and *La Voz* share not only a radio license but also some content and frequently break bread together, with *La Voz* president Norma Rodriguez-Reyes presiding over an annual joint Thanksgiving dinner. A dozen or so years ago, Rodriguez-Reyes and Bass were talking about a more integrated approach—one newsroom, essentially, that would provide coverage to both publications. In late 2021, that idea still hadn't gotten past the talking stage. Bass was seeking funds to pay for a bilingual reporter who would write about what was taking place on WNHH, both the English-language programming and *La Voz*'s Spanish-language shows. By the spring of 2022, though, that still hadn't happened.[35]

La Voz is a free for-profit weekly newspaper with a print run of about thirty thousand that circulates in New Haven and eight other Connecticut communities. The paper was founded in 1993, and Rodriguez-Reyes became the co-owner in 1998. She handles the business side; the other co-owner, Abelardo King, is the editor. The *Independent*'s nonprofit financial model allowed it to survive the early months of the COVID pandemic relatively unscathed. By contrast, *La Voz*, dependent on ads from mom-and-pop stores, nearly went under. "When they canceled the St. Paddy's parade, I knew we were headed to uncharted territory," Rodriguez-Reyes said. "At that time I owed—how much?—$40,000 to the printer. I had a $10,000 credit-card payment. So I'm saying, 'Oh, my goodness.'" Two issues were canceled. But then the situation began to turn around, mainly because of advertisements taken out by health-care providers who were trying to reach the Spanish-speaking population. "I was really concerned about these people who have worked for me for all these years," she said. "But thank goodness that they all managed to stay and help out."[36]

Sixty-eight at the time of our interview, Rodriguez-Reyes—who, like Harry Droz, is Puerto Rican—describes herself as "traditional." She wears fashionable dresses in the office and uses "Hispanic" and "Latino" interchangeably; she doesn't like "Latinx." She said that she and her staff (*La Voz* employs five full-timers and about twenty independent contractors) had to adjust to working alongside *Independent* journalists, who were more politically progressive than they were; she admonished her employees to stop disparaging LGBTQ folks, and they switched to real plates and flatware when they ate at the office in order to be more environmentally friendly.

Like Bass, Rodriguez-Reyes expressed some exasperation at how little had been accomplished in bringing the two operations together. *La Voz* runs one *Independent* article a week, translated from English to Spanish. She'd like more, but translation is expensive and time-consuming. The *Independent*, in turn, runs translated political cartoons from *La Voz* in its daily newsletter. She was also frustrated with the radio station. Under the terms of the license that the *Independent* and *La Voz* received from the FCC, WNHH is on the air weekdays from 4 a.m. to 4 p.m. Another operation, WONH, uses the frequency from 4 p.m. to 4 a.m. Rodriguez-Reyes had hoped to work out a content-sharing arrangement. Instead, WONH broadcasts music during its entire twelve hours, squeezing *La Voz* into the 2–to–4 p.m. slot on weekdays, after the *Independent*'s programming for the day has wrapped up. *La Voz* has more hours available on weekends, when it runs public-affairs programs such as *Hechos y Opiniones* ("Facts and Opinions") and *La Voz del Inmigrante* ("The Immigrant Voice"). But she said that New Haven's Spanish-language community hasn't embraced streaming, even though *La Voz*'s programming—live and archived—is available on its website, on Facebook, and on YouTube. "That's where we want to go," she said. "That's what we want to do. But we have to do a marketing campaign."

Rodriguez-Reyes wears two hats. In addition to helping run *La Voz*, she is the chair of the Online Journalism Project, the blandly named 501(c)(3) set up by Bass that serves as the umbrella operation for the *Independent*, the *Valley Independent Sentinel*, and WNHH. The way Rodriguez-Reyes describes it, her job is to put her foot down in situations where Bass might be reluctant—such as pushing employees to return to the office after the worst of the pandemic had abated. "I think I'm a little tougher," she said. "They need to be here. Paul's a little bit more nice." Bass agreed that the *Independent* and *La Voz* get story ideas from each other by working in the same offices. "She's a really good chair," he said, with "incredible social intelligence." He added: "She notices. She never says, 'You should do this, you should do this,' but she always notices."[37]

Two other developments in the *Independent*'s growth and evolution are worth noting. The first is coverage of the arts. New Haven has a vibrant arts scene, and cultural reporting ought to be part of any local news organization's mission—not just because there are good stories to be had but because it's a way to build a sense of community. Alternative weeklies such as the *New Haven Advocate* were known for their strong arts coverage, but such stories were something of an afterthought during the *Independent*'s early years. That has changed. Today the *Independent* publishes eight to ten arts stories each week and then gathers them all into a Sunday arts newsletter. There is a substantial amount of cultural programming on WNHH as well.

Brian Slattery, a musician who's the *Independent*'s part-time arts editor, writes about four stories a week and has a stable of freelancers to get to events he can't attend. In an interview at his home in Hamden, Slattery described his approach. "When Paul and I first talked about it," he said, "Paul said that I think our gimmick right now is that we like to report on the arts like it's news. It's not so much that you need to have pieces of criticism so much as just what's going on. I thought it was a great idea."[38]

The second development is that the *Independent* has expanded its geographic reach by adding Hamden to its coverage area. With a population of about 61,000, approximately 58 percent white and 26 percent Black,[39] Hamden is regarded as something of a destination for Black middle-class families in New Haven who want to leave the city and buy their own homes. The two cities are tightly integrated.

On a sunny afternoon, Nora Grace-Flood, twenty-three, was tramping around an industrial property in North Hamden, looking for people to interview about proposed zoning changes that would ease governmental regulations.[40] She hit paydirt with Peter Nizen, the owner of the Nizen Machine Shop, who was pleased with what he heard. "For some reason Hamden has something against machine shops," he told her. "I know we had to jump through hoops to get the machine shop in here."[41] Later on, Grace-Flood said, "I think it's really important to go to these things rather than covering them in an abstract sense."[42]

Grace-Flood had been Bass's intern, then became a full-time *Independent* reporter covering Hamden when she was accepted as a corps member with Report for America. "The reason I originally was drawn to Report for America was because it seemed like they really cared about local news as the pinnacle of what news could be," she said. "It's not secondary to national coverage." One of the lessons of Grace-Flood's and Maya McFadden's experiences at the *Independent* is the stereotype that young journalists aren't interested in local news may be false. Give them an opportunity to work for a first-rate news organization with good mentoring, and they may discover that community journalism is their calling.

Paul Bass sat down with us at the *La Voz* offices one afternoon in late 2021 and reflected on the past and the future of the *Independent* and his own place in the New Haven media environment. Bass had accomplished a lot. Compared to ten years earlier, he said, "I think we're broader. We cover more things. We have arts every day. And we have Hamden pretty much every day. We go deeper than we used to."[43] Sixty-one when we spoke, Bass's enthusiasm for the job seemed undiminished.

Still, he admitted to having less energy than he once did. He and his wife are observant Jews and do not work during the twenty-five hours of Shabbos. Other than that, though, he's grinding away. "I don't have enough boundaries," he said. "Almost every Saturday night I'm editing something. And then, Sunday, I'm editing stuff, getting ready for the week, running out covering stuff." He had a serious health challenge in 2020. Although he recovered, he was starting to wonder about what would happen to the *Independent* if he decided to step away. He was hoping to work until he was about seventy. Could the *Independent* be sustained after that?

"He's built something that's crucial to the way the town functions," said Michelle Chihara, an English professor at Whittier College who got to know Bass at the *New Haven Advocate* when she was a student at Yale and is now part of his board, attending meetings remotely from the West Coast. "I'm not sure how the model outlasts him. And that's my concern as a board member."[44]

One person who could pay a significant role in any succession is Karen Pritzker, a wealthy philanthropist whose Seedlings Foundation has been part of the *Independent* almost from the beginning and who continues to provide about a fifth of Bass's budget. Seedlings, according to its website, "supports programs that nourish the physical and mental health of children and families, and foster an educated and engaged citizenship."[45] It was Pritzker who pushed Bass to gather the *Independent*'s arts reporting into a weekly newsletter so that it didn't get lost in the crush of daily coverage. Bass has also talked with her about setting up an endowment that could fund the *Independent* long-term. Pritzker, though, wasn't ready to go down that road. "There isn't an industry and there isn't an enterprise that doesn't have succession issues," she said. "I know Paul's concerned about it, but it's working right now. It needs to work. He should absolutely be training people so that there is a future. But if someone at *The Texas Tribune* is being trained and ends up coming here when Paul goes, that's good too."[46]

Although Bass worries that his success as a fundraiser could not easily be replicated by someone else, he believes the *Independent* could sustain itself as a news organization because of the talent he's been able to attract over the years—such as Tom Breen, who jumped from Yale University Press to a full-time reporting position at the *Independent* in 2018 and later became the managing editor. That made him part of an extended *Independent* family: his wife, Lucy Gellman, was the first station manager at WNHH. She continues to host an arts show on the station and runs *Arts Paper*, which is published by the Arts Council of Greater New Haven. The council, in turn, was also Markeshia Ricks's employer for several years.

We met Breen on the front porch of Babz Rawls Ivy's house and then headed out on foot into the neighborhood, where Breen knocked on the doors of two houses that had been foreclosed on recently.[47] It was a regular practice for Breen, who sits through housing court proceedings and pores over foreclosure records. While the *New Haven Register* was using an outside vendor called United Robots to generate automated foreclosure stories from public documents, as was becoming a common practice at several newspaper chains, Breen was looking for the stories behind those documents.[48] On one occasion it led to his being attacked and badly bitten in the leg by a pit bull owned by the tenants Breen was interviewing. "The son is screaming about how upset he is that the mom forgot about the pit bull," Breen said. "It was a good reminder not to walk blithely into a stranger's apartment without checking to see if there is a dog waiting on the other end."[49]

Fortunately, there were no pit bulls to greet us at the two houses we stopped at. Unfortunately, neither was there anyone else. Breen wrote notes with his contact information and slipped them near their front doors. "A lot of these homes are being bought by investors, usually locally based, who then immediately flip the property to another investor, usually based out of New York or New Jersey," Breen explained later. "The middleman makes a big profit. Sometimes the tenants get hit with rent increases that force them out."

Breen described his job as being Bass's second-in-command. He's in charge when Bass is observing Shabbos and the Jewish holidays, and he helps with editing and assigning stories. Bass and Breen both use what they call "angling" when they deal with reporters—talking through what will be the most important angle in the story, which helps them craft a compelling lead paragraph. "I think what distinguishes an *Independent* article is not just the empathy and care that we have toward the subjects that we write about," Breen said, "but the attitude, the chops that we have as reporters—just the focus and coherence of it."

Bass said he considered Breen someone who could take over the *Independent* someday. Was that a possibility? Breen was thirty-three at the time of our interview. He said he and Lucy had talked about what their next steps might be. "It's difficult to imagine a job that I derive more meaning and purpose and joy from," Breen said. "It really is my favorite thing to do. It's just the best possible fit for me. So I've no interest in leaving anytime soon. But if we have kids, is this a sustainable way to parent? It's difficult to imagine running off to as many assignments and spending as much time and reporting as I do now." (As noted in the epilogue, Breen did, in fact, succeed Bass as editor in late 2022, with Bass continuing to serve as executive director of the *New Haven Indy*, the *Valley Indy*, and WNHH.)

It is the perpetual dilemma of community journalism. Even those who have a passion for it sometimes hit the wall—they need to earn more money or carve out more time for themselves. But it's also the way a news organization like the *Independent* renews itself. It is probably fair to say that New Haven is among the best-covered medium-sized cities in the country. That's to Bass's credit, but it also says something about the random distribution of local news. A community's media ecosystem shouldn't be so dependent on one founder with a vision and philanthropic leaders who are willing to pay for that vision.

Even so, in the years since the *Independent*'s founding, hundreds of digital news projects have sprung up to serve their cities and towns. Some are better than others. The *Independent* has shown how to do it the right way.

CHAPTER EIGHT

STORM LAKE, IOWA

A Print Newspaper with a
Voice Fights for Survival

On a July day in 2021, pickups, RVs, and panel trucks hauling cargo stream south along Interstate 35 from the Minnesota border through Iowa. The highway runs in a north-south line through a landscape of paintbox colors. Green fields of soybeans and corn line both sides of the highway, and brown cows and horses graze in fenced-in pastures. A few black clouds move in, holding rain in advance of a summer storm.

The highway also provides a view of Iowa's multiple economies. Wind turbines churn in a southerly breeze, hallmark of a state where wind accounts for 57 percent of the electrical grid.[1] Semi-trailers loaded with hogs lumber along, most likely headed for the meatpacking plants in Denison or Storm Lake, where the Tyson Foods plant is the town's major employer. Sun-scorched gray barns and lone silos stand as testimony to a more timeless way of scraping a living from the rich black soil ("Iowa gold," newspaper editor Art Cullen calls it).

To get to Storm Lake, home to Cullen's paper, the *Storm Lake Times Pilot*, a car, or a hog truck, must exit west off the interstate and navigate two-lane roads that pass through small towns and even smaller dots on the map. The paper's tongue-in-cheek address: Times Square, also known as 220 West Railroad Street. The newspaper-strewn office has a lived-in feel, not totally unexpected in an industrial-looking building Cullen once called "Storm Lake's finest machine shed."[2]

A newsroom visit in July 2021 finds Art and his wife, Dolores, plotting out the next day's front page, discussing stories and headline sizes as Dolores deftly clicks through design options on a computer. Their twenty-eight-year-old son, Tom, a general assignment reporter, works the phones nearby. Peach, a ginger and white "newshound," ambles around in search of a friendly hand, then sits quietly at Dolores's feet.

If the scene seems somewhat familiar, it's because the Cullens and the *Storm Lake Times Pilot* were featured in the 2021 documentary *Storm Lake.* The film, co-directed by Jerry Risius and Beth Levison, tracks two years in the life of the twice-weekly print *Times Pilot* and its ten-person staff. Risius brings a kind of muddy-boot credibility to the production: he grew up on a hog farm outside Buffalo Center, Iowa, and "knows this northwest corner of the state as few do."[3] Or, as Cullen put it in our *What Works* podcast in 2021, "[He] really understands the vernacular, and there's no learning curve with him. If you're out interviewing a farmer, Jerry understands what a barrow is and what a gilt is. Those are hogs, by the way."[4]

The award-winning film is noteworthy in its focus on the role a small-town newspaper can play in stitching together the social fabric of rural communities through sharp, knowledgeable (not to mention truthful) reporting.[5] It also depicts how tough it was for the newspaper to scrap it out in the face of a decline in advertising made unimaginably steeper by the uncertainty of the COVID-19 pandemic.

Like many newspapers, the *Times Pilot* is working to make up that gap through targeted digital advertising, events, and subscriber revenue. The paper is also the beneficiary of an entirely new model for funding journalism in the state. A recently formed nonprofit organization called the Western Iowa Journalism Foundation (WIJF) raises money to fund grants for a small network of for-profit newspapers that serve rural communities in nearby Denison, Carroll, and Greene.[6]

These grants help keep the *Times Pilot* and three other papers afloat: *La Prensa* in Denison, which serves the Hispanic population, the *Carroll Times Herald*, and *The Greene Recorder*.[7] Newspapers in rural communities fill a unique role in a state where "about one-third of the population lives in very small towns," according to Christopher

R. Martin, a professor of digital journalism at the University of Northern Iowa.[8] Small local newspapers like the *Times Pilot* and the *Carroll Times Herald*, which has been owned by the Burns family since 1929, play a critical role in cementing community identity in a state marked by a growing divide between Democratic-leaning urban areas and deeply Republican rural towns.[9]

The WIJF is new, but the problem it is trying to solve is decades old. The story of legacy newspapers in Iowa follows a familiar arc: the loss of print and digital advertising over the last twenty-five years led to closures or bargain-basement sales to chains and hedge funds. Corporate consolidation, layoffs, and real estate sales typically followed—along with steep declines in circulation. A 2020 study by the Center for Journalism & Liberty, a nonprofit organization that advocates against monopoly control, found that only 33 percent of Iowa newspapers have in-state owners. (One out-of-state owner named in the study is Lee Enterprises. While the headquarters are in Davenport, Iowa, it's a national chain, and 87 percent of its newspapers are outside the state.)[10]

Even the *Des Moines Register*, once the state's authoritative newspaper of record, has lost circulation and reach under Gannett's ownership. The paper, founded in 1903 by Iowa banker Gardner Cowles Sr., had a statewide circulation of 240,000 in 1985 when it was sold for $200 million to Gannett and reached all ninety-nine of Iowa's counties.[11] The sale of the *Register* made headlines in *The New York Times*; the *Register* had been propelled to national attention by its bowtie-wearing editor, Michael Gartner, and was renowned for astute political coverage of the first-in-the-nation Iowa national caucuses, which have been held every four years since 1972.

For the *Register*, the Gannett era has been marked by retreat. By 2022, the *Register*'s paid combined print and digital circulation was just 38,000 on weekdays and 51,000 on Sundays.[12] In 1997, the *Register* fielded a newsroom of 205 people. By mid-2020, it had 56 editorial employees.[13] When the Center for Journalism & Liberty analyzed the "dimensions of resilience in Iowa news organizations," measuring "historic reputation and civic institution status," it designated the *Register* as an "at risk" paper.

Committed local ownership, combined with focused community coverage, seems to contribute to the long-term resilience of local news organizations—although, to be sure, those ingredients are only part of the overall strategy needed to stay in the black. "Part of the resiliency of the *Storm Lake Times Pilot* is that [it is] run by the Cullen family," the Center for Journalism & Liberty study reported in 2020. "It has eight employees, and half of them have the last name Cullen." Editor Art Cullen and his brother John, who is publisher, acknowledge that the newspaper is run like a family enterprise, where the hours can be long and everyone pitches in. In his 2018 book *Storm Lake: Change, Resilience, and Hope in America's Heartland*, Art Cullen writes that, after many trials, the family took a stand. "We all agreed: The newspaper is the family. If it goes down, the family goes down with it."[14]

Although the Cullens skirted disaster once or twice, that downfall never happened. They won the newspaper war in Storm Lake, where the editorial page remains a progressive voice in a state that has largely embraced right-wing candidates—a shift that *New York Times* political reporter R. W. Apple noted in 1995: "The state's economy has gone from bust to boom, the religious right has seized control of the Iowa Republican Party, and the moderates who used to dominate it have lost most of their influence."[15] Becky Vonnahme, the executive director of the WIJF, who works from her family farm in Breda, adds: "Politically in Iowa, we've shifted quite a bit to the right as a state. We used to be middle-of-the-road, but we really aren't any more."

In her view, Donald Trump's 2016 political campaign "kept feeding it and feeding it. He'd say, 'You've got to fight back; these people think they know more than you.' And it worked, and that's where we are right now. The majority [of local residents] don't look at small-town newspapers as promoting and protecting democracy. They don't see that at all. For them, they still want to see the newspaper stay open, but it's more protecting the identity of the community."

In other words, local leaders may not want to give to the WIJF, which attained 501(c)(3) nonprofit status in early 2021, in order to bolster the First Amendment or to save democracy. "But they don't want to see the newspaper go under either," Vonnahme said. "That's where it hits home for them in these small towns when they see that the newspaper is going to go broke. The first thought is more about 'Well, who's going to cover the school?'"

Kyle Munson, a veteran journalist who is president of the WIJF, said he became a "local-news zealot" during his twenty-four years at the *Des Moines Register* when it was owned by the Cowles family. As a reporter and then as a columnist who roamed the state, he saw how the *Register* played a crucial role in the lives of Iowans. "I wouldn't expect modern audiences to have any notion of why local newsrooms of a bygone era were so central to a sense of community—especially in Iowa, a state with agricultural, educational, and political infrastructure that I would argue made us somewhat unique," Munson said. "I fear that in today's world increasingly we're in a business of trying to fill leaky buckets—clawing back sheer numbers of local reporters and their coverage to try to distribute through fractured or broken (or politically polarized) networks that just won't yield the results we want. I don't expect members of the average Facebook group or the average TikTok viewer to care what the local newsroom says. That's not their job; it's the newsroom's job to entice them to care. Hence, I see the work of WIJF as tackling root causes of problems."[16]

The rules that govern nonprofits are complex. If the *Times Pilot* were a nonprofit, Cullen would not be able to endorse candidates or ballot measures on the editorial page. The WIJF allows Cullen to apply for grants while retaining his full-throttle editorial voice.

The WIJF, which launched in August 2020, started by focusing on a subset of counties in western Iowa. Munson and others at the foundation are still ramping up, setting up full-time infrastructure and trying to get more funding. "We can't be the Paycheck Protection Program for newspapers," Munson said. "But we've been able to grant tens of thousands of dollars to some of these newsrooms, and the *Storm Lake* documentary has been a huge help in visibility."[17] The *Times Pilot*, *La Prensa*, and *The Carroll Times Herald* have all received grants.

In the summer of 2021, a $4,000 grant from the WIJF proved transformational for Lorena López, editor and publisher of *La Prensa*. López, originally from Estelí, Nicaragua, launched *La Prensa* in 2006 to serve Spanish-speaking immigrants from Mexico and Central America who were flocking to Denison, Iowa, to work in the meatpacking plants. (Denison, a city of eight thousand, is 48 percent Hispanic, according to the 2021 US Census.)[18] A former television broadcaster in Nicaragua, López fled to the United States after a documentary she produced angered the Somoza government.

"They were looking for me, and the government was starting to put what we call 'the white hand' on doors—that means that if your house was marked with a white hand, the military and paramilitary, would come for you and your family," she told us.[19] She began *La Prensa* in 2006, naming it in honor of journalist Pedro Joaquín Chamorro Cardenal, whose assassination in 1978 was a signal event leading up to the Nicaraguan revolution and the overthrow of the Somoza regime a year later. Her twice-weekly newspaper's print circulation has climbed in recent years from two thousand to six thousand copies, and though her readers skew older and prefer print, she is experimenting with digital as well. The WIJF grant allowed her to hire two interns for a ten-week period, freeing her to focus on advertising sales. During that period her advertising sales increased 40 percent, she said. López, fifty-eight at the time of our conversation, hopes to secure more grant funding. "This is not just for the Latino community," she said. "All the minority cultures in our rural areas are in need of media to learn about things in their community." Her goal for the coming decade: "To educate myself as much as I can about all these new platforms and to transition to digital."

During our newsroom visit in July 2021, Art and Dolores Cullen took time away from deadline to recount to us the newspaper's history, their deep roots in Iowa, and their scramble to "float the boat," as Art put it. Standing around a table in a back room of the *Times* office, they flipped through the newspaper archives—the old-fashioned kind that smell of newsprint, ink, and more than a few dust motes. Copies that dated back to the paper's founding in 1990 were neatly clipped into big binders.

The focus was relentlessly local, with profiles, features, and news stories recounting local events. The newspaper confined opinions on national politics and debates to the editorial page. That, said Art, cools off some of the most ardent partisan debates: "I can help create common conversations." That day, Art and Dolores were chasing a tip that a local fisherman had caught a long-nosed gar. "We take pride in writing about local people," Dolores said. "It's a strange fish, with a snout, and that will probably be on our front page, along with the people who caught it. I've learned to squeeze tidbits out of people that are doing interesting things, to go out and get pictures with the idea that this is the first draft of history." Another feature story, with photos, was about a trip to Omaha and a reunion of old friends.

Art's elegantly crafted editorials don't pull punches—after Joe Biden won the 2020 presidential election, he called out "President Trump's last gasps" as the former president attempted to contest the vote through the courts.[20] Because of his progressive voice on the editorial page, "people want to say, 'You're fake news,'" Art said. "But look at that front page." It's all local, and it's all news. Opinion is clearly labeled inside. And local news seems to sell papers. "Community journalism is about babies and weddings and pies and bars," Art said. "And obituaries and school board meetings. . . . It's about what happens in a little farming community in the middle of nowhere. We are the primary source of vital information."

Concerned about the damaging impact that misinformation on Facebook had during the 2020 Iowa caucuses, Douglas Burns, vice president for news at the twice-weekly *Carroll Times Herald* in Carroll, Iowa, applied for a Facebook Accelerator grant, a program that supplies training and tools to Facebook Group administrators in order to deepen community impact.[21] One of the smallest papers accepted into the program, the *Times Herald* received $150,000. Burns donated $30,000 of that to *La Prensa* and put the rest of the grant to work setting up the WIJF. Two years later, he said, grants from the WIJF were helping to keep his own newsroom alive. In 2013, the *Times Herald* was a daily newspaper with a circulation of seventy-five hundred in Carroll, a city with a population of ten thousand, and was named Newspaper of the Year by the Iowa Newspaper Association. But the ensuing years had been hard, Burns said. The paper is now published twice a week and has a circulation of about three thousand, including about three hundred to four hundred digital subscriptions.

Burns said that although the federal Paycheck Protection Program (PPP) signed into law in March 2020 during the COVID-19 pandemic allowed him to keep most of his five-person staff on the payroll, it was only a temporary reprieve. In a phone interview conducted as he drove across the state to a meeting, he noted that he was $250,000 in debt the first quarter of 2022 because he refused to implement steep job cuts, and he was worried that he'd have to sell the building that houses the newspaper and shut down if he couldn't pay off his bank loan.

Like many editors and owners, he's scrambling. "We've started a company called Mercury Boost, which is a digital advertising and marketing company," he said. "The profits from that all funnel back into the paper. So, basically, I have to run a digital marketing company, and I have to walk around almost like I'm president of a small college and fundraise, just to be able to cover the Carroll City Council. Here's the dilemma I'm running into: Seventy percent of our county went for Trump, and I just can't beat the Facebook algorithms here. . . . If we go away, community newspapers like ours are the last bastion of collective truth."

The pandemic brought into sharp focus the critical role that a local news outlet can play during a public health crisis—disseminating authoritative information from experts and discrediting misinformation. An analysis by the Brookings Institution found that in early April 2020, half of the 2,485 counties in the US that reported cases of coronavirus had either no local newspaper or only one surviving paper.[22] Two-thirds were rural. As the pandemic undermined the faltering advertising model even further, newspaper closures continued. In a 2019–20 directory, the Iowa Newspaper Association counted 273 newspapers in Iowa. By September 2020, five of those had closed.

Three were owned by Community Newspaper Holdings Inc. (CNHI), a national chain based in Montgomery, Alabama, and two were owned by Mid-America Publishing, a small chain based in Iowa.

"The closings left Marion County as the first of Iowa's 99 counties without a newspaper," researcher Martin wrote in his 2020 study of resilience.[23] "The moves by CNHI, which is owned by the Retirement Systems of Alabama, demonstrates the dangers in having a newspaper owner that is not local and for which journalism is not central to its business model. The centerpiece investments of CNHI are in real estate, including the Robert Trent Jones Golf Trail and several resorts in Alabama. Newspapers are almost an afterthought in CNHI's webpage listings, under 'other investments' along with movie theaters and outlet stores."

The *Storm Lake Times Pilot*'s print circulation dropped by 9.1 percent in the sixteen-year period recorded by the study (2002–18), from 3,154 to 2,868. But it is climbing again, demonstrating that local owners who know their community intimately are nimble enough to spot trends quickly and can stress-test different strategies for boosting circulation. Rather than working with a generic product template spawned at a distant corporate headquarters for a sprawling chain of papers, local editors, publishers and ad salespeople can experiment in real time, sometimes walking door to door to talk with residents and business owners.

While Art Cullen delivers a dose of straight news on the front page of the *Times Pilot*, his editorial page is another matter. He is unabashed about staking out positions that he characterizes as "New Deal Democrat," grounding his fierce editorials about polarizing subjects like agriculture and climate change in pragmatic logic that springs from his knowledge of Iowa and the way farmers pull their living from the soil. When Art won the Pulitzer Prize for Editorial Writing in 2017, the Pulitzer board wrote that his editorials were "fueled by tenacious reporting, impressive expertise and engaging writing that successfully challenged powerful corporate agricultural interests in Iowa."[24]

In his prize-winning series of ten editorials, Art drew a direct line between agricultural practices and water contamination, and pushed farm owners and state and federal regulators alike to find solutions that bolster the public's interest in having clean water flowing in the Raccoon River. It's not both-sides-ism; it's advocacy for preservation of the environmental resources that are foundational to Iowa's economic future.

As he wrote: "We believe that federal and state governments must work with landowners and farmers by giving cash inducements for conservation, and by setting rules of the road. Such as: You will keep a 20-foot or 50-foot grass buffer between your field and the river. We understand why agriculture objects."[25]

Because of his editorials—and his Pulitzer—Art Cullen "has a shot at building a bigger digital subscription base than almost any other rural newspaper in Iowa, for sure, and maybe even nationally," Burns observed. "Because he has a nationally recognized editorial voice. I think a lot of people in Austin, Boston, New York City would subscribe to the *Storm Lake Times Pilot* just to read him. It's sort of like being a Substack subscriber; you're subscribing to Art Cullen."

The documentary film shows the stark contrast of before and after the pandemic, as newsroom bustle and door-to-door hustling for advertising gives way to working from home, Zoom calls, and empty streets. By the summer of 2021, the Cullens were scrambling to find the funds to make up a $70,000 budget gap. Art and John do not draw salaries—both took early Social Security. Dolores works on a "nun's salary," the couple jokes. Art estimated that he needs "to fill a $110,000 hole annually" through circulation revenue and fundraising in order to publish the newspaper twice a week.

Even before the pandemic shut down storefronts in Storm Lake, retail advertising revenue had begun to plummet, and Art, like many newspaper executives, was transitioning to a business model that relied primarily on paid subscriptions. In 2017, the year the paper won the Pulitzer, he said, "Detroit decided they didn't want to advertise in print anymore, so we lost $70,000 worth of auto advertising."

Art said that readership was growing in the summer of 2021, "partly because we have a bit of dim celebrity from the movie." The newspaper's circulation had dropped to twenty-eight hundred but climbed back up to three thousand. "If we can get to four thousand at our current rate, we can float the boat, mainly through circulation revenue," he said. "Frankly, Donald Trump did wonders for the newspaper industry. It really did wake people up to the fact that freedom isn't free, democracy has a price, and it costs just about as much as a cup of coffee. Readers have started paying that price."

When Art's brother John launched the paper in 1990, Art was already working for daily newspapers. A native of Storm Lake, he had received a bachelor's degree in journalism from the University of St. Thomas, in St. Paul, Minnesota. In an interview with National Public Radio's *Fresh Air* in 2021, Art said that he had been working his way "up Interstate 35 in hopes of getting a job at the Minneapolis *Star Tribune*."[26] When John called Art about starting his own paper in Storm Lake, Art was news editor at the daily *Globe Gazette* in Mason City, Iowa, part of the Lee Enterprises chain.[27] "I was kind of tired of corporate journalism, working for a large, publicly traded company," he said. "And John wanted to start this newspaper in our hometown. And, so, I came home."

It was, he said, "about the worst time you could imagine starting a print publication in rural Northwest Iowa." Family farms were hard-pressed. Pressured by the tight federal monetary policy of the 1980s, the Iowa farm economy bottomed out in 1983.[28] Federal assistance helped trigger a slow recovery of farm income, but, even with that help, an average of two thousand Iowa farms went out of business each year between 1980 and 1986. Some farmers decided to pack up and move, driving a population decline. According to one study, "By 1990 Iowa's rural counties had lost over 227,000 residents during the 1980s, compared with 136,977 for the state as a whole. . . . Lower population meant lower representation both at the state and federal levels, lower amounts of federal aid for cities, counties, and school districts, and a lower tax base to work with on the road to economic recovery."[29]

The *Times* got off to an ambitious if costly start, launching a free weekly publication supported by advertising, which racked up $500,000 in debt, according to Christopher Martin. An award-winning

competing paper, the *Storm Lake Pilot-Tribune*, had served the town
since the late 1800s. On April 1, 2022, the Cullens announced that
they had purchased the *Pilot-Tribune* and were merging it into theirs.
The purchase, according to John Cullen, ended a "32-year contest"
with the town's oldest continuing business.[30] No layoffs were reported.

Asked what lessons he took from the pandemic, Art Cullen said
that although he needed PPP funding to get through the early
days, he found that readers were eager to find out what "the straight
facts were" about how COVID-19 was affecting the Tyson Foods plant.
Faced with a dearth of information about the number of COVID-19
cases from Tyson, Art, Dolores, and Tom combed Facebook and
walked the streets to find out who was sick and who had died. "I
would write one story," Dolores said, "and people would call and
say, 'Oh, yeah, I had it, and I survived too.' We'd get calls from people saying, 'Keep it up, keep it up.' It really bothered me that people
were dying, and the official response [from Tyson] was sort of like,
'Oh, let's just go on, nothing to see here.'"

The news section reported the facts, but Art let loose on the editorial page. "I was excoriating [Tyson] for their cynical approach to the
way they treated vulnerable people," he said. "On the editorial page,
I was hollering, but Tom, our general assignment reporter, was being
very diligent and straight about it," Art said. In December 2020, the
Times Pilot partnered with *ProPublica* on an investigation into how
COVID-19 ravaged Waterloo, Iowa.[31]

As the *ProPublica* story, which also ran in the *Times Pilot*, put it:
"To understand how things got to this point—how American cities
came to be held hostage to global meat corporations—there may be
no better place to go than Waterloo, where the outbreak at Tyson's
pork plant took a stunning toll on both workers and the community.
The damage left behind illustrates what's at stake as key Republicans
push for granting widespread immunity to corporations, shielding
them from repercussions related to COVID-19."

The *Times Pilot* also conducted a twenty-year editorial campaign
to dredge the lake that gives Storm Lake its name. The lake, a tourist

attraction and recreation area, was clogged by "150 years of sedimen-
tation from when [pioneers] broke the prairie," Art said. "It worked:
we removed seven hundred thousand cubic yards of silt—Iowa black
gold—from the bottom of the lake. It wouldn't have happened but
for our editorials."

Asked how his news reporting—not to mention his editorials—
went over with powerful institutions in the Storm Lake area, Art
Cullen chuckled. "Well, it doesn't matter much anymore," he said,
noting that advertising collapsed during the pandemic. "Tyson isn't
going to buy any ads with us anyway. I used to be a little more shy."

He had no plans to cut back on editorials. "One of the things I've
noticed in my research is that if you're doing an email newsletter,
the strongest response rate is on opinion pieces. I've noticed that to
be true on the email newsletter we do. People want opinion. They
don't want snark, I don't think, but they want well-informed opinion
or well-written sarcasm," he said. In fact, he believes, "a lot of the
future of local journalism is going to be in investigative journalism
and, again, informed, not snarky analysis of very complex issues like
climate change and agriculture."[32]

Because of the Tyson plant, Storm Lake has attracted workers from
abroad, and immigrant families from Mexico, Malaysia, Africa, and
elsewhere are settling in, attending school and starting businesses.
(According to the 2021 US Census, 39 percent of Storm Lake's population is Hispanic, 15 percent is Asian, and 4 percent is Black.)[33] But
because many immigrants do not speak English as a first language,
building up paid circulation can be a challenge, Art said. He also
hopes to expand his digital presence. "We're dedicated to our print
edition because of an aging demographic, and that drains all our attention and resources. We don't have the same kind of resources and
attention to devote to our digital products. We're going to have to
do that," he said.

Even before the pandemic, he added, "we could see the freight
train coming down the tracks at us. We were already losing advertising, simply because newspapers are not the middleman, the advertising broker, between the reader and the advertiser. Social media is.
We have to find a different way to raise money, and we've turned to

philanthropy through the WIJF. It achieved nonprofit status through the Internal Revenue Service in January of 2021. It was just in the nick of time."

In 2021, said Becky Vonnahme of the WIJF, a donor wanted to bestow $60,000 on the Cullens' newsroom. Art Cullen put together a proposal to request the funds and must report back on how the money is being spent, tracking staff salaries and the number of articles being written. "This was huge for a small newspaper like this," Vonnahme said in a telephone interview. It is, she noted, the difference between staying open and shutting down. "Now all of a sudden, your reporters who haven't gotten a raise in five years can get a raise."

The WIJF is beginning to explore how funds can help with succession planning. "It can be very difficult to get someone to come to take over a newspaper in a small town," she said, "especially if they don't have experience growing up in a rural area." If she can crack the code, she can help to build a model for future local ownership. "Because if you don't get a new editor in to that small weekly, you have a chain that comes in or a hedge fund. They buy it, they gut it, they keep the legal ads. And then there's just nothing else in it, so what's the point? Because you have a paper, but it's not providing that watchdog coverage, it's not there at the city council meeting, asking questions, not interviewing the school board candidates. We've lost so much in our rural communities. If you lose the newspaper, you have almost completely lost your identity."

ELIZABETH HANSEN SHAPIRO, PHD

A scholar and serial entrepreneur
looks to the future.

Elizabeth Hansen Shapiro is the CEO and co-founder of the National Trust for Local News, a nonprofit that is dedicated to "keeping local news in local hands." She was also a senior research fellow at the Tow Center for Digital Journalism at the Columbia Journalism School in New York. At the Tow Center, Dr. Hansen Shapiro's work focused on the future of local journalism and the policies needed to assure that future. Her research involved audience engagement and revenue strategies as well as the relationship between news and social platforms. Prior to her work at the Tow Center, Dr. Hansen Shapiro led the news sustainability research initiative at the Shorenstein Center on Media, Politics and Public Policy at the Harvard Kennedy School. She holds a doctorate in organizational behavior from Harvard Business School.

The Trust works with local news publishers, philanthropists, and socially conscious investors "to conserve, transform, and sustain community news outlets across the U.S.," as its mission statement puts it. The goal is to help local news thrive and have a demonstrable impact in their community.

In 2021, the Trust and other collaborators purchased twenty-four weekly and monthly newspapers in the suburbs of Denver, Colorado (the purchase is covered in chapter 4 of this book), owned by a couple who wanted to retire from the news business but didn't want to sell to a corporate owner that would slash costs and eliminate jobs. A new public benefit corporation, the Colorado News Conservancy, was set up to run the cluster of papers. The Conservancy is owned jointly by the Trust and *The Colorado Sun*, a digital news organization.

Our podcast interview with Dr. Hansen Shapiro was posted on August 4, 2022. This transcript has been condensed and lightly edited for clarity.

DAN: You've compiled data showing that $300 million would be enough money to save most of the independent newspapers at risk in the United States put together. Can you walk us through the numbers? What steps are you taking to raise that money? How many independent papers are we talking about, and how does that compare with the number of chain newspapers that are out there?

ELIZABETH: Dr. Penny Muse Abernathy's recently updated "news deserts" study shows that the picture has gotten much bleaker since her first report in 2020. Almost four hundred papers have been lost—something like two a week, she estimates, between the early months of the pandemic and the spring of 2022. As of this moment, she estimates there are 6,377 papers left. There are 4,600 or so titles that are owned by what you could call sub-large chains. Of those, about 4,100 are weekly papers. How might we value those? If you think about those approximately 4,100 weekly independent titles, how do you value an individual paper or a chain of papers? There are some industry-standard multiples, but it really is particular to the community. We took a back-of-the-envelope of $75,000 per title, understanding that the range can vary widely. That's how we, by multiplication, got to something like $300 million for the estimated value of remaining independent titles in the country.

DAN: Are you making efforts to raise that money? Where would the money come from to do that?

ELIZABETH: We're currently in the process of raising funds that would allow us to make a significant dent in that number. When you are philanthropic fundraising or impact-investment fundraising for a new organization like ours, testing out new financing models, new ownership models, the funders want to see a robust proof of concept. We are raising $15 million to make our first set of acquisitions. This is a scratch on the surface of the need. But the strategy here is to prove that this is possible and that it's possible in a range of circumstances so that we can then go raise that bigger fund.

ELLEN: Could you tell us what the National Trust is doing not just to save newspapers but to foster the next generation of community news projects?

ELIZABETH: As a national organization, we absolutely do not want to be the final arbiter of what's worth saving in any given community. Those are community decisions that need a lot of context and discussion. What that has meant for us so far is partnering with local funders, local publishing partners, state press associations, universities, and academics to understand the community demographics in this region or state and the economic trends. What kinds of social resources are available where these newspapers are based? What's the philanthropy that's available statewide or locally? What is the history of these papers like? What other sources of news are available? I think it's important to say that the National Trust for Local News is building nonprofit conservancies that are meant to be the next generation of community news institutions that can become the context for new kinds of community news projects.

DAN: One of the National Trust's highest profile moves to date was to purchase twenty-four weekly and monthly newspapers owned by Colorado Community Media in the Denver suburbs. Could you tell us how that came about?

ELIZABETH: We were so lucky to have the opportunity to work with the folks in Colorado in our launch phase when the National Trust for Local News was just a concept paper back in October of 2020. We connected with the folks at the Colorado Media Project, and Melissa Milios Davis there shared that they had been working with the family owner of a chain of papers. He had a next-generation entrepreneurial buyer lined up, but she couldn't find financing. We started to brainstorm around financing options, trying to understand what she was potentially buying, what strategy she wanted to bring. And through that series of discussions, it became clear for her as a solo, entrepreneurial, first-time publisher, this was a bigger opportunity than she wanted to bite off. She ended up dropping out of the sales process.

We said to ourselves, look, OK, our mission is local news in local hands. Then it's our job to push this forward and find the local ownership solution that's going to realize our mission. From that moment forward, the National Trust became the buyer. At the same time, we looked for a strong local operating partner who could really start to step into that role. Our cofounder, Lillian Ruiz, had been at Civil Media. [The Civil Media Company and the Civil Foundation, a nonprofit, were founded in 2016 in an effort to create a blockchain-based media platform for journalism owned and operated by the public. That effort raised some crucial startup funding but ultimately fell short.] They had helped seed *The Colorado Sun*. We were lucky that the *Sun* was willing to take a chance on this completely unproven model. It has been a fantastic learning journey for all of us since then about how to make this work.

ELLEN: I've heard comments during my reporting that too many people involved in preserving local journalism focus their efforts on affluent communities. I want to hear your take on how the National Trust is involved in saving local news coverage in rural areas, in communities of color, and other places that are perhaps more challenging than the suburbs.

ELIZABETH: It's absolutely critical that journalism funders and organizations like ours move beyond supporting local news in major metro areas and reach out into rural communities and communities of color and the wide variety of places. My goal for the Conservancy in Colorado is to come out with a strategic plan and a set of resources and fundraising commitments so that we can go out with our partners and expand beyond our base and start to meet the need in some of those tiny communities across the state that are in dire straits and need strengthening. More broadly, we are keen to understand how issues of succession and capital needs are playing out in publishers serving communities of color.

DAN: This may be beyond what the National Trust is able to wrap its arms around, but ultimately it's going to be very difficult to solve the local news problem if we can't do something about the big chain owners, especially Gannett and Alden Global Capital. Do you have any ideas about what could be done to encourage chain owners to sell their papers to local interests, maybe through tax incentives or disincentives?

ELIZABETH: It's a difficult problem, and it would absolutely be a game changer to transform some of these metro chains into a system of local ownership. Ultimately, as I've rolled around this question in my head, I think it's actually going to take a concerted institutional funder-led effort to intervene at that scale. The Gannett market capitalization is $440 million. The Lee market cap is like $100 million. Chatham took McClatchy private for $300 million. Those are big dollars. To tackle chain ownership you really have to be thinking at a much different scale than the nonprofit news funders thinking, "Well, I'll give you $100,000 a year for three years." It's just a much different kettle of fish.

But I think the advantage at that scale is that there is profitability in the sector. These businesses still generate quite a bit of cash, still generate margins. This doesn't have to be philanthropy. Mission-related investments, program-related investments like impact investing could be usefully wrangled in that chain-paper space. But I think it would take leadership on behalf of some big institutional funders to say, "We want to take another shot at this because it's not something a single funder could do alone." And it would take some serious capital.

CHAPTER NINE

TEXAS

A High-Profile Behemoth
Prepares for Its Second Act

It was June 2022, and Evan Smith, cofounder and CEO of *The Texas Tribune*, was glad to be back in front of an audience, behind a mic, brimming with purpose and ready for a reboot. Smith was traveling the state, hosting a slate of live *Texas Tribune* events. He was renewing discussions and debates he described as "perfectly aligned with the *Tribune*'s now-thirteen-year-old public service mission, which is to raise the level of civic engagement and to civilize these kinds of conversations in the state of Texas," as he told a live audience at the University of Texas El Paso who had come to hear him quiz three state legislators onstage about their priorities.[1]

Their conversation touched on events that were still raw: the mass shooting that left nineteen children and two adults dead at Robb Elementary School in Uvalde, Texas, and the US Supreme Court decision overturning *Roe v. Wade*. Smith didn't mince words—or stint on explaining the mission that has long motivated him. "We know how polarized policy debates and political fights are," he told the audience. "But Texas is better when we all come together, find the things that we can agree on." This "reboot" of *The Texas Tribune*'s live events was overdue, and he was an exuberant presence, happy to be back where he had always been, poking and probing issues at the core of some of the state's most pressing public-policy challenges. The El Paso event was quintessential Smith and quintessential *Tribune*. "I have always believed in journalism in real time," he told us later.[2] And he made sure to thank the sponsors—in this case, ranging from the Paso del Norte Community Foundation to El Paso Community College—who are a core of the *Tribune*'s strategy of diversified funding.

Once a pioneering upstart, *The Texas Tribune*, based in Austin, the state capital, is now arguably one of the most well-known—and most successful—digital newsrooms in the country. The *Tribune* was launched in November 2009 during a crippling economic downturn that triggered layoffs and thwarted ambitions at mainstream newsrooms nationwide, and prompted reporters who feared being laid off at their for-profit papers to consider making the leap to a nonprofit startup.[3] The very concept of a digital nonprofit news outlet was so novel back then that when he wrote about Smith's plans, *New York Times* reporter Richard Pérez-Peña had to explain it was a website: a "nonprofit news web site devoted to government and politics in the Lone Star State."[4]

Dubbed "the poster child of the nonprofit [journalism] models emerging over the past few years" in a study published by the Harvard Shorenstein Center on Media, Politics and Public Policy, *The Texas Tribune* carries the imprint of its visionary founders.[5] Despite—or because of—the crisis at legacy newspapers across the state, Smith and his colleagues effectively made the case for journalism as a public good, adapting the National Public Radio nonprofit model that relies on member donations and sponsorships to a statewide digital newsroom covering government, politics, and public policy.

In October 2021, Sewell Chan, editorial page editor at the *Los Angeles Times* and a former *New York Times* journalist, was named editor-in-chief of the *Tribune*. In January 2022, Smith announced that he intended to "step down from this most enviable of all jobs no later than Dec. 31," prompting a search for a successor as CEO.[6] Now, as the founding generation moves on, *The Texas Tribune* is leading the way again, arguably writing the script about how a digital project can continue to innovate and build for the future.

The three cofounders, Smith, John Thornton, and Ross Ramsey, were already steeped in the lore and folkways of Texas politics, culture, and business when they combined forces in 2009. Thornton was a longtime venture capitalist based in Austin. (In 2018, he went on to cofound the American Journalism Project, which aims to help launch and build local news organizations through a funding concept it calls "venture philanthropy.")[7] When Smith announced in January 2022 that he intended to step down from *The Texas Tribune* after thirteen years, he paid tribute: "There's no way for me to quantify my debt to our founder, John Thornton, who changed my life when he finally persuaded me, after many months of resisting, to join him in his selfless effort to save what he called 'capital-J journalism.' He does not get nearly the credit he deserves for choosing to make the world better when he did not have to."[8]

Ramsey, who retired as executive editor in 2022 (his LinkedIn profile says "off the leash"[9]), brought years of experience as a political reporter and broadcaster in prominent Texas newsrooms, including those of the *Houston Chronicle*, the now-defunct *Dallas Times Herald*, and KBOX/KMEZ radio.

Smith was the longtime editorial chief at *Texas Monthly*, the city magazine with a storytelling bent based in Austin. He joined *Texas Monthly* as a senior editor in 1992 and was named editor and then president and editor in chief. By the time he left to start *The Texas Tribune* in 2009, *Texas Monthly* had received sixteen nominations for National Magazine Awards and won the National Magazine Award for General Excellence twice.[10]

But Smith, Thornton, and Ramsey had watched as the once-robust statehouse reporting corps in Austin's imposing granite capitol building shrank due to layoffs, buyouts, and attrition at the state's major daily newspapers.[11] As Smith told us in an interview at his *Tribune* office near the capitol on a sweltering day in July 2022, that left "white space" in journalism, a gap in the "existential if not literal" responsibility in journalism to hold powerful interests accountable and serve the public interest.[12] He knew the history, he assessed the reality, and he saw an opportunity.

"We have a Restoration Hardware problem in this country," he said. "We're nostalgic for a time that never actually existed. That is also the case in journalism. We have romanticized the old days completely out of proportion with what they actually were. We talk about, 'Oh, in the old days, public service journalism was so much in evidence and in abundance, and now it's gone.' I'm not sure that it was ever in abundance in the way that people think it was."

The cofounders raised $4 million in private contributions as seed funding, assembled a small team of talented journalists and computer programmers, and flipped the switch on November 3, 2009. A month before launch, Smith and his collaborators apprised the editors of the state's "big five" papers of their plans in a meeting with the *Morning News*, the *Chronicle*, the *Austin American-Statesman*, the *San Antonio Express-News*, and the *Fort Worth Star-Telegram*. "I refer to this in the telling all these years later as the Easter Island meeting," Smith said, "because they looked at us across the conference room table like the statues on Easter Island: stone-faced."

Smith said that the message he and his cofounders got from the five editors was that their newspapers had cut back accountability reporting on state government because "nobody cares." "And I said, 'You have it right, but you have it backwards. Nobody cares because you've stopped doing this stuff.' As I think back on it, we were not wrong. The news business in Texas had not entirely stopped serving the public interest, but it had gotten mostly out of the business of doing that. And so, for us, jumping in where they had largely jumped out was the point. That was a feature and not a bug."

From the outset, Smith knew he would be "building the plane while in flight." "It was absolutely gut. There was no feasibility study, there were no focus groups, there was no research," he said. His nascent newsroom, set up in an office building in downtown Austin, was infused with a sense of adventure and experimentation and determined to repeatedly publish, measure, and iterate. Sitting in his office in the mostly vacant *Tribune* newsroom in the summer of 2022, Smith recalled: "In the course of the first day, we would learn that we had done these things right and these things wrong, and on the second day we would revise the plan from the first day—and then on and on and on. And eventually we would find our feet, we would find our rhythm, and our path would become clear to us. We were not in those days, and still in these days are not, afraid of taking chances. The thing that is killing legacy media is aversion to risk because the cost of failure is too great. We have never been afraid to fail."

Since the days of Smith's "Easter Island meeting" with leaders of other Texas newsrooms, more and more legacy media titles have struggled for survival—and that struggle has brought with it new collaboration. Projects that cross institutional boundaries are pro-liferating, often with high-impact results. In 2021, for example, the Pulitzer Prize for National Reporting was awarded for a year-long investigation into the use of police dogs—and the injuries they can inflict—by a wide-ranging team of journalists from the Marshall Project; AL.com in Birmingham, Alabama; *The Indianapolis Star* in Indiana; and the Invisible Institute in Chicago.[13]

"If you view everybody else who is doing this work as your com-petitor, then you foreclose on the possibility that working together can produce work that is more important and more meaningful and more impactful than the work that either of you can produce individually," Smith observed. The *Tribune*, which now has one of the largest statehouse bureaus of any news organization in the United States, provides all of its content for free to print, digital, and broadcast outlets throughout Texas, and to its national partner, *The Washington Post*.[14] It's a strategy that initially worked to spread the word that the *Tribune* was a serious player, and that over the years has allowed legacy media to keep a grip on their public ser-vice mission and maintain accountability reporting as the econom-ics of the news business collapsed. In 2021, there were 422 *Texas Tribune* stories that appeared on the front pages of twenty different Texas newspapers.[15]

The *Tribune* leadership hopes to seed new ventures. Just before the pandemic lockdown in March 2020, the *Tribune* launched the RevLab, a journalism support organization housed in the *Tribune*, to share lessons learned and to help train other would-be news en-trepreneurs around the country. Emily Dresslar, who moved to the *Tribune* from the Compass Experiment at the McClatchy newspaper chain in 2021, is working on "creating cohorts or communities of practice in order to really build support networks—and then be able to support each other as [they] move on a road to sustainability." To start with, these cohorts focused on news organizations covering an entire state, such as *SpotlightPA*, *CalMatters*, and *VTDigger*. The interest, she said, is building. "Today, after we've just begun, we have twenty-seven news organizations participating, with half of US states represented. Hopefully, there will be fifty someday."[16]

The *Tribune*'s much-envied events strategy was an idea that preceded the *Tribune* itself. As Smith tells it, he was inspired by the New Yorker Festival, a live forum with a mix of presentations, talks, and screenings, back when he was running *Texas Monthly*: "I said, 'We need one of these here. And by here, I meant Austin, not Texas. Because Austin is the kind of community where we have the intersection of politics, media, culture, high-level college athletics, academia, and, more broadly, ideas and technology." He discussed the idea for a general-interest festival with Roland Swenson, cofounder and managing director of the South by Southwest Festival, and the late president of the University of Texas (UT), Bill Powers.[17]

Although the subprime mortgage crisis forced them to shelve those plans, the idea returned as Smith took his first office space in September 2009 to found *The Texas Tribune*. Swenson called him to ask if he was still thinking about events. Swenson connected Smith to Tanya Erlach, who had worked on live events at *The New Yorker*.[18] Smith hired Erlach as his first-ever events director, starting small with one-off discussions, leading ultimately to a schedule of as many as fifty events per year and the first Texas Tribune Festival in 2011.

In 2021, the festival—the *Tribune*'s biggest event of the year—featured 191 speakers and drew 1.7 million session views. That year, the *Tribune*'s digital platforms attracted 3.8 million unique visitors monthly, 41.5 million site users, and more than 9,000 paying members. Newsletters had 172,000 subscribers.

"Live journalism is where you put people in a room, on a stage, where you have an elected official, a newsmaker, a policymaker, on the record, cameras rolling," Smith told us in his office in 2022. "It has the benefit of building branding, it makes news, it's a lead generator for audience, it's a lead generator for membership—it's all those things. To me, it's a perfect way to accomplish, with innovation and creativity and a real sense of purpose, the mission of this organization."

E ven before it launched, *The Texas Tribune* attracted notice and talent. In August 2009, three award-winning Texas journalists jumped from large mainstream media outlets to join Smith's project, giving the young newsroom credibility. Elise Hu moved over from KVUE-TV in Austin, where she had been covering the Texas legislature. Matt Stiles arrived from the *Houston Chronicle*, where he had covered government and politics and delved into what was then called "computer-assisted reporting."

Emily Ramshaw left *The Dallas Morning News* to join Smith's staff and stayed for more than ten years. She served as an investigative reporter, editor, and editor in chief before leaving in January 2020 to cofound *The 19th* along with Amanda Zamora, who held jobs as digital editor and audience strategist at *ProPublica* and a number of publications, including *The Texas Tribune* and *The Washington Post*.[19] *The 19th*, an independent nonprofit organization and digital news platform, is named after the 19th Amendment of the Constitution, which afforded women the right to vote. The site focuses on gender, politics, LGBTQ+ rights, and policy. Ramshaw, who still lives in Austin, is also a member of the Pulitzer Prize Board at Columbia University.

By all accounts, Ramshaw was a rising star at the *Morning News*, so we asked her about her assessment of risk of jumping from a major metro daily to an online startup at that time. "I had survived multiple rounds of layoffs in my first few years as a working professional journalist," she told us, "and, to be perfectly frank with you, legacy media felt very unstable and felt very risky. People I loved and cared deeply about were getting laid off right and left. And it was hard as a young journalist to see a future where I would withstand those repeated rounds of cuts. I was thinking about what I might do next. I took the LSAT and started applying to law school. Then the founders of *The Texas Tribune* approached me and said they had this idea for a nonprofit startup, that they had the funding to at least make a go of it for the first couple of years. And in many ways that felt more stable than legacy media did. So I decided that it was worth the risk, that I deeply believed that there ought to be a new and functional business model for American media. And I took the plunge."[20]

The nonprofit news sector wasn't entirely unfamiliar for Ramshaw, whose father, Gregg Ramshaw, was managing producer and news editor for a public broadcasting show: PBS's *NewsHour* with Jim Lehrer.[21] "I had always seen journalism as a public service worth supporting," she said. "So I thought that the way they laid it out with a diversified revenue model had legs." Ramshaw made a deep imprint as a writer and editor at the *Tribune*, of course, but she also leaves a more concrete legacy. A plaque affixed to the conference room in the newsroom in downtown Austin declares, "Welcome to Ramshaw, in honor of Emily Ramshaw, Editor-in-Chief, 2016–2019."

Cofounder Ross Ramsey, a longtime political reporter and analyst, yearned early in his career to be part of the pack of "ninety to ninety-five credentialed journalists covering the Texas capital. That was the heyday, everyone was banging, they were making a lot of money." He worked in the Austin bureau of the *Times Herald*, then became statehouse bureau reporter for the *Houston Chronicle*. "You had a vibrant political news culture," he said."[22] Ramsey, who later bought the *Texas Weekly* newsletter, which fed scoops to political insiders and lobbyists, served as bureau chief to the legendary columnist Molly Ivins when both were at the *Times Herald* Austin bureau: "A highly theoretical position! But you had a really vibrant columnist culture. And it evolved into something less than that." Eventually the number of reporters covering the state legislature— which meets every other year but does plenty of business in interim sessions—dwindled to the point where "there weren't enough ants at the picnic," Ramsey told us. He retired as executive editor of *The Texas Tribune* in May 2022.

Texas arguably is a state-sized laboratory for national politics, minting presidential candidates and making headlines with its policies on border crossings. In the 1990s, Ramsey said, Texas was indeed emerging as a national political laboratory "in a way that California had been for the previous ten or twenty years. And that has only developed since then." The team that the cofounders gathered to launch the *Tribune* surveyed the state's media and political landscape to assess where the gaps in information were. As Emily Ramshaw put it:

What was missing in that media landscape was deep-dive and fast-paced reporting on what was happening in the Texas legislature inside the state capitol. As a lot of state news organizations [and] a lot of regional news organizations started to face cutbacks in the for-profit space, often one of the first things to go was their capitol coverage. We saw that there weren't very many eyes on that prize. Our vision was to be kind of like a hybrid between *Politico* and *ProPublica* for Texas. Yes, it was to provide that daily drumbeat of news and information that we believed Texans needed and that people who worked in and around the capitol needed to do their jobs. But also to ensure there was a really strong accountability piece. There were a lot of things happening behind the scenes that simply hadn't been covered enough, and we wanted to expose those things.[23]

The state's political ferment, and the crisis in legacy media that once covered it, intersected with an era of digital transformation, in Austin and throughout Texas. By 2007, about 60 percent of Texans used the internet, according to data from the US Census Bureau. Broadband access had widened across the US, with 82 percent of households reporting that they used a high-speed connection; only 17 percent used dial-up.[24] By 2015, internet use in Austin was higher than the national average, according to a joint report by the city and the University of Texas at Austin.[25] The report, based on a survey of 1,908 Austin residents, found that 92 percent of Austin households were connected to the internet—higher than the national average of 72 percent.

As a purely digital site, *The Texas Tribune* could present news, investigations, and data-driven reporting in packages that were blazingly urgent, highly visual, and eminently searchable—without shouldering the burden of ending a century-old industrial print process. Stiles had been rustling scoops as a budding data journalist in the statehouse bureau of the *Houston Chronicle* when he attended a party at Smith's house. "I had never met him before but obviously was a huge admirer," Stiles told us.[26] He had also watched newsroom cutbacks claim valued colleagues. Then the home office called to ask him to return to Houston because of layoffs. Stiles, who felt settled in Austin, determined that he wasn't going back. "I called Evan and said, 'Look, I don't want to leave Austin. Can I come work for you?' He said, 'It's going to be fine; we're going to figure something out. You're not going to have to go back.' It was very vague. And I just trusted him."

Stiles was already assembling data sets of public records at the *Chronicle* by making requests under the Texas Public Information Act. He wanted to share his data more widely, and he would do just that as employee number two at *The Texas Tribune*. (Employee number one was Abby Rapoport, now publisher of the *Stranger's Guide* travel guides, who signed on as an administrator and reporter.) Stiles spent the months before the *Tribune*'s official launch date in November 2009 gathering gigabytes of data and planning products that the *Tribune* would offer on its site and that he hoped would engage a new audience: an expansive salary database that covered nearly five hundred thousand state employees, a legislative bill tracker, and a database tracking controversial remote cameras that logged red-light violations. All of these drew readers, who could conduct research with these products on their own.

Ramsey said, "[In hindsight] it looks easy. From there, it looked like a real roll of the dice. If you were starting a news organization and it was 1880, you'd start a newspaper. In the '20s and '30s, you might start a radio station. In the '50s, you might start TV. The year before we started, the iPhone came out. The technology was blossoming, there was a market need, and people were getting news on their phone, not from something delivered to their front porch. All those things came together at the same time." Ramsey added, "If you thought about the internet and digital media in a particular way, it was like being in your twenties with a garage band and an uncle sent you a box full of guitar pedals. It was like: We have all these toys, let's make new noises!"

When Ramsey helped fuel the liftoff of the *Tribune*, he brought years of experience and credibility as a political reporter, first for metro newspapers and then as owner and editor of the *Texas Weekly*, a newsletter that was printed and mailed on Friday afternoons. Within four years of purchasing the newsletter in 1998, Ramsey said, he had moved it completely online as an emailed publication tied to a sub-scription-based website. He charged somewhere north of $200 a year and had 1,500 subscribers—primarily lobbyists and political insid-ers—when he moved it to *The Texas Tribune*. Now published three times a week, the newsletter has been renamed *The Blast*. It remains a paid product, costing subscribers $349 yearly, with a discount for nonprofits and government agencies.[27]

The core idea at the *Tribune* was to be the central place for Texas political, governmental, and policy coverage, according to Ramsey. "That's expanded somewhat. If you start with an idea that every sin-gle person you hire is an amendment, because they have ideas of their own, over time that's how you evolve."

As *The Texas Tribune* newsroom focused on taking the state's po-litical temperature, a key partner was Dr. James Henson, a polit-ical science professor at the University of Texas Austin, founder and codirector of the University of Texas/*Texas Tribune* Poll, launched in 2009. Indeed, the poll, which he describes as "the only open-access public survey of public opinion in Texas," seems adept at measuring the political fevers that sweep through this sprawling state of thirty million people.[28] The crosstabs of data and methodology are freely available on the *Tribune's* website for those who want to delve into the finer points of the 2022 gubernatorial race between Republican governor Greg Abbott and Democratic challenger Beto O'Rourke—or anyone who wants to understand why "potential candidate Matthew McConaughey is not universally beloved by Texans."[29]

Henson, who holds a PhD from UT in government, had been col-laborating with colleagues on statewide polling for the Texas Lyceum, a civic club and networking organization. He connected with Ramsey and others who noticed "there was no more statewide polling being done regularly in Texas," Henson told us.[30] Henson also wanted to tap into the nascent power of the internet. "Evan talked to me pretty early about the idea of the *Tribune*," he said. Henson noted Smith's natural "political junkie-ness" and added, "I've known Evan since before he was Evan Smith. He and I were in a poker game here in Austin when I was in graduate school. It was all musicians and media people, writers. It was one of my refuges from academic life."

The poll breaks news and garners national attention, such as the survey that found 30 percent of those questioned believed dinosaurs and humans roamed the earth at the same time.[31]

In January 2022, when Smith announced that he intended to step away at the end of the year, the *Tribune*'s foundational precepts hadn't wavered—the mission of transparency, nonpartisanship, and public service journalism is still core to daily coverage. His news resonated throughout independent newsrooms across the country, nonprofit, for-profit, and in between. Asked why, Smith offered a thoughtful answer that illustrated how he has kept the spirit of innovation and experimentation alive in the newsroom for thirteen years.

"This organization is in the best shape it's ever been," he told us. "There is never a better time to leave than when things are going really well. A second reason: A founder is by definition wedded to the origin story of an organization, is nostalgic and sentimental. Nostalgia and sentimentality are the enemies of progress. Every organization needs to change and evolve and grow." He continued: "For me, I've had two jobs in thirty-one years, with a weekend between. It's time for me to do something else. The world still needs to be saved. Journalism still needs to be saved. I'm up to the task. I'm just going to do it in a different way. But I want to be very clear about this: I don't love this place any less. If anything, I love it as much in the thirteenth year as I did on the first day. But I love it enough to know when it's time to leave."

An inveterate multitasker, Sewell Chan checks messages and email at the standup desk in his office just off *The Texas Tribune* newsroom before sitting down at a small round table to recount his journey from a childhood in Queens, New York, to Harvard University, and through the newsrooms of *The Washington Post*, *New York Times*, and *Los Angeles Times*. When he started at the *Tribune*, in October 2021, disinformation, the role of media, and the state of democracy in twenty-first-century America were all very much on his mind.

"I really feel that the crisis in our democracy is not going to be fixed from the coasts," he told us. "We need to help restore America from the inside out, if you will, and from the bottom up." Chan is clear-eyed about his goals. Number one, he said, is to enlarge and diversify the *Tribune*'s audience. Number two is "re-centering the Texas part of the *Tribune*. We're not *The Austin Tribune*; we're the *Texas Tribune*. Texas has a very urban population, but it is also important that we remember that the rural areas continue to be decisive, especially in statewide contests. But even outside of the political dimensions, there are a lot of issues—from broadband access to health care—that are particular to rural areas. A lot of publications don't cover them very well."[32]

To that end, Chan had just hired a reporter to cover the Texas Panhandle and South Plains and announced the first-ever East Texas reporter, who would live in Lufkin, a city of thirty-five thousand, "covering a big and diverse part" of the state. Chan's third goal, he said, was "to say . . . at a time of great turmoil and upheaval in our politics, that we stand for something. We are nonpartisan, and we are nonprofit. But we're not non-thinking, as Evan Smith says."

The entire organization is "resolutely pro-democracy," he said, adding more specifically, "That means we favor pluralism and diversity of views and perspectives, recognizing that we live in complex times. We are not here to support any party, sect, or faction. We are not trying to change Texas. We would like, however, to improve the functioning of democracy in Texas, and we do that by shining the light of accountability and by holding power to account."

Chan, the only child of parents who immigrated from China, attended Hunter College High School, a publicly funded school that is chartered by the City University of New York, administered by Hunter College, and known as a crucible for bright and creative students. His first brush with the power of the press occurred when he was fourteen and attending the 1992 Democratic National Convention in

New York as part of the staff of the now-shuttered *Children's Express* magazine and news service. He interviewed educator Marian Wright Edelman and Democratic National Convention chair Ron Brown and was hooked. "It was fascinating," he said, "this idea of bearing witness to history and watching power at work."

Chan holds a degree in social studies from Harvard and a master's in political science from Oxford, where he studied on a Marshall Scholarship. He began his professional career as a local reporter at *The Washington Post* in 2000 and moved on to a lengthy career at *The New York Times*, where he was a metro reporter, Washington correspondent, deputy op-ed editor, and international news editor. In 2018, he moved west to become a deputy managing editor of the *Los Angeles Times*. Chan ultimately became editorial page editor at the *Times*, where he directed coverage that won the Pulitzer Prize for Editorial Writing in 2021 for editorials on the California criminal justice system.[33] While in Los Angeles, Chan and his staff published a noteworthy editorial that apologized for past failures in coverage on race, as part of a larger series.[34]

Chan was realistic about the political climate in Texas, where Lieutenant Governor Dan Patrick announced in spring of 2022 that he wanted to prioritize legislation that would mirror the Florida bill referred to as the "don't say gay" law, which prohibits teachers from teaching sexual orientation or gender identity to children below the fourth grade.[35] "As someone who is gay," Chan said, "I am troubled, of course, by the direction that public policy is taking. But I also feel that it is important to remember that we as journalists are among the most empowered and privileged people in America. That doesn't mean we don't have feelings; I want to be very clear. But, ultimately, we're not telling stories about ourselves; we're telling stories about vulnerable people."

Texas, he added, really matters, "because the future of America really matters, and it is being shaped in states like this, like Georgia, Florida, North Carolina, Tennessee, Arizona, whether we like it or not." Chan is passionate about American history—our interview continued the next day as we toured the Lyndon Baines Johnson Presidential Library, lingering in front of a replica of LBJ's Oval Office and watching old television footage of civil rights movement marches and antiwar demonstrations. Chan knows that in Texas he is in the heart of a momentous, continually unfolding story—of demographic change, of climate change, of heated partisan debate. But he is passionate about the fact that feisty, independent newsrooms—newsrooms like his own—are an essential part of telling it.

THE FUTURE IS ALREADY HERE

The final days of 2022 were a reality check for struggling local news organizations whose leaders had hoped that politicians in Washington might come to their rescue. Two pieces of legislation that had been bandied about for several years failed to make it into the $1.7 trillion omnibus spending bill that was passed by Congress and signed into law by President Joe Biden.[1] With the House of Representatives about to flip from Democratic to Republican control, the prospects for reviving either bill appeared unlikely, even though both had some measure of bipartisan support.

One of those bills, the Journalism Competition and Preservation Act, would have granted an antitrust exemption to the news business so that it could negotiate collectively with Google and Facebook for a share of their advertising revenues. Although the measure was enthusiastically supported by the newspaper industry, including its two largest players, Gannett and Alden Global Capital, it also sparked considerable opposition. Critics argued that a similar law in Australia had served mainly to further enrich that country's leading press baron, Rupert Murdoch, and that startup digital publishers were likely to be excluded from sharing in the benefits. Chris Krewson, the executive director of LION (Local Independent Online News) Publishers, wrote to the organization's three hundred or so members that the main beneficiaries would be "the largest legacy publishers—including those who have strip-mined reporters from communities in the name of 20–30 percent profit margins, sending more money out of those towns and boroughs in order to boost profits for a corporate bottom line elsewhere."[2]

The other bill was less controversial, yet it too fell short. The Local Journalism Sustainability Act would have created three tax credits for a five-year period. One would have allowed people to write off the cost of subscriptions and donations to local news outlets. The second would have done the same for businesses that advertised in those outlets. The third would have provided tax benefits to the owners of local news organizations for hiring and retaining journalists. As proponents pointed out, that last provision might shame corporate chain owners into doing the right thing since they wouldn't be able to take advantage of it unless they stopped eliminating jobs and began to restore some of their reporting capacity. And because the governmental assistance would be indirect, the bill also elided concerns that it would interfere with journalistic independence. "This clever, bipartisan bill would provide more help for local news than any time in about a century, yet it's done in a very First-Amendment-friendly way," wrote Steven Waldman, cofounder of Report for America and president of Rebuild Local News, a coalition that comprises media and public interest organizations.[3]

Whatever the merits of these two proposals, their demise may have a salutary effect. Rather than waiting for a bailout from Google and Facebook, which after years of meteoric growth were starting to run into financial challenges, or from the whims of politicians, local news organizations were going to have to figure out a path to sustainability on their own.[4] As we have seen, many of them are doing just that.

The second half of 2022 was also a time of transition for several of the outlets that we've profiled in this book. Perhaps the most significant was at the *New Haven Independent*, whose founder and editor, Paul Bass, was among the first wave of local news entrepreneurs. On November 1, the *Independent* announced that Bass was stepping aside as editor, with managing editor Tom Breen moving up. It was a change that Bass and Breen had been toying with when we interviewed them a year earlier. Not that Bass was cutting back all that much: he would continue to report for the *Independent*, host a program on WNHH, and serve as executive director of the Online

Journalism Project, the nonprofit that serves as the umbrella organization for those projects as well as the *Valley Independent Sentinel* in New Haven's northwest suburbs. "The transition has been seamless," Bass told us in an email. "Tom's an excellent editor, always with good ideas for coverage and questions I wouldn't have thought of asking," he said, adding: "I also enjoy not working at night and on Sundays anymore!" Said Breen: "Paul's still a force of nature, and in my years of working with him, I've never seen him as happy on the job as he is now diving back into his true professional love of writing and reporting local news." One unfortunate side effect of the transition: because Breen would be writing less, Report for America corps member Nora Grace-Flood was reassigned from Hamden to New Haven, leaving Hamden without coverage. Bass said he hoped to restore the Hamden position at some point.[5]

In Minneapolis, *MinnPost* and the *Star Tribune* weathered several comings and goings. At *MinnPost*, the most high-profile of those changes took place in June 2022, when Elizabeth Dunbar, a twelve-year veteran of Minnesota Public Radio News, was hired as editor. Dunbar replaced Andrew Putz, who had joined *MinnPost* in 2014 and had served in the top position since 2016. "The organization is as strong as it's ever been," Putz told *MinnPost*, "which is one of the reasons why this felt like the right time to do this—to get out of the way and let somebody else lead the newsroom." Shortly after she arrived, Dunbar told her readers that one of her goals was to take part in an ongoing conversation with them, saying, "Local news organizations have an opportunity to help connect people with resources and with each other in unique ways. Engaging readers in helping shape local journalism is one of the best trends that's reached local news organizations around the country."[6]

At the *Star Tribune*, publisher and CEO Mike Klingensmith, who led the regional daily's turnaround during his thirteen-year run, announced that he would retire in January 2023. In an interview with *Poynter Online*, Klingensmith said, "The newsroom is behind all the success we have had." He was hopeful, despite an economic downturn in 2022. "There are some clouds now, not only clouds, but rain this year—inflation that's driving up our costs and a shaky economy. . . .

But I am overall an optimist; this is a very rough patch, but we will work through it."[7]

In October 2022, *The Texas Tribune*'s board of directors announced that Sonal Shah would become the new CEO as of January 1, 2023, replacing legendary CEO and founder Evan Smith. Shah, who had more than two decades of experience in nonprofit and government work, told *The New York Times*: "I'm a Texan so the *Tribune* matters to me." Smith, who said he would continue to advise the *Tribune*, would also become a senior adviser to the Emerson Collective, the nonprofit founded by Laurene Powell Jobs that helps fund nonprofit newsrooms, among many other projects. Smith, who built live events into an art form at the *Tribune*, would also advise Jobs on AtlanticLIVE events at *The Atlantic* magazine, of which Jobs is the majority owner. Shah brings deep-rooted experience in innovation and technology. She founded Georgetown University's Beeck Center for Social Impact and Innovation and worked in the Obama administration on issues such as technology, civic participation, and governmental reform. Before joining the White House, Shah worked at Google, where she led global development initiatives for Google.org. She also cofounded Indicorps, which offers fellowships for the Indian diaspora around the world to work on development projects in India.[8]

Following Julie McCay Turner's departure as managing editor of *The Bedford Citizen* in the summer of 2022, the news organization hired its first outside editor. The choice underscored the extent to which the fate of local news coverage in Bedford was entangled with Gannett. Turner and her fellow cofounders had launched the *Citizen* a decade earlier in response to what they saw as poor coverage by the local weekly, owned by GateHouse Media, which later morphed into Gannett. The *Citizen* was left as the only news source in the town after Gannett's *Bedford Minuteman* was shut down in the spring of 2022. And in October 2022, the *Citizen* announced that its new editor would be Wayne Braverman, who had been the editor of a Gannett real estate publication, *Boston Homes*, before it was closed in September. "I am well aware that I am stepping into the very big shoes of Julie Turner, Founder and Managing Editor, who has worked with extraordinary diligence to shape The Citizen into the outstanding resource it has become," Braverman wrote in introducing himself to the *Citizen*'s readers. "The bar is high." The original plan for replacing Turner, as discussed in chapter 3, was to bring in a part-time editor and a part-time content manager. Instead, the *Citizen* was able to make Braverman's position full-time. Executive director Teri Morrow said the additional funds came in part from unspent money and in part from continued success in soliciting donations.[9]

In an interview with PBS's *Frontline* in 1996, the media critic Ben Bagdikian was asked about the First Amendment to the US Constitution, which specifically mentions the press. Bagdikian observed that while the First Amendment allows newspapers to print unpopular views without government interference, the framers had more in mind. "There's an implied moral obligation," he said. "Because you have unusual power, . . . you have an obligation to serve the whole community, because the First Amendment was framed with the supposition that there would be multiple sources of information."[10]

Bagdikian, a former *Washington Post* editor and academic who died in 2016 at age ninety-six, spent much of his career warning of the dangers of monopoly, where a few powerful corporations control media outlets across the country. In his oft-updated book *The Media Monopoly*, he decried the concentration of media ownership in the television, film, book, and newspaper industries—including, yes, Gannett, which in the 1970s was running up profit margins of 30 to 50 percent at some of its papers.[11] As we've argued in this book, the business model for local news is broken, and chain ownership by a few powerful corporations has compounded the damage and prevented the investment needed to chart a new path.

The startups we've profiled are part of an emerging movement that we hope can sustain multiple local sources of information nationwide. This movement is still unfolding. If we are to save our democracy, it has to begin at the grassroots level. The paramount precondition for that is trustworthy news and information so that citizens can participate in civic affairs and make informed decisions. More than twenty years ago, in his classic book *Bowling Alone*, the Harvard sociologist

Robert D. Putnam identified a strong link between news consumption and civic engagement, writing, "Compared to demographically identical nonreaders, regular newspaper readers belong to more organizations, participate more actively in clubs and civic associations, attend local meetings more frequently, vote more regularly, volunteer and work on community projects more often, and even visit with friends more frequently and trust their neighbors more."[12] What Putnam described was a two-way dynamic: newspaper readers are more likely to be immersed in civic life; but civic life is not possible in the first place without newspapers and other sources of community journalism.

In meeting and talking with dozens of local news leaders for this book as well as for our podcast, we came away profoundly optimistic. In hundreds of communities across the country, independent news organizations are providing news and information of the quality and quantity that Bagdikian and Putnam would recognize as vital to living in a neighborhood, a village, a city, or a state. These news organizations are fulfilling the vision of our country's founders, who believed in a well-informed citizenry taking charge of their own affairs. As a quote often attributed to the science fiction writer William Gibson would have it, "The future is already here. It's just not evenly distributed yet."[13] News deserts are not going to disappear in the immediate future; indeed, the problem may get worse before it gets better. In the long run, though, we believe that it's possible for communities of all types—urban, suburban, and rural; affluent and not so affluent; alike and diverse—to take part in what we hope will be a news revolution.

ACKNOWLEDGMENTS

We knew we wanted to write a book together even before we had a topic. Ellen was retiring as editorial-page editor of *The Boston Globe*. Dan had wrapped up his book about how the *Globe*, *The Washington Post*, and the *Orange County Register* were faring under wealthy individual ownership. We'd known each other for quite a while, and the thought of collaborating was appealing to both of us. After considering and casting aside an idea or two, we hit upon writing a book about how a new generation of independent local news projects was demonstrating that there are alternatives to the bottom-line mentality of corporate chain ownership. Writing on a whiteboard one afternoon in the School of Journalism at Northeastern University, we came up with a list of projects and divided them up. It's been a lot of work, with our travel plans continually bumping up against the limits imposed by the COVID-19 pandemic. But it's also been a lot of fun.

Our heartfelt thanks go to Catherine Tung, our editor at Beacon Press, who was enthusiastic about our project as soon as we proposed it to her, and who cheerfully endorsed our decision to put everything on hold during the worst of the pandemic, when travel was impossible. Others at Beacon who deserve our thanks include managing editor Susan Lumenello; production manager Beth Collins; Chris Dodge, our diligent copyeditor; Carol Chu, the designer; and Alyssa Hassan and Bev Rivero, who are handling marketing and publicity. We also appreciate the support we received from Jonathan Kaufman, director of Northeastern's journalism program. Ellen thanks her wife, Ellen Zucker, and two sons, Jonathan Gagen and Jake Zucker, for tolerating the chaotic intersection of long-form writing, stop-start travel, and a pandemic lockdown. Dan thanks his wife, Barbara Kennedy, and children, Tim and Becky Kennedy, for their love and support throughout the uncertain, time-consuming process of writing a book. And we both thank the journalists, thinkers, scholars, and entrepreneurs who generously agreed to talk about their vision.

NOTES

INTRODUCTION

1. Rick Edmonds, "Gannett Reports Disastrous Financial Results; Layoffs Are Coming," *Poynter Online*, August 4, 2022, https://www.poynter.org/reporting-editing/2022/gannett-reports-disastrous-financial-results-layoffs-are-coming.

2. "*Grafton News* Editor Laid Off in Gannett Cuts; Newspaper May No Longer Print," *Grafton Common*, August 13, 2022, https://graftoncommon.com/grafton-news-editor-laid-off-in-gannett-cuts-newspaper-may-no-longer-print; Angela Fu, "Gannett Lays Off More Than 50 Journalists after Dismal Second Quarter Results," *Poynter Online*, August 16, 2022, https://www.poynter.org/business-work/2022/gannett-lays-off-journalists-after-dismal-second-quarter-results.

3. Jeong Park, Twitter thread, August 13, 2022, 12:47 a.m.; later deleted but available at https://web.archive.org/web/20221117142044/https://twitter.com/JeongPark52/status/1558314155676823554.

4. Rick Edmonds, "Gannett Tells Its News Division That More Layoffs Are Coming Dec. 1," *Poynter Online*, November 17, 2022, https://www.poynter.org/business-work/2022/gannett-tells-its-news-division-that-more-layoffs-are-coming-dec-1.

5. Penny Abernathy, *The State of Local News: The 2022 Report*, Northwestern/Medill Local News Initiative, June 29, 2022, https://localnewsinitiative.northwestern.edu/research/state-of-local-news/report.

6. Gannett Company proxy statement to shareholders, April 27, 2022, https://s1.q4cdn.com/307481213/files/doc_downloads/annual_meeting/2022/Gannett-2022-Definitive-Proxy-Statement.pdf.

7. Ken Doctor, "Newsonomics: Alden Global Capital Is Making So Much Money Wrecking Local Journalism It Might Not Want to Stop Anytime Soon," *Nieman Lab*, May 1, 2018, https://www.niemanlab.org/2018/05/newsonomics-alden-global-capital-is-making-so-much-money-wrecking-local-journalism-it-might-not-want-to-stop-anytime-soon.

8. Cara Lombardo and Jeffrey A. Trachtenberg, "GateHouse Media Parent to Buy Gannett for $1.4 Billion," *Wall Street Journal*, August 5, 2019, https://www.wsj.com/articles/gatehouse-media-parent-to-buy-gannett-for-1-4-billion-11565031875; Tali Arbel, "Alden Puts Its Stamp on Tribune with

New Debt and Leadership," Associated Press, May 26, 2021, https://apnews.com/article/business-a1ddfd98054a1e77175cf62fec4d2718.

9. John Reinan, "How Craigslist Killed the Newspapers' Golden Goose," *MinnPost*, February 3, 2014, https://www.minnpost.com/business/2014/02/how-craigslist-killed-newspapers-golden-goose.

10. Sara Lebow, "Google, Facebook, and Amazon to Account for 64% of US Digital Ad Spending This Year," *Insider Intelligence*, November 3, 2021, https://www.insiderintelligence.com/content/google-facebook-amazon-account-over-70-of-us-digital-ad-spending.

11. Doug Muder, "Expand Your Vocabulary: News Desert," *The Weekly Sift* (blog), December 5, 2011, https://weeklysift.com/2011/12/05/expand-your-vocabulary-news-desert. Muder traces the term back to Laura Washington, writing in *In These Times*, who discussed "communications deserts." *Chicago Is the World*, a blog covering Chicago's "ethnic media landscape," written by Steve Franklin, then shortened it to "news desert"; http://chicagoistheworld.org/2011/04/the-news-desert-we-live-in-please-come-and-visit.

12. Josh Stearns, "How We Know Journalism Is Good for Democracy," Local News Lab, June 20, 2018, https://localnewslab.org/2018/06/20/how-we-know-journalism-is-good-for-democracy.

13. Priyanjana Bengani, "Hundreds of 'Pink Slime' Local News Outlets Are Distributing Algorithmic Stories and Conservative Talking Points," *Columbia Journalism Review*, December 18, 2019, https://www.cjr.org/tow_center_reports/hundreds-of-pink-slime-local-news-outlets-are-distributing-algorithmic-stories-conservative-talking-points.php.

14. Henry David Thoreau, *Walden* (New York: Cosimo, 2009), 34.

15. Walter Lippmann, *Public Opinion* (New York: Harcourt, Brace, 1922), 248; Jay Rosen, *What Are Journalists For?* (New Haven, CT: Yale University Press, 1999), 65.

16. Nikki Usher, *News for the Rich, White, and Blue: How Place and Power Distort American Journalism* (New York: Columbia University Press, 2021), 17.

17. The *What Works* website and podcast are at https://whatworks.news; the podcast can also be found on all the major podcast platforms.

CHAPTER ONE: NEW JERSEY

1. Dave Caldwell, "Robbinsville, N.J.: A Diverse Community 'at the Center of It All'" *New York Times*, January 26, 2022, https://www.nytimes.com/2022/01/26/realestate/robbinsville-nj.html.

2. Micah Rasmussen spoke on March 2, 2022, at an event called "Warehouse Growth in New Jersey: Impacts and Opportunities." Video online at Jon Hurdle, "Stakeholders Advocate Solutions for How to Manage NJ's Warehouse Surge," *NJ Spotlight News*, March 8, 2022, https://www.njspotlightnews.org/2022/03/nj-warehouse-growth-control-opportunities-truck-traffic-tax-revenue-jobs-some-strong-opposition.

3. Steven Shalit, video interview by Dan Kennedy, March 24, 2022.

4. Richard Prince, "*Star-Ledger* to Lose 40% of Newsroom," *Journal-isms*, November 1, 2008, https://www.journal-isms.com/2008/11/archive-348.

5. John Mooney, in-person interview by Kennedy, March 28, 2022.

6. Aaron Fischer, "WNET Acquires *NJ Spotlight*, Fosters Closer Partnership with NJTV," *NJ Spotlight News*, March 5, 2019, https://www.njspotlight news.org/2019/03/19–03–04-wnet-acquires-nj-spotlight-fosters-closer -partnership-with-njtv.

7. "Population Estimate for 2021," *StatsAmerica*, https://www.statsamerica .org/sip/rank_list.aspx?rank_label=pop1, accessed July 25, 2022.

8. Neal Shapiro, video interview by Kennedy, March 31, 2022.

9. Elizabeth Hansen, "The Public Media Mergers Playbook," Public Media Merger Project, January 14, 2021, https://medium.com/the-public-media -merger-project/the-public-media-mergers-playbook-b576be1a0356.

10. David Sachsman and Warren Sloat, *The Press and the Suburbs: The Daily Newspapers of New Jersey* (New Brunswick, NJ: Center for Urban Policy Research, Rutgers University, 1985), 3.

11. Sachsman and Sloat, *The Press and the Suburbs*, 4–7, 28–33.

12. Sachsman and Sloat, *The Press and the Suburbs*, 78–84, 113–19.

13. "NAMI Condemns Trenton Newspaper for 'Roasted Nuts' Headline About Fire at Psychiatric Hospital," National Alliance for the Mentally Ill, July 16, 2002, https://www.nami.org/Press-Media/Press-Releases/2002 /NAMI-Condemns-Trenton-Newspaper-for-Roasted-Nuts.

14. Circulation figures for the six-month period ending March 31, 2022, as reported to the Alliance for Audited Media, https://auditedmedia.com.

15. "NJ Advance Media Names 2 Veteran Journalists as New General Manager, VP Content," NJ.com, October 14, 2022, https://www.nj.com/news /2022/10/nj-advance-media-names-2-veteran-journalists-as-new-general -manager-vp-content.html.

16. Chris Kelly, in-person interview by Kennedy, March 30, 2022. Kelly was also the source of the NJ.com newsroom count of 115 and of the daily-visits figure of 1.5 million.

17. Katherine Landergan, video interview by Kennedy, April 1, 2022.

18. "About Us," *New Jersey Globe*, https://newjerseyglobe.com/about-us, accessed August 26, 2022; Dana Rubinstein and Ryan Hutchins, "Kushner-Allied Editor Joins Forces with Bridgegate Mastermind," *Politico*, March 1, 2018, https://www.politico.com/states/new-york/city-hall/story /2018/03/01/kushner-allied-editor-joins-forces-with-bridgegate -mastermind-288086.

19. Rick Edmonds, "After Shrinking for Years, Statehouse Coverage Has Started Modestly Growing," *Poynter Online*, April 5, 2022, https://www .poynter.org/reporting-editing/2022/after-shrinking-for-years-statehouse -coverage-has-started-modestly-growing.

20. Elahe Izadi, "The Troubling New Void in Local Journalism—and the Nonprofits Trying to Fill It," *Washington Post*, December 6, 2021, https:// www.washingtonpost.com/media/2021/12/06/media-states-newsroom -government.

21. "Find a Newsroom in Your State," States Newsroom, https://states newsroom.com/newsrooms, accessed July 26, 2022.

22. Stefanie Murray, in-person interview by Kennedy, March 29, 2022.

23. Sarah Stonbely, "What Makes for Robust Local News Provision?," Center for Cooperative Media, Montclair State University, February 2021, https:// centerforcooperativemedia.org/wp-content/uploads/sites/5/2021/02/what -makes-for-robust-local-news-provision-2021.pdf.

24. "Local News Map—NJ," April 2020, Center for Cooperative Media, Montclair State University, https://newsecosystems.org/njmap.

25. Sarah Stonbely, in-person interview by Kennedy, March 29, 2022.

26. Joe Amditis, in-person interview by Kennedy, March 29, 2022.

27. Cassandra Etienne, in-person interview by Kennedy, March 29, 2022.

28. "About the Consortium," New Jersey Civic Information Consortium, https://njcivicinfo.org/about, accessed July 27, 2022; "NJ Civic Information Consortium Announces 2022 State Appropriation," New Jersey Civic Information Consortium, July 20, 2022, https://njcivicinfo.org/wp-content /uploads/sites/11/2022/07/Consortium-2022-Budget-Press-Release.pdf.

29. Laura Hazard Owen, "The State of California Will Fund $25 Million in Local Reporting Fellowships," *Nieman Lab*, September 8, 2022, https:// www.niemanlab.org/2022/09/the-state-of-california-will-fund-25-million -in-local-reporting-fellowships.

30. "Public Radio Finances," NPR.org, https://www.npr.org/about-npr /178660742/public-radio-finances, accessed November 7, 2022.

31. Molly de Aguiar, in-person interview by Kennedy, March 27, 2022.

32. Michael Shapiro, video interview by Kennedy, March 17, 2022; "A Network of Community News Franchises: Mike Shapiro on What Makes TAPinto Click," *What Works* (podcast), April 27, 2022, https://whatworks .news/2022/04/27/a-network-of-community-news-franchises-mike-shapiro -on-what-makes-tapinto-click.

33. Rick Rojas, "Software Engineer Starts an Unlikely Business: A Weekly Newspaper," *New York Times*, March 27, 2017, https://www.nytimes .com/2017/03/27/nyregion/new-newspaper-prompts-war-of-weeklies-in -new-jersey-suburb.html.

34. Stephen Engelberg and Jonathan Alter, in-person interview by Kennedy, March 29, 2022; "*Montclair Local* Merges with *Baristanet* to Become a Digital-Only News Organization," *Montclair Local*, April 21, 2023, https://montclairlocal.news/montclair-local-merges-with-baristanet-to -become-a-digital-only-news-organization/.

35. Lou Hochman, video interview by Kennedy, April 8, 2022.

36. John McAlpin, video interview by Kennedy, July 21, 2022.

37. Lilo Stainton, video interview by Kennedy, March 22, 2022.

38. John Reitmeyer, in-person interview by Kennedy, March 28, 2022.

39. Bob Feinberg, in-person interview by Kennedy, March 28, 2022.

40. "NJTV Announces Jamie Kraft to Assume New Role as Senior Managing Editor for NJTV News and *NJ Spotlight*," *Insider NJ*, October 28, 2019, https://www.insidernj.com/njtv-jamie-kraft-editor-njtv-spotlight. Kennedy visited the NJ PBS newsroom on July 20, 2022.

41. Jamie Kraft, in-person interview by Kennedy, July 20, 2022.
42. "Joseph Lee Appointed New General Manager of NJ PBS," NJ PBS, August 18, 2021, https://www.njtvonline.org/blog-post/joseph-lee-general -manager-nj-pbs; Joseph Lee, in-person interview by Kennedy, July 20, 2022.
43. Briana Vannozzi, "Rep. Watson Coleman on Arrest, Reshaping Top Court, Continuing Fight for Women's Rights," *NJ Spotlight News*, July 20, 2022, https://www.njspotlightnews.org/video/rep-watson-coleman-on-arrest -reshaping-top-court-continuing-fight-for-womens-rights.
44. Briana Vannozzi, in-person interview by Kennedy, July 20, 2022.
45. "Briana Vannozzi Elevated to Full-Time Anchor for *NJTV News* on New Jersey Public Television," *Insider NJ*, September 9, 2020, https://www .insidernj.com/press-release/briana-vannozzi-elevated-full-time-anchor -njtv-news-new-jersey-public-television.

CHAPTER TWO: MINNEAPOLIS, MINNESOTA
1. Jennifer A. Delton, "The Black Communities in Minnesota," in *Making Minnesota Liberal: Civil Rights and the Transformation of the Democratic Party* (Minneapolis: University of Minnesota Press, 2002), 61–78.
2. "Staff of the Star Tribune, Minneapolis, Minn.," 2021 Pulitzer Prize Winner in Breaking News Reporting, Pulitzer Prizes, https://www.pulitzer.org /winners/staff-star-tribune-minneapolis-minn.
3. "Darnella Frazier," 2021 Pulitzer Prize Winner in Special Citations and Awards, Pulitzer Prizes, https://www.pulitzer.org/winners/darnella-frazier.
4. Mukhtar Ibrahim, telephone interview by Ellen Clegg, July 23, 2021.
5. Minnesota Department of Health, *Weekly COVID-19 Report*, July 22, 2021, https://www.health.state.mn.us/diseases/coronavirus/stats/covid weekly2921.pdf.
6. Minnesota State Demographic Center statistics based on 2018 population estimates from the US Census Bureau, https://mn.gov/admin/demography /data-by-topic/age-race-ethnicity, accessed August 18, 2022.
7. Burl Gilyard, "New Report Touts Importance of Immigrants to Minnesota's Economy," *MinnPost*, March 24, 2021, https://www.minnpost.com /twin-cities-business/2021/03/new-report-touts-importance-of-immigrants -to-minnesotas-economy.
8. Anduin Wilhide, "Somali and Somali American Experiences in Minnesota," *MNopedia*, February 27, 2018, https://www.mnopedia.org/somali -and-somali-american-experiences-minnesota.
9. "Eid Al-Adha Prayer at Huntington Bank Stadium," photo gallery, *Star Tribune*, July 20, 2021, https://www.startribune.com/eid-al-adha-prayer -at-huntington-bank-stadium/600079778.
10. Mukhtar Ibrahim, telephone interview by Clegg, March 22, 2019.
11. Giulia Paravicini, "Ethiopian Who Demanded Justice Now Has Half a Year to Deliver It," Reuters, January 28, 2020, https://www.reuters.com /article/us-ethiopia-justice/ethiopian-who-demanded-justice-now-has-half -a-year-to-deliver-it-idUSKBN1ZR10K.

12. Nancy Cassutt, "Editor's Note: Racial Bias in MPR's Work? We Want to Know," *Inside MPR News*, January 22, 2019, https://www.mprnews.org/story/2019/01/18/mpr-news-changing-racial-narratives.

13. Nancy Cassutt, in-person interview by Clegg, April 8, 2019.

14. Glen Nelson Center at American Public Media website, https://www.glennelson.org, accessed April 9, 2019.

15. 2007 Peabody Awards, "Speaking of Faith: The Ecstatic Faith of Rumi," https://peabodyawards.com/award-profile/speaking-of-faith-the-ecstatic-faith-of-rumi.

16. Mukhtar Ibrahim, "Editor's Note: Welcome to Sahan Journal," *Sahan Journal*, August 11, 2019, https://sahanjournal.com/changing-the-narrative/welcome-to-sahan-journal.

17. Ibrahim Hirsi, "Young, Educated and Black: Here's How Minnesota's Politicians with African Roots Are Reshaping the State's Politics," *Sahan Journal*, August 30, 2020, https://sahanjournal.com/democracy-politics/black-immigrants-minnesota-elections.

18. "About Ilhan Omar," House.gov, https://omar.house.gov/about, accessed December 29, 2021.

19. Carol Guensburg and Betty Ayoub, "Somali American Lawmaker in Minnesota Sees Role as Bridge Builder," Voice of America, November 15, 2021, https://www.voanews.com/a/somali-american-lawmaker-in-minnesota-sees-role-as-bridge-builder/6313557.html.

20. Minnesota Legislature, Legislative Coordinating Commission, American Community Survey Profile Report for Senate District 62, https://www.gis.lcc.mn.gov/php/profiles/senate.php?district=62&section=dp05, accessed December 29, 2021.

21. "Columbia Journalism School Names 2022 Alumni Award Winners," Columbia Journalism School, Columbia University, December 14, 2021, https://journalism.columbia.edu/columbia-journalism-school-names-2022-alumni-award-winners.

22. Katie Hawkins-Gaar, "How *Sahan Journal* Built Community Support to Grow Revenue by 50% in One Year," Institute for Nonprofit News, September 8, 2021, https://inn.org/sahan-journal-increased-revenue.

23. "Shaking the Trees: How 15 Newsrooms Grew Sponsorship Revenue by 250%," Institute for Nonprofit News, March 15, 2022, https://inn.org/news/shaking-the-trees-how-15-newsrooms-grew-sponsorship-revenue-by-250.

24. "*Sahan Journal* Receives $1.2 Million Grant from American Journalism Project to Expand Diverse News Coverage in Minnesota," *Sahan Journal*, January 11, 2022, https://sahanjournal.com/inside-sahan-journal/sahan-journal-american-journalism-project-grant-minnesota.

25. "Reporters Committee Announces 2022 Freedom of the Press Award Honorees," Reporters Committee for Freedom of the Press, June 7, 2022, https://www.rcfp.org/awards-2022-honorees.

26. Aala Abdullahi, "Inside *Sahan Journal*: When a Charter School Closed in Cedar Riverside, We Realized We Had a Lot to Learn," *Hiiraan Online*, June 3, 2021, https://hiiraan.com/news4/2021/Jun/182798/inside_sahan

_journal_when_a_charter_school_closed_in_cedar_riverside_we_realized_we_
had_a_lot_to_learn_about_getting_the_news_to_immigrant_parents.aspx.

27. Kimiko de Freytas-Tamura, "In Minneapolis, Somali-Americans Find Unwelcome Echoes of Strife at Home," *New York Times*, June 7, 2020, https://www.nytimes.com/2020/06/07/us/minneapolis-somalis-george-floyd.html.

28. "Quick Facts: Minnesota," US Census Bureau, July 22, 2022, https://www.census.gov/quickfacts.

29. Troy Patterson, "The Tiny Media Collective That Is Delivering Some of the Most Vital Reporting from Minneapolis," *New Yorker*, https://www.newyorker.com/culture/culture-desk/the-tiny-media-collective-that-is-delivering-some-of-the-most-vital-reporting-from-minneapolis.

30. Dan Feidt, telephone interview by Clegg, April 28, 2021

31. "About *Unicorn Riot*," Unicorn Riot, https://unicornriot.ninja/about-unicorn-riot, accessed August 18, 2022.

32. "Donate," https://unicornriot.ninja/donate/.

33. Feidt interview; John Hilliard, Sara Wu, and Brian MacQuarrie, "Protesters Jeer Straight Pride Parade Marchers along Route to City Hall," *Boston Globe*, August 31, 2019, https://www.bostonglobe.com/metro/2019/08/31/counterprotesters-rally-across-city-from-straight-pride-parade-starting-point/qFStqXFPcWoOWAaxkDyDfI/story.html.

34. *Unicorn Riot* IRS Form 990 for 2020, available at GuideStar, http://guidestar.org/.

35. Adam Gabbatt, "*Unicorn Riot*: The Tiny Media Outlet on the Frontlines of US Protests," *The Guardian*, July 1, 2020, https://www.theguardian.com/media/2020/jul/01/unicorn-riot-george-floyd-protests.

36. Emici Thug, "Brazil: The People, at Last, Took to the Streets," *Unicorn Riot*, June 3, 2021, https://unicornriot.ninja/2021/brazil-the-people-at-last-took-to-the-streets.

37. Katharine Q. Seelye and Andrew Ross Sorkin, "Knight Ridder Newspaper Chain Agrees to Sale," *New York Times*, March 12, 2006, https://www.nytimes.com/2006/03/12/archives/knight-ridder-newspaper-chain-agrees-to-sale.html.

38. John Vomhof Jr., "*Star Tribune* Circulation Slips 2.9%" *Minneapolis/St. Paul Business Journal*, May 8, 2006, https://www.bizjournals.com/twincities/stories/2006/05/08/daily9.html.

39. Briana Bierschbach and Greta Kaul, "The Five Reasons Why Voter Turnout in Minnesota Is So High," *MinnPost*, September 29, 2016, https://www.minnpost.com/politics-policy/2016/09/five-reasons-why-voter-turnout-minnesota-so-high.

40. Jim Romenesko, "McClatchy Sells *Star Tribune* to Private Equity Firm for $530M," *Poynter Online*, December 26, 2006, https://www.poynter.org/reporting-editing/2006/mcclatchy-sells-star-tribune-to-private-equity-firm-for-530m; "McClatchy to Sell *Star Tribune* Newspaper," *TheStreet*, December 26, 2006, https://www.thestreet.com/investing/stocks/mcclatchy-to-sell-star-tribune-newspaper-10329713.

41. Joe Kimball, "10 at 10: An Oral History of the Birth of *MinnPost*," *MinnPost*, December 28, 2017, https://www.minnpost.com/inside-minnpost/2017/12/10-10-oral-history-birth-minnpost.

42. Martin Moylan, "Mainstream Journalists Launch Online News Site," Minnesota Public Radio, November 8, 2007, https://www.mprnews.org /story/2007/11/08/mainstream-journalists-launch-online-news-site.

43. Andrew Putz and Susan Albright, in-person interview by Clegg, April 9, 2019.

44. Erin Coghlan, Lisa McCorkell, and Sara Hinkley, "What Really Caused the Great Recession?," policy brief, Institute for Research on Labor and Employment, University of California, Berkeley, September 19, 2018, https://irle.berkeley.edu/what-really-caused-the-great-recession.

45. Kimball, "10 at 10."

46. Jon Pratt and Edson W. Spencer, "Dynamics of Corporate Philanthropy in Minnesota," *Daedalus* 129, no. 3 (2000): 269–92.

47. Kimball, "10 at 10."

48. "About Us," 2020 IRS 990 form, *Voice of San Diego*, https://voiceofsan diego.org/wp-content/uploads/2022/06/Voice-of-San-Diego-990–2020 -FYE-06–30–21-PUBLIC-DISCLOSURE.pdf, accessed August 14, 2022.

49. Kathleen Gilsinin, "Not for Profit? The *Voice of San Diego* Experiment," Knight Case Studies Initiative, Graduate School of Journalism, Columbia University, https://ccnmtl.columbia.edu/projects/caseconsortium/casestudies /51/casestudy/www/layout/case_id_51.html, accessed August 18, 2022.

50. Kimball, "10 at 10."

51. Jeremy W. Peters, "*Times*'s Online Pay Model Was Years in the Making," *New York Times*, March 20, 2011, https://www.nytimes.com/2011/03/21 /business/media/21times.html.

52. Putz and Albright interview.

53. Kimball, "10 at 10."

54. Moylan, "Mainstream Journalists Launch Online News Site."

55. Kimball, "10 at 10."

56. Taylor Soper, "Report: Amazon Takes More Digital Advertising Market Share from Google-Facebook Duopoly," *GeekWire*, February 20, 2019, https://www.geekwire.com/2019/report-shows-amazon-taking-digital -advertising-market-share-google-facebook-duopoly.

57. Putz and Albright, in-person interview by Clegg, April 9, 2019.

58. Rick Edmonds, "Looking for a Sustainable Business Model for a Regional Newspaper? Start at the *Minneapolis Star Tribune*," *Poynter Online*, May 19, 2016, https://www.poynter.org/business-work/2016/looking -for-a-sustainable-buisness-model-for-a-regional-newspaper-start-at-the -minneapolis-star-tribune; Rick Edmonds, "Why Does the *Star Tribune* Outperform the Pack of Metros? An Update," *Poynter Online*, May 2, 2018, www.poynter.org, https://www.poynter.org/business-work/2018 /why-does-the-star-tribune-outperform-the-pack-of-metros-an-update; Kristen Hare, "At the *Minneapolis Star Tribune*, a Newsroom That's Gone from Surviving to Thriving," *Poynter Online*, November 2, 2016, www.poynter.org/tech-tools/2016/at-the-minneapolis-star-tribune-a-news room-thats-gone-from-surviving-to-thriving.

59. "Michael T. P. Sweeney, Executive Profile," Bloomberg, https://www .bloomberg.com/profile/person/5927523, accessed June 5, 2019.

60. Eric Black, "Selling *Star Tribune* to Koch Some Day 'Could Happen,' Chairman Says," *MinnPost*, June 12, 2013, https://www.minnpost.com/eric-black-ink/2013/06/selling-star-tribune-koch-some-day-could-happen-chairman-says.
61. Black, "Selling *Star Tribune* to Koch."
62. Lori Sturdevant, telephone interview by Clegg, May 22, 2019.
63. Black, "Selling *Star Tribune* to Koch."
64. Michael J. Klingensmith biography, *Star Tribune*, https://www.startribune.com/michael-klingensmith-bio/80963562, accessed June 5, 2019; David Brauer, "*Star Tribune* Names Klingensmith Publisher," Braublog, *MinnPost*, January 7, 2010, https://www.minnpost.com/braublog/2010/01/star-tribune-names-klingensmith-publisher.
65. Pulitzer Prize winners by year, Pulitzer Prizes, https://www.pulitzer.org/prize-winners-by-year.
66. "Staff of the Star Tribune, Minneapolis, Minn.," 2021 Pulitzer Prize Winner in Breaking News Reporting, Pulitzer Prizes, https://www.pulitzer.org/winners/staff-star-tribune-minneapolis-minn.
67. Adam Belz, "Glen Taylor Finalizes Purchase of *Star Tribune*," *Star Tribune*, July 1, 2014, https://www.startribune.com/july-1–2014-glen-taylor-finalizes-purchase-of-star-tribune/265223641.
68. Curt Brown, "From Farm Boy to Billionaire, Glen Taylor Steers His Own Course," *Star Tribune*, June 29, 2014, https://www.startribune.com/june-29–2014-from-farm-boy-to-billionaire-taylor-steers-own-course/265057261.
69. Brown, "From Farm Boy to Billionaire."
70. Sturdevant interview.
71. Janet Moore, "*Star Tribune* to Move Headquarters to Capella Tower in 2015," *Star Tribune*, May 13, 2014, https://www.startribune.com/star-tribune-to-move-to-capella-tower-in-2015/253801281.
72. Jean Taylor, LinkedIn profile, https://www.linkedin.com/in/jean-taylor, accessed June 6, 2019; Sturdevant interview.
73. Dana Thiede, "*Star Tribune* Buys *City Pages*, Retires *Vita.mn*," KARE-11, May 6, 2015, https://www.kare11.com/article/news/star-tribune-buys-city-pages-retires-vitamn/89–105520664, accessed June 5, 2019.
74. Joy Summers, "*City Pages*, Minneapolis' Alternative Weekly Paper, Ceased Production Today," *Eater Twin Cities*, October 28, 2020, https://twincities.eater.com/2020/10/28/21538395/city-pages-minneapolis-best-of-star-tribune-shut-down-closed.
75. "From Northeastern to the North Country: Em Cassel's Entrepreneurial Journey," *What Works* (podcast), April 5, 2022, https://whatworks.news/2022/04/05/from-northeastern-to-the-north-country-em-cassels-entrepreneurial-journey.
76. Sturdevant interview.
77. Sean, "How Big Is Minneapolis? A Local's Opinion on the Numbers," *Discover the Cities*, March 1, 2022, https://discoverthecities.com/how-big-minneapolis-city; metropolitan area: Suki Dardarian, telephone interview by Clegg, June 29, 2022.
78. Annie Baxter, "More Cutbacks at Star Tribune," Minnesota Public Radio News, May 7, 2007, https://www.mprnews.org/story/2007/05/07/strib.

79. Circulation numbers as reported to the Alliance for Audited Media, http://auditedmedia.com/.

80. Adam Platt, "*Star Tribune* Publisher Mike Klingensmith on the *Pioneer Press*, the Ad Biz and the Future of Print and Digital Media," *MinnPost*, July 13, 2018, https://www.minnpost.com/twin-cities-business/2018/07/star-tribune-publisher-mike-klingensmith-pioneer-press-ad-biz-and-futur; Tim McGuire, telephone interview by Clegg, May 24, 2019.

81. "How Diverse Are US Newsrooms?," American Society of News Editors, https://googletrends.github.io/asne/?view=4, accessed June 30, 2022.

82. "*Star Tribune* Names Suki Dardarian Editor and Senior Vice President," Star Tribune Media Company press release, February 10, 2022, https://www.startribunecompany.com/learn-about-us/news/press-release/star-tribune-names-suki-dardarian-editor-and-senior-vice-president; Paul Farhi and Elahe Izadi, "'The Norms Have Broken Down': Shock as Journalists Are Arrested, Injured by Police While Trying to Cover the Story," *Washington Post*, May 31, 2020, https://www.washingtonpost.com/lifestyle/media/journalists-at-several-protests-were-injured-arrested-by-police-while-trying-to-cover-the-story/2020/05/31/bfbc322a-a342-11ea-b619-3f9133bbb482_story.html.

83. *Police on Trial (Full Documentary)*, *Frontline*, PBS, May 31, 2022, available at YouTube, https://www.youtube.com/watch?v=Ggxiylkvuq0.

84. "What Is the Table Stakes Program?," Table Stakes, https://www.tablestakes.org/about, accessed August 18, 2022.

CHAPTER THREE: BEDFORD, MASSACHUSETTS

1. Dan Kennedy accompanied Mike Rosenberg on July 26, 2021; Mike Rosenberg, "Walking Tour of Bedford's Cultural District Reveals Town's Treasures," *Bedford Citizen*, July 29, 2021, https://www.thebedfordcitizen.org/2021/07/walking-tour-of-bedfords-cultural-district-reveals-towns-treasures.

2. "A Chronology of Bedford's Railroad History," Friends of Bedford Depot Park, August 30, 2012, https://www.bedforddepot.org/history/RRHistory.html.

3. Julie McCay Turner, "Bedford Minutemen Re-enact 1775 Breakfast at Fitch Tavern," *Bedford Citizen*, April 24, 2015, https://www.thebedfordcitizen.org/2015/04/bedford-minutemen-re-enact-1775-breakfast-at-fitch-tavern.

4. The 2016 revenue figure is from *The Bedford Citizen*'s Form 990-EZ, filed with the Internal Revenue Service and available through *ProPublica*'s Nonprofit Explorer database, https://projects.propublica.org/nonprofits; the 2021 revenue figure is from *The Bedford Citizen 2021 Annual Report*, https://drive.google.com/file/d/12uernmQfsqhlU9HOSRT4JpBuNBd917AM/view, accessed April 11, 2022.

5. "Bedford, Massachusetts," City-Data.com, http://www.city-data.com/city/Bedford-Massachusetts.html, accessed April 21, 2022.

6. Katharine Q. Seelye, "When the Local Paper Shrank, These Journalists Started an Alternative," *New York Times*, June 20, 2021, https://www

.nytimes.com/2021/06/20/business/media/when-the-local-paper-shrank
-these-journalists-started-an-alternative.html; Gal Tziperman Lotan, "In
New Bedford, Career Journalists Looking to Shine a New Light," *Boston
Globe*, April 10, 2021, https://www.bostonglobe.com/2021/04/10/metro
/new-bedford-career-journalists-looking-shine-new-light.

7. Laura Bullock, "Ask Aunt Laura—How to Make the Perfect Hard Boiled
Egg," *Bedford Citizen*, April 5, 2022, https://www.thebedfordcitizen.org
/2022/04/ask-aunt-laura-how-to-make-the-perfect-hard-boiled-egg-inbox.

8. *Bedford Citizen* 2021 annual report.

9. Dan Kennedy, "Gannett Goes on a Massive Spree of Closing and Merging
Weekly Newspapers," *Media Nation* (blog), March 17, 2022, https://dan
kennedy.net/2022/03/17/gannett-goes-a-massive-spree-of-closing-and
-merging-weekly-newspapers.

10. The *Bedford Minuteman*'s circulation is from a report Gannett filed with
the Alliance for Audited Media for the six months ending September
30, 2021, https://www.auditedmedia.com/; Bedford's population is from
"QuickFacts" for Bedford, MA, US Census Bureau, https://www.census
.gov/quickfacts/, accessed August 26, 2021.

11. Julie McCay Turner, email message to Kennedy, April 26, 2022.

12. Email message to Kennedy from Gannett's corporate communications office, August 30, 2021.

13. Kenneth Gordon, telephone interview by Kennedy, January 13, 2021.

14. Katie Duval, in-person interview by Kennedy, March 11, 2022.

15. "*Bedford Minuteman* Goes Digital Only; Suspends Print Publication,"
Bedford Minuteman, March 16, 2022, https://www.wickedlocal.com/story
/bedford-minuteman/2022/03/16/bedford-minuteman-focuses-digital-only
-suspends-print-publication/7066200001.

16. Gene Kalb, "What's Going On in Bedford? Or More to the Point, How Do
You Find Out What's Going On in Bedford?," *Bedford Citizen*, March 16,
2022, https://www.thebedfordcitizen.org/2022/03/whats-going-on-in
-bedford-or-more-to-the-point-how-do-you-find-out-whats-going-on-in
-bedford. A search of the *Bedford Minuteman*'s website confirmed Kalb's
assertion that the paper did not cover the town election.

17. Dan Kennedy, "Gannett's Mass. Weeklies to Replace Much of Their Local
News with Regional Coverage," *Media Nation*, February 16, 2022, https://
dankennedy.net/2022/02/16/gannetts-mass-weeklies-to-replace-much-of
-their-local-news-with-regional-coverage.

18. Around 2019–20, about 68 percent of adults in Bedford were college
graduates. The per capita income of $68,113 was nearly 50 percent higher
than the statewide average of $45,555. "QuickFacts" for Bedford, MA,
US Census Bureau, https://www.census.gov/quickfacts/, accessed April 11,
2022.

19. Erin Karter, "As Newspapers Close, Wealthier Communities Are Hit Hard-
est by the Decline in Local Journalism," *Northwestern Now*, June 29,
2022, https://news.northwestern.edu/stories/2022/06/newspapers-close
-decline-in-local-journalism.

20. Julie McCay Turner, in-person interview by Kennedy, December 8, 2021.

21. Kim Siebert, video interview by Kennedy, August 5, 2020.
22. Meredith McCulloch, video interview by Kennedy, August 18, 2020.
23. Turner interview, December 8, 2021; Siebert interview, August 5, 2020.
24. David Dahl, video interview by Kennedy, February 28, 2022.
25. Eric Convey, "*Boston Globe* Lays Off Hyper-Local *Your Town* Correspondents," *Boston Business Journal*, March 6, 2014, https://www.bizjournals.com/boston/news/2014/03/06/boston-globe-lays-off-hyper-local-your.html.
26. "Bedford Citizen," GuideStar, https://www.guidestar.org/profile/46-0777549, accessed April 12, 2022.
27. Mike Rosenberg, in-person interview by Kennedy, July 26, 2021.
28. "Alan Adams, Lexington Publisher" (obituary), *Boston Globe*, March 10, 1975.
29. Howard M. Ziff, "Practicing Responsible Journalism: Cosmopolitan versus Provincial Models," in *Responsible Journalism*, ed. Deni Elliott (Beverly Hills, CA: Sage, 1986), 155.
30. "Alan Adams, Lexington Publisher"; Richard Kollen, *Lexington: From Liberty's Birthplace to Progressive Suburb* (Charleston, SC: Arcadia Publishing, 2004), 138.
31. Dorothy Bergin, video interview by Kennedy, February 11, 2022.
32. Turner interview, December 8, 2021; Bergin interview.
33. Jon Marcus, "Older Adults Are Stepping Up to Help Cover Local News," AARP, April 5, 2022, https://www.aarp.org/work/careers/older-adults-journalism-careers.
34. Lincoln Millstein, video interview by Clegg and Kennedy, *What Works*, February 16, 2022, https://whatworks.news/2022/02/16/lincoln-millstein-talks-about-his-journey-from-high-powered-media-executive-to-hyperlocal-journalist.
35. Salary information from the *Citizen*'s Forms 990-EZ.
36. Teri Morrow, email message to Kennedy, April 11, 2022.
37. "QuickFacts" for Bedford, MA, US Census Bureau, https://www.census.gov/quickfacts, accessed April 11, 2022.
38. "NewsGuild-CWA Study of Pay Equity in 14 Gannett Newsrooms," April 27, 2021, 15, 20, https://newsguild.org/wp-content/uploads/2021/04/Gannett-Pay-Equity-Study-at-14-Newsrooms-2021-0427.pdf.
39. Confidential reporting by Kennedy.
40. Julie Turner, "Ten Years—a Note from Julie Turner," *Bedford Citizen*, June 24, 2022, https://www.thebedfordcitizen.org/2022/06/ten-years-a-note-from-julie-turner.
41. "Jobs," *Bedford Citizen*, https://www.thebedfordcitizen.org/jobs, accessed August 9, 2022.
42. Teri Morrow, interviews by Kennedy, August 18, 2020 (via video), and December 6, 2021 (in person).
43. Morrow interview, December 6, 2021; *The Bedford Citizen 2021 Annual Report*.
44. *The Bedford Citizen 2021 Annual Report*; Gene Kalb, telephone interview by Kennedy, January 12, 2022.
45. Gene Kalb, email message to Kennedy, January 12, 2022.

46. Gene Kalb, "Introducing the *Bedford Explained* Podcast—Episode One: Pole Capping Day," *Bedford Citizen*, April 8, 2022, https://www.thebedford citizen.org/2022/04/introducing-the-bedford-explained-podcast-episode -one-pole-capping-day; Mike Rosenberg, "Pole-Capping Ceremony Returns on Saturday, April 9; First Time in Three Years," *Bedford Citizen*, March 26, 2022, https://www.thebedfordcitizen.org/2022/03/pole-capping -ceremony-returns-on-saturday-april-9-first-time-in-three-years.

47. Chloe Kizer, "Research Report," Project Oasis, March 2021, https://www .projectnewsoasis.com/sites/default/files/2022–02/project-oasis-report -2021–1.pdf. The report was sponsored by the Center for Innovation and Sustainability in Local Media, part of the Hussman School of Journalism and Media at the University of North Carolina; the Google News Initiative; LION Publishers; and Douglas K. Smith.

48. Chloe Kizer, video interview by Kennedy, March 3, 2022.

49. Kara Meyberg Guzman, video interview by Kennedy, March 7, 2022.

50. "About," Tiny News Collective, https://tinynewsco.org/about, accessed April 20, 2022; Cassandra Balfour, "Meet the Winners of the 2021 LION Publishers Local Journalism Awards," LION Publishers, November 16, 2021, https://www.lionpublishers.com/meet-the-winners-of-the-2021-lion -publishers-local-journalism-awards.

51. "*Lookout Local*: Ken Doctor's False Narrative about Santa Cruz," *Good Times*, November 9, 2020, https://www.goodtimes.sc/lookout-local-ken -doctor-false-narrative.

52. Ken Doctor, video interview by Clegg and Kennedy, *What Works*, March 2, 2022, https://whatworks.news/2022/03/02/the-doctor-is-in-why-a -respected-media-analyst-decided-to-start-a-local-news-site.

53. "Bedford's 2022 Town Election—Preliminary Election Results and a Possible Record Turnout," *Bedford Citizen*, March 12, 2022, https://www .thebedfordcitizen.org/2022/03/bedfords-2022-town-election-preliminary -election-results-and-a-possible-record-turnout.

54. "QuickFacts" for Bedford, MA, US Census Bureau, accessed January 15, 2023, https://www.census.gov/quickfacts.

55. Heather Galante, principal of Bedford High School, email message to Kennedy, January 9, 2023; "What Is METCO?," Metropolitan Council for Educational Opportunity, https://metcoinc.org/apply/what-is-metco, accessed January 15, 2023.

56. Video interview by Kennedy, January 6, 2023.

57. Mike Rosenberg, "Board of Health Votes 3–2 to Rescind Bedford's Mask Mandate," *Bedford Citizen*, February 14, 2022, https://www.thebedford citizen.org/2022/02/board-of-health-votes-3–2-to-rescind-bedfords-mask -mandate.

58. Mike Rosenberg, "Town Meeting Approves 139 The Great Road as Site for New Fire Station," *Bedford Citizen*, March 31, 2022, https://www .thebedfordcitizen.org/2022/03/town-meeting-approves-139-the-great -road-as-site-for-new-fire-station.

59. Mike Rosenberg, "The Minuteman Bikeway Extension—Annual Town Meeting 2022," *Bedford Citizen*, March 29, 2022, https://www.thebedford

citizen.org/2022/03/the-minuteman-bikeway-extension-annual-town
-meeting-2022.

60. Julie McCay Turner, in-person interview by Kennedy, February 23, 2022.
61. Joan Bowen, video interview by Kennedy, February 15, 2022.
62. Ginni Spencer spoke at *The Bedford Citizen*'s editorial board meeting, held via video, on March 22, 2022.
63. Julie McCay Turner, video interview by Kennedy, June 28, 2021.
64. In October 22, about 60 percent of registered voters in Massachusetts were "unenrolled," or independent; about 29 percent were Democrats; and fewer than 9 percent were Republicans, according to the Massachusetts Secretary of the Commonwealth. Accessed November 25, 2022, https://www.sec.state.ma.us/ele/eleenr/enridx.htm.
65. In-person reporting by Dan Kennedy supplemented by "September 18, 2021—What a Day It Was!," *Bedford Citizen*, September 20, 2021, https://www.thebedfordcitizen.org/2021/09/september-18–2021-what-a-day-it-was.
66. Turner email, April 26, 2022.
67. Morrow interview, December 6, 2021.
68. Ginni Spencer, video interview by Kennedy, February 15, 2022.

CHAPTER FOUR: DENVER, COLORADO
1. *News Matters: Inside the Fight to Save American Journalism*, dir. Brian Malone, Fast Forward Films, 2020.
2. Jennifer Brown, "Families Kept in the Dark about Children's Safety in Colorado's Child Welfare System" (first of three parts), *Colorado Sun*, May 19, 2021, https://coloradosun.com/2021/05/19/colorado-residential-center-abuse-neglect-death; Brown, "10 Moves in 4 Months: Following One Homeless Couple's Endless Migration around Denver," *Colorado Sun*, June 27, 2021, https://coloradosun.com/2021/06/27/homeless-denver-sweeps-pandemic; Brown, "Wild Horse Roundup in Northwest Colorado Begins as BLM Tries to Gather 733 Mustangs," *Colorado Sun*, September 5, 2021, https://coloradosun.com/2021/09/05/wild-horse-roundup-blm-sand-wash-basin.
3. Jennifer Brown, video interview by Dan Kennedy, October 21, 2021.
4. The estimate of sixty full-time journalists at *The Denver Post* was provided by several sources inside and outside the *Post*.
5. Brown interview.
6. "As Vultures Circle, *The Denver Post* Must Be Saved," *Denver Post*, April 8, 2018, https://www.denverpost.com/2018/04/06/as-vultures-circle-the-denver-post-must-be-saved.
7. Chuck Plunkett, video interview by Kennedy, September 29, 2021.
8. Larry Ryckman, email message to Kennedy, June 29, 2022.
9. Larry Ryckman, in-person interview by Kennedy, September 20, 2021.
10. Laura Hazard Owen, "Civil's Token Sale Has Failed. Now What? Refunds, for One Thing—and Then Another Sale," *Nieman Lab*, October 16, 2018, https://www.niemanlab.org/2018/10/civils-token-sale-has-failed-now-what-refunds-for-one-thing; Joshua Benton, "'I Had to Borrow Money to Pay My Rent': Civil's Tokenomics Has Left Some of Its Journalists Wondering

Where Their Salary Is," *Nieman Lab*, November 27, 2018; Rick Edmonds, "R.I.P. Civil—Lessons from a Failed Startup," *Poynter Online*, June 2, 2020, https://www.poynter.org/business-work/2020/r-i-p-civil-lessons-from -a-failed-startup.

11. Nathan Schneider, "Broad-Based Stakeholder Ownership in Journalism: Co-ops, ESOPs, Blockchains," *Media Industries* 7, no. 2 (2020): 56.
12. "Become a Member," *Colorado Sun*, https://coloradosun.com/membership, accessed June 8, 2022; "*Colorado Sun* Newsletters," https://coloradosun .com/newsletters, accessed June 8, 2022.
13. Ryckman email.
14. Dan Kennedy, *The Return of the Moguls: How Jeff Bezos and John Henry Are Remaking Newspapers for the Twenty-First Century* (Lebanon, NH: ForeEdge, 2018), 189–91; Peter Dobrin, "H. F. 'Gerry' Lenfest" (obituary), *Philadelphia Inquirer*, August 5, 2018, https://www.inquirer.com/obituaries /inq/hf-gerry-lenfest-philadelphia-philanthropist-dies-88–20180805.html.
15. Holly Ensign-Barstow, video interview by Kennedy, September 15, 2021.
16. Dan Kennedy, *The Wired City: Reimagining Journalism and Civic Life in the Post-Newspaper Age* (Amherst: University of Massachusetts Press, 2013), 107–9.
17. Carol Wood, in-person by Kennedy, September 20, 2021.
18. David Gilbert, in-person interview by Kennedy, September 20, 2021.
19. Elizabeth Hansen Shapiro, video interview by Clegg and Kennedy, September 16, 2021; Corey Hutchins, "All Eyes on Colorado Again," *Inside the News in Colorado*, May 4, 2021, https://coloradomedia.substack.com/p /-a-new-newspaper-ownership-model.
20. "FJC Loan Preserves Community Stewardship of Local News in Colorado," FJC, May 3, 2021, https://fjc.org/news/fjc-loan-preserves-community -stewardship-of-local-news-in-colorado.
21. Jerry and Ann Healey, in-person interview by Kennedy, September 17, 2021.
22. Linda Shapley, in-person interview by Kennedy, September 22, 2021.
23. Alliance for Audited Media, news media statement for the six-month period ending September 30, 2021, http://www.auditedmedia.com/.
24. Bill Hosokawa, *Thunder in the Rockies: The Incredible Denver Post* (New York: William Morrow, 1976), 16–17, 96–107, 138–47, 307–15.
25. Deirdre Carmody, "Sale of *Denver Post* for $95 Million Set," *New York Times*, October 23, 1980, https://timesmachine.nytimes.com/timesmachine /1980/10/23/111302926.html; Geraldine Fabrikant, "Texan Is Buying His 29th Daily, *The Denver Post*," *New York Times*, September 15, 1987, https://www.nytimes.com/1987/09/15/business/texan-is-buying-his-29th -daily-the-denver-post.html; Renee McGaw, "MediaNews Group Parent Files Chapter 11," *Denver Business Journal*, January 22, 2010, https:// www.bizjournals.com/denver/stories/2010/01/18/daily95.html; Emily Chassen, "MediaNews Owner Files Prepackaged Bankruptcy," Reuters, January 22, 2010, https://www.reuters.com/article/industry-us-affiliated media-bankruptcy/medianews-owner-files-prepackaged-bankruptcy -idUSTRE60M01920100123.

26. Michael Roberts, "Dean Singleton on Resigning from the *Post:* 'They've Killed a Great Newspaper,'" *Westword*, May 7, 2018, https://www.westword.com/news/dean-singleton-on-resigning-from-the-denver-post-theyve-killed-a-great-newspaper-10287146.

27. Dean Singleton, telephone interview by Kennedy, October 4, 2021.

28. "QuickFacts" for Denver, US Census Bureau, https://census.gov/quickfacts, accessed March 7, 2023.

29. Lee Ann Colacioppo, email message to Kennedy, September 7, 2021; Matt Sebastian, email message to Kennedy, September 14, 2021.

30. John Wenzel, "The Gutting of *The Denver Post* Is a Death Knell for Local News," *Atlantic*, May 11, 2018, https://www.theatlantic.com/entertainment/archive/2018/05/denver-post/560186.

31. John Wenzel, telephone interview by Kennedy, October 1, 2021.

32. "Colorado Public Radio Acquires News Website *Denverite*," CPR News, March 6, 2019, https://www.cpr.org/2019/03/06/colorado-public-radio-acquires-news-website-denverite.

33. Kevin Dale, in-person interview by Kennedy, September 21, 2021.

34. Patty Calhoun, in-person interview by Kennedy, September 23, 2021.

35. Vince Bzdek, telephone interview by Kennedy, October 14, 2021.

36. John Frank, email message to Kennedy, January 5, 2022.

37. "About Us," *Colorado Newsline*, https://coloradonewsline.com/about, accessed June 21, 2022.

38. "QuickFacts" for Denver; "Denver Metro Area Population 1950–1922," Macrotrends, accessed June 15, 2022, https://www.macrotrends.net/cities/22972/denver/population; "QuickFacts" for Colorado, US Census Bureau, https://www.census.gov/quickfacts, accessed June 15, 2022.

39. "QuickFacts" for Pueblo, CO, US Census Bureau, https://www.census.gov/quickfacts, accessed June 21, 2022.

40. Abe Streep, "What Happened When John Rodriguez, a Local Publisher, Sought Public Funding," *Columbia Journalism Review* (Winter 2020), https://www.cjr.org/special_report/for-pueblo.php.

41. Corey Hutchins, in-person interview by Kennedy, September 22, 2021.

42. Dana Coffield, telephone interview by Kennedy, October 13, 2021.

43. Melissa Milios Davis, in-person interview by Kennedy, September 23, 2021.

44. Laura Frank, video interview by Kennedy, September 28, 2021.

45. Kennedy accompanied Erica Breunlin and Olivia Sun on September 20, 2021; Erica Breunlin, "Denver High School Students Protest Outside DPS Offices Calling for Removal of Board Member Tay Anderson," *Colorado Sun*, September 20, 2021, https://coloradosun.com/2021/09/20/tay-anderson-denver-public-schools-student-walkout.

46. Erica Breunlin, in-person interview by Kennedy, September 20, 2021.

47. Olivia Sun, in-person interview by Kennedy, September 20, 2021.

CHAPTER FIVE: MEMPHIS, TENNESSEE

1. Wendi C. Thomas, telephone interview by Ellen Clegg, June 28, 2021.

2. "Our Story," *MLK50*, https://mlk50.com/our-story, accessed April 23, 2022.

3. "Memphis Sanitation Workers' Strike," Martin Luther King Jr. Research and Education Institute, Stanford University, https://kinginstitute.stanford .edu/encyclopedia/memphis-sanitation-workers-strike, accessed April 23, 2022.

4. Thomas, telephone interview.

5. Elena Delavega and Gregory M. Blumenthal, "2020 Memphis Poverty Fact Sheet," University of Memphis, https://www.memphis.edu/benhooks /programs/pdf/2020povertyfactsheet.pdf, accessed April 23, 2022.

6. "Republish Our Stories," *MLK50*, https://mlk50.com/republish-our -stories, accessed April 20, 2022.

7. "*MLK50*'s Thomas Wins Selden Ring Award for Her Work on the Series 'Profiting from the Poor,'" *MLK50*, March 3, 2020, https://mlk50.com /2020/03/03/mlk50s-thomas-wins-selden-ring-award-for-her-work-on-the -series-profiting-from-the-poor.

8. Wendi C. Thomas, "Profiting from the Poor: Methodist Le Bonheur Healthcare and Debt Collection," *MLK50*, https://mlk50.com/profiting -from-the-poor, accessed August 17, 2022.

9. Wendi C. Thomas, "Why Is Journalism Failing Democracy?," panel discussion, International Journalism Festival, Perugia, Italy, April 9, 2022, https://www.journalismfestival.com/programme/2022/why-is-journalism -failing-democracy.

10. Thomas, telephone interview.

11. Victor Trammell, "May 27: Angry White Mob Ransacked Ida B. Wells' News Office On This Date In 1892," Blackthen.com, May 27, 2022, https://blackthen.com/may-27-angry-white-mob-ransacked-ida-b-wells -news-office-on-this-date-in-1892.

12. "Membership Standards: Best Practices for Strengthening Public Service Journalism and Encouraging Public Trust," Institute for Nonprofit News, https://inn.org/about/membership-standards, accessed April 24, 2022.

13. For instance, see Carrington J. Tatum, "Council Holds City-County Pipeline Ordinance, Passes on Second Reading Proposed Permitting Process Law," *MLK50*, August 3, 2021, https://mlk50.com/2021/08/03/will-the -memphis-city-council-take-steps-to-keep-byhalia-and-other-pipelines-out.

14. "88th National Headliner Award Winners," National Headliner Awards 2022, https://www.headlinerawards.org/wp-content/uploads/2022/04 /2022-headliner-winners.pdf, accessed April 28, 2022.

15. Carrington J. Tatum and Hannah Grabenstein, "'A Victory for Us': Southwest Memphis Residents Elated as Developers Drop Byhalia Pipeline Project," *MLK50*, July 2, 2021, https://mlk50.com/2021/07/02/byhalia -connection-pipeline-pulls-project.

16. Carrington J. Tatum, "Loans Got Me into Journalism. Student Debt Pushed Me Out," *MLK50*, June 13, 2022, https://mlk50.com/2022/06/13 /loans-got-me-into-journalism-student-debt-pushed-me-out.

17. Wendi C. Thomas, "When Student Loans and the Housing Crisis Force Journalists Out of the Business," *MLK50*, June 13, 2022, https://mlk50.com /2022/06/13/when-student-loans-and-the-housing-crisis-force-journalists -out-of-the-business.

18. Wendi C. Thomas, email message to Clegg, June 28, 2021.
19. Thomas, telephone interview.
20. Evan Smith, "T-Squared: 2022 Will Be My Last Year as *The Texas Tribune's* CEO," *Texas Tribune*, January 12, 2022, https://www.texastribune.org/2022/01/12/evan-smith-texas-tribune-ceo.
21. Wendi C. Thomas, Twitter thread, January 12, 2022, 7:16 p.m., https://twitter.com/wendi_c_thomas/status/1481419969141395463.
22. Borealis Philanthropy, https://borealisphilanthropy.org, accessed April 24, 2022.
23. Thomas, telephone interview.
24. Wendi C. Thomas, "A Temp Worker Died on the Job after FedEx Didn't Fix a Known Hazard. The Fine: $7,000," *MLK50* in partnership with *ProPublica*, December 22, 2022, https://mlk50.com/2020/12/22/fedex-prioritizes-packages-over-employee-safety-workers-and-experts-say.
25. Wendi C. Thomas, "The Police Have Been Spying on Black Reporters and Activists for Years. I Know Because I'm One of Them," June 9, 2020, *ProPublica*, https://www.propublica.org/article/the-police-have-been-spying-on-black-reporters-and-activists-for-years-i-know-because-im-one-of-them.
26. Thomas, "The Police Have Been Spying."
27. "Making Memphis and Shelby County a Safer Place," Memphis Shelby County Crime Commission, https://memphiscrime.org, accessed May 1, 2022.
28. Thomas, telephone interview.
29. "Supporting Just and Sustainable Communities," Surdna Foundation, https://surdna.org, accessed May 1, 2022.
30. "*MLK50* Among 11 Nonprofit Newsrooms to Receive First-Ever American Journalism Project Grants," *MLK50*, December 10, 2019, https://mlk50.com/2019/12/10/mlk50-among-11-nonprofit-newsrooms-to-receive-first-ever-american-journalism-project-grants.
31. Anne Marie Lipinski, Twitter post, December 10, 2019, 12:49 p.m., https://twitter.com/amlwhere/status/1204458087236554752.
32. Christine Schmidt, "Here are the American Journalism Project's First 11 Recipients, Taking Home $8.5 Million to Grow Their Business Operations," *Nieman Lab*, December 10, 2019, https://www.niemanlab.org/2019/12/here-are-the-american-journalism-projects-first-11-recipients-taking-home-8-5-million-to-grow-their-business-operations.
33. "Our Supporters," *MLK50*, https://mlk50.com/our-supporters, accessed May 26, 2022.
34. Kathleen Kingsbury, email message to Clegg, May 11, 2022.
35. Thomas, telephone interview.
36. Otis Sanford, telephone interview by Clegg, May 4, 2022.
37. Richard Thompson, telephone interview by Clegg, May 31, 2022.
38. Matthew Leake, Marina Adami, Federica Cherubini, Eduardo Suarez, and Caithlin Mercer, "International Journalism Festival 2022: What We Learnt in Perugia About the Future of News," Reuters Institute, University of Oxford, April 8, 2022, https://reutersinstitute.politics.ox.ac.uk/news/international-journalism-festival-2022-what-we-learnt-perugia-about-future-news.

39. Andrea Morales, in-person interview by Clegg, June 10, 2022.

40. Adrienne Johnson Martin, in-person interview by Clegg, June 10, 2022.

41. "Reporters Committee Announces 2022 Freedom of the Press Award Honorees," Reporters Committee for Freedom of the Press, June 7, 2022, https://www.rcfp.org/awards-2022-honorees.

42. "QuickFacts" for Memphis, US Census Bureau, https://www.census.gov /quickfacts/, accessed May 2, 2022.

43. Otis Sanford, telephone interview by Clegg, May 4, 2022; Ed Frank, "Memphis *Commercial Appeal*," *Tennessee Encyclopedia*, https://tennessee encyclopedia.net/entries/memphis-commercial-appeal, accessed May 2, 2022.

44. "1923 Pulitzer Prizes," https://www.pulitzer.org/prize-winners-by-year /1923.

45. "*Memphis Press-Scimitar*, The History," https://memphispressscimitar. com/THE_HISTORY.html, accessed May 2, 2022.

46. James Fallows, "In Memphis, a Lab Experiment for Local News," *The Atlantic*, November 8, 2019, https://www.theatlantic.com/ideas/archive /2019/11/the-lab-experiment-for-the-fourth-estate/622137.

47. Tom Charlier, "Mark Russell Named Executive Editor of *The Commercial Appeal*," *Commercial Appeal*, June 28, 2017, https://www.commercial appeal.com/story/news/2017/06/28/mark-russell-named-executive-editor -commercial-appeal/435074001.

48. "Newsroom Directory," *Commercial Appeal*, https://www.commercial appeal.com/contact/staff, accessed May 2, 2022.

49. Cassandra Stephenson, "*Jackson Sun, Commercial Appeal* Printing Operations to Move to Mississippi," *Jackson Sun*, January 6, 2021, https://www .jacksonsun.com/story/news/local/2021/01/06/jackson-sun-commercial -appeal-move-printing-operations-mississippi/6553382002.

50. Brandon Richard, "Memphis Overflow Hospital Among Most Expensive in Country," WMC ActionNews5, May 20, 2020, https://www.actionnews5 .com/2020/05/20/memphis-overflow-hospital-among-most-expensive -country.

51. Gabrielle Masson, "$51M Tennessee COVID-19 Overflow Hospital Closes Without Treating Any Patients," *Becker's Hospital Review*, July 21, 2021, https://www.beckershospitalreview.com/patient-flow/51m-tennessee-covid -19-overflow-hospital-closes-without-treating-any-patients.html.

52. "*Commercial Appeal* Unveils New Home Delivery Schedule, More Digital Services," *Commercial Appeal*, January 13, 2022, https://www.commercial appeal.com/story/news/2022/01/12/commercial-appeal-ceases-home -delivery-single-copy-sales-on-saturdays/9186388002.

53. Circulation figures as reported to the Alliance for Audited Media, https:// auditedmedia.com.

54. Ken Doctor, "Newsonomics: In Memphis' Unexpected News War, *The Daily Memphian*'s Model Demands Attention," *Nieman Lab*, February 20, 2020, https://www.niemanlab.org/2020/02/newsonomics-in-memphis -unexpected-news-war-the-daily-memphians-model-demands-attention.

55. "Tennessee Newspaper Legend Otis Sanford on the Rise of a New Media Ecosystem in Memphis," *What Works* (podcast), June 2, 2022, https://whatworks.news/2022/06/02/tennessee-newspaper-legend-otis-sanford-on-the-rise-of-a-new-media-ecosystem-in-memphis.
56. Eric Barnes, in-person interview by Clegg, June 11, 2022.
57. Andy Cates, video interview by Clegg, April 25, 2022.
58. Eric Barnes, LinkedIn profile, https://www.linkedin.com/in/ericbarnes, accessed May 29, 2022.
59. Doctor, "Newsonomics."
60. Eric Barnes, video interview by Clegg, March 21, 2021.
61. Doctor, "Newsonomics."
62. "INN Mission and History," Institute for Nonprofit News, https://inn.org/about/who-we-are, accessed January 25, 2023.
63. Cates video interview.
64. Doctor, "Newsonomics."
65. "The Knight Foundation Supports The Daily Memphian with $250,000 Grant," *Daily Memphian*, August 16, 2022, https://dailymemphian.com/article/30359/knight-foundation-250000-grant-to-daily-memphian.
66. David Arant, "Department Engaged in Efforts to Improve Local News Reporting," *Meeman Matters: Newsletter of the Department of Journalism and Strategic Media* (University of Memphis), August 2018, https://www.memphis.edu/jrsm/news/news_pdfs/meemanmattsummer18.pdf.
67. Marc Perrusquia, "A Dim View: Critics Assail TVA's Secrecy, Marketing," Institute for Public Service Reporting, June 2, 2022, https://www.psrmemphis.org/secret-salaries-tva-again-declines-to-release-employee-pay-records; Reporters Committee for Freedom of the Press, *Perrusquia v. The City of Memphis*, Case Number CH-22–0595, https://www.rcfp.org/litigation/perrusquia-v-memphis-pip-plans, accessed August 17, 2022.
68. Marc Perrusquia, video interview by Clegg, May 27, 2022.
69. Barnes in-person interview by Clegg.
70. John Beifuss, "'Elvis' at Graceland: Tom Hanks Joins Director, Stars, Presley Family for Movie Premiere," *Commercial Appeal*, June 13, 2022, https://www.commercialappeal.com/story/entertainment/movies/2022/06/12/elvis-movie-graceland-tom-hanks-austin-butler-baz-luhrmann-memphis/7487735001.

CHAPTER SIX: MENDOCINO COUNTY, CALIFORNIA
1. Dan Kennedy attended *The Mendocino Voice*'s event at the Ukiah Brewing Company, March 3, 2020.
2. Kennedy attended the coronavirus news conference, held March 5, 2022.
3. Kristen Hare, "More Than 100 Local Newsrooms Closed During the Coronavirus Pandemic," *Poynter Online*, December 2, 2021, https://www.poynter.org/locally/2021/the-coronavirus-has-closed-more-than-100-local-newsrooms-across-america-and-counting.
4. Kate Maxwell, video interview by Kennedy, July 1, 2022.
5. W. Jeffrey Brown, video interview by Kennedy, June 30, 2022.
6. Kate Maxwell and Adrian Fernandez Baumann, in-person interview by Kennedy, March 5, 2020.

7. "QuickFacts" for Mendocino County, CA, US Census Bureau, https://www.census.gov/quickfacts/, accessed July 5, 2022.

8. Patrick McGreevy, "Voters Legalize Pot in California. Here's What Will Happen Next," *Los Angeles Times*, November 8, 2016, https://www.latimes.com/politics/la-pol-ca-proposition-64-california-legalizes-marijuana-snap-20161108-story.html.

9. Maxwell interview, March 5, 2020.

10. Kate Fishman, "Fort Bragg Shows Out for Salmon Restoration, Good Time at World's Largest Salmon BBQ," *Mendocino Voice*, July 6, 2022, https://mendovoice.com/2022/07/fort-bragg-shows-out-for-salmon-restoration-good-time-at-worlds-largest-salmon-bbq; Fishman, "Nome Fire in Covelo Reaches 20% Containment (Updated 10 PM)," *Mendocino Voice*, July 5, 2022, https://mendovoice.com/2022/07/fire-crews-responding-to-vegetation-fire-in-covelo; Fishman, "'We Are the Overwhelming Majority': Huffman Addresses Dozens Rallying in Fort Bragg for Reproductive Rights," *Mendocino Voice*, July 6, 2022, https://mendovoice.com/2022/07/we-are-the-overwhelming-majority-huffman-addresses-dozens-rallying-in-fort-bragg-for-reproductive-rights; Lucy Peterson, "A Guide to Public Participation at Mendocino County Government Meetings," *Mendocino Voice*, June 21, 2022, https://mendovoice.com/2022/06/a-guide-to-public-participation-at-government-meetings.

11. Kate B. Maxwell, "Khadijah Britton Has Been Missing for Four Years—an Online Vigil Is Happening Feb. 5," *Mendocino Voice*, January 30, 2022, https://mendovoice.com/2022/01/khadijah-britton-has-been-missing-for-four-years-an-online-prayer-event-is-happening-feb-5.

12. "McGourty Wins Potter Valley Straw Poll; Watch the District 1 Candidates Forum (Video)," *Mendocino Voice*, February 23, 2020, https://mendovoice.com/2020/02/mcgourty-wins-potter-valley-straw-poll-watch-the-district-1-candidates-forum-video.

13. "The Mounting Mental Health Toll of Disasters," Center for Public Integrity, August 25, 2020, https://publicintegrity.org/environment/hidden-epidemics/the-mental-toll-of-disaster.

14. Kristen Lombardi, telephone interview by Kennedy, January 26, 2022.

15. *The Mendocino Voice*'s Facebook page was accessed July 5, 2022, https://www.facebook.com/MendoVoice.

16. Alyssa Ballard, email message to Kennedy, June 24, 2021; "Contact Us," *Ukiah Daily Journal*, https://www.ukiahdailyjournal.com/contact-us; *Mendocino Grapevine*, January 1973, accessed July 7, 2022.

17. See chapter 4 on Colorado.

18. Circulation figures for MediaNews Group's newspapers in Mendocino County are not reported to the Alliance for Audited Media.

19. K. C. Meadows, in-person interview by Kennedy, March 4, 2020.

20. K. C. Meadows, email message to Kennedy, July 7, 2022.

21. Alicia Bales, in-person interview by Kennedy, March 4, 2020.

22. Katie Kilkenny, "Freelance Writers Cautiously Optimistic About CA Gig Economy Law Amendment: 'Work Has Picked Up,'" *Hollywood Reporter*, September 17, 2020, https://www.hollywoodreporter.com/news/general

-news/freelance-writers-cautiously-optimistic-about-ca-gig-economy-law
-amendment-work-has-picked-up-4062319.

23. Jennifer Poole, in-person interview by Kennedy, March 5, 2020.

24. Kym Kemp, telephone interview by Kennedy, December 10, 2022.

25. "QuickFacts" for Haverhill, MA, US Census Bureau, https://www.census
.gov/quickfacts/, accessed July 6, 2022.

26. Dan Kennedy, *The Wired City: Reimagining Journalism and Civic Life
in the Post-Newspaper Age* (Amherst: University of Massachusetts Press,
2013), 147–50.

27. Dan Kennedy, "In Haverhill, WHAV Lives—but a Long-Planned Co-op for
News Folds Up Shop," *Media Nation*, January 9, 2020, https://dankennedy
.net/2020/01/09/in-haverhill-whav-lives-but-a-long-planned-co-op-for
-news-folds-up-shop.

28. Dan Kennedy, "New Directions in Local News," YouTube, October 23,
2014, 6:31, https://www.youtube.com/watch?v=IpICTdiVbuE&t=193s.

29. It should be noted that Kennedy has been a featured speaker at two fundraising events for WHAV.

30. Dan Kennedy, "Can Perennial Hopes for Local News Co-ops Ever Turn
into Reality?," *Nieman Lab*, January 27, 2020, https://www.niemanlab
.org/2020/01/can-perennial-hopes-for-local-news-co-ops-ever-turn-into
-reality.

31. Tom Stites, video interview with Kennedy, June 30, 2022.

32. Laura Hazard Owen, "Lauded 'Local News Co-op' Shuts Down Without
Warning, Leaving Its Co-owners in the Dark," *Nieman Lab*, October 19,
2021, https://www.niemanlab.org/2021/10/lauded-local-news-co-op-shuts
-down-without-warning-leaving-its-co-owners-in-the-dark; Kabir Bhatia,
"Akron's *Devil Strip* Comes to an End with Resignation of Final Board
Members," WKSU.org, January 7, 2022, https://www.wksu.org/community
/2022–01–07/akrons-devil-strip-comes-to-an-end-with-resignation-of-final
-board-members.

33. Olivia Henry, telephone interview by Kennedy, January 26, 2022.

34. Dan Kennedy, "Are Cooperatively Owned News Projects an Idea Whose
Time Has Finally Come?," *Media Nation*, June 22, 2021, https://dan
kennedy.net/2021/06/22/are-cooperatively-owned-news-projects-an-idea
-whose-time-has-finally-come.

35. Maxwell and Baumann interview, March 5, 2020; Maxwell clarified that
she might seek to hire more than seven employees in her interview with
Kennedy on July 1, 2022.

36. Adrian Fernandez Baumann, email message to Kennedy, July 13, 2022.

37. s. e. smith, email messages to Kennedy, November 25, 26, and 28, 2022;
Lucy Peterson, email message to Kennedy, November 26 and 29, 2022.

38. Maxwell, interview via Zoom, November 30, 2022.

39. Maxwell interview, July 1, 2022; "Become a Member," *Mendocino Voice*,
https://mendovoice.app.neoncrm.com/np/clients/mendovoice/membership
Join.jsp#single-contribution, accessed July 7, 2022.

40. *The Mendocino Voice*'s home page, https://mendovoice.com, was accessed
December 19, 2022.

CHAPTER SEVEN: NEW HAVEN, CONNECTICUT

1. Dan Kennedy observed the broadcast of *LoveBabz LoveTalk* on WNHH on a visit to Babz Rawls Ivy's apartment on November 16, 2021, 9 to 11 a.m. The first hour, featuring Rawls Ivy's conversation with Harry Droz, is at YouTube, https://www.youtube.com/watch?v=NbMh4oLgQfo.
2. Paul Bass, email message to Kennedy, June 6, 2022.
3. Dan Kennedy, "In New Haven, a Low-Power FM Experiment Seeks Local Conversation—and Financial Sustainability," *Nieman Lab*, August 4, 2015, https://www.niemanlab.org/2015/08/in-new-haven-a-low-power-fm-experiment-seeks-local-conversation-and-financial-sustainability; Bass, email message to Kennedy, November 30, 2022.
4. "QuickFacts" for New Haven, CT, US Census Bureau, https://www.census.gov/quickfacts/, accessed May 2, 2022.
5. Babz Rawls Ivy, in-person interview by Kennedy, November 16, 2021.
6. Maaisha Osman with Zhaozhou Dai, "How a Nonprofit Digital Newsroom Tracked the 2021 Local Elections Live, Online, and Over the Air," *What Works*, December 23, 2021, https://whatworks.news/2021/12/23/how-a-nonprofit-digital-newsroom-tracked-the-2021-local-elections-live-online-and-over-the-air.
7. Paul Bass, in-person interview by Kennedy, November 15, 2022.
8. Melissa Bailey, "Former Alderwoman Gets 30 Days in Prison," *New Haven Independent*, July 26, 2007, https://www.newhavenindependent.org/index.php/article/former_alderwoman_gets_30_days_in_prison.
9. Rawls Ivy interview.
10. New Haven Independent, "LoveBabz LoveTalk with Babz Rawls-Ivy," streamed live November 8, 2021, YouTube, https://www.youtube.com/watch?v=1HvDnenFx1Q.
11. Rawls Ivy interview.
12. Dan Kennedy, *The Wired City: Reimagining Journalism and Civic Life in the Post-Newspaper Age* (Amherst: University of Massachusetts, 2013), 10.
13. Bass interview; Paul Bass, email message to Kennedy, May 17, 2022; Facebook and Twitter numbers are as of May 17, 2022.
14. Bass interview.
15. Bass interview; Bass email, May 17, 2022.
16. Bass interview; Bass email, May 17, 2022.
17. Bass email, May 17, 2022; Harry Droz, in-person interview by Kennedy, December 14, 2022.
18. "Governor Lamont Signs Bill Legalizing and Safely Regulating Adult Use Cannabis," press release, Office of Governor Ned Lamont, June 22, 2021, https://portal.ct.gov/office-of-the-governor/news/press-releases/2021/06-2021/governor-lamont-signs-bill-legalizing-and-safely-regulating-adult-use-cannabis.
19. Thomas Breen, "Shafiq Abdussabur Resigns as Alder," *New Haven Independent*, June 9, 2022, https://www.newhavenindependent.org/article/shafiq_abdussabur_resigns.
20. Bass interview.

21. Droz interview.

22. Paul Bass, "Hearst Buys *New Haven Register*," *New Haven Independent*, June 6, 2017, https://www.newhavenindependent.org/article/hearst_buys _new_haven_register; Hearst's holdings are from the company's website, https://www.hearst.com/, accessed November 30, 2022.

23. Alliance for Audited Media, news media statement for the six-month period ending March 31, 2022, http://www.auditedmedia.com/.

24. The newsroom job count and combined print and digital circulation numbers as well as quotes are from Wendy Metcalfe, email message to Kennedy, June 2, 2022; digital-only circulation numbers are from confidential reporting by Kennedy; "Hearst CT Media Group Shifts Printing Press Operations to Albany," *Connecticut Post*, May 24, 2022, https://www.ctpost .com/business/article/Hearst-CT-Media-Group-shifts-printing-press -17194700.php.

25. David Folkenflik, "'Vulture' Fund Alden Global, Known for Slashing Newsrooms, Buys Tribune Papers," NPR.org, May 21, 2021, https://www .npr.org/2021/05/21/998730863/vulture-fund-alden-global-known-for -slashing-newsrooms-buys-tribune-papers.

26. Flemming Norcott Jr., in-person interview by Kennedy, November 17, 2021.

27. Paul Bass, "*New Haven Advocate*, 1975–2013," *New Haven Independent*, December 4, 2013, https://www.newhavenindependent.org/article/new _haven_advocate_1975–2013.

28. Kennedy, *The Wired City*, 25–38.

29. New Haven is 43.6 percent white, 33.6 percent Black, and 30.8 percent Hispanic or Latino; "Quick Facts" for New Haven, CT, US Census Bureau, https://www.census.gov/quickfacts, accessed May 19, 2022.

30. Rawls Ivy interview.

31. Bass interview.

32. Markeshia Ricks, in-person interview by Kennedy, November 17, 2021.

33. Markeshia Ricks, LinkedIn post, May 2022, https://www.linkedin.com/ feed/update/urn:li:activity:6941726601978007552.

34. Maya McFadden, in-person interview by Kennedy, November 17, 2021; Maya McFadden, "Basketball's Back at Farnham," *New Haven Independent*, December 9, 2021, https://www.newhavenindependent.org/article /farnam_basketball.

35. Paul Bass, email message to Kennedy, May 19, 2022.

36. Norma Rodriguez-Reyes, in-person interview by Kennedy, December 16, 2021.

37. Bass interview.

38. Brian Slattery, in-person interview by Kennedy, December 15, 2021.

39. "QuickFacts" for Hamden, CT, US Census Bureau, https://www.census .gov/quickfacts, accessed May 19, 2022.

40. Nora Grace-Flood, "Zoning 'Gobbledygook' Zapped," *New Haven Independent*, December 20, 2021, https://www.newhavenindependent.org /article/hamden_amends_zoning_regulations_rewrites_gobbledygook.

41. Kennedy accompanied Nora Grace-Flood on December 16, 2021.

42. Nora Grace-Flood, in-person interview by Kennedy, December 16, 2021.
43. Bass interview.
44. Michelle Chihara, telephone interview by Kennedy, January 20, 2022.
45. Seedlings Foundation, https://www.seedlingsct.org, accessed November 30, 2022.
46. Karen Pritzker, in-person interview by Kennedy, December 15, 2021.
47. Kennedy accompanied Tom Breen on November 16, 2021.
48. Dan Kennedy, "The Latest Bad Idea for Chain Newspapers: Robot Reporting on Real Estate," *Media Nation*, January 27, 2022, https://dan kennedy.net/2022/01/27/the-latest-bad-idea-for-chain-newspapers-robot -reporting-on-real-estate.
49. Tom Breen, in-person interview by Kennedy, November 16, 2021.

CHAPTER EIGHT: STORM LAKE, IOWA
1. "Wind Energy in Iowa," Office of Energy Efficiency & Renewable Energy, https://windexchange.energy.gov/states/ia#capacity, accessed February 21, 2022.
2. Mike Kilen, "How a Small-Town Newspaperman 'Raised Hell' and Became a Critical Voice for Iowa," *Des Moines Register*, October 5, 2018, https://www.desmoinesregister.com/story/life/2018/10/05/iowa-newspaper- writer-art-cullen-pulitzer-prize-storm-lake-times/1510101002.
3. *Storm Lake: A Newspaper. A Family. A Community*, ITVS, 2021, https:// itvs.org/films/storm-lake.
4. "Our Latest Podcast Features an Interview with Art Cullen, Editor of the *Storm Lake Times*," *What Works* (podcast), November 15, 2021, https:// whatworks.news/2021/11/15/our-latest-contest-features-an-interview -with-art-cullen-editor-of-the-storm-lake-times.
5. *Storm Lake*, https://stormlakemovie.com, accessed February 21, 2022.
6. "Who We Serve," Western Iowa Journalism Foundation, https://www .westerniowajournalismfoundation.com/who-we-serve, accessed March 12, 2022.
7. *La Prensa de Iowa*, https://www.laprensaiowa.com; *Carroll Times Herald*, https://www.carrollspaper.com/news; *Greene Recorder*, https://www.greene recorder.com, accessed March 12, 2022.
8. Christopher R. Martin, telephone interview by Clegg, March 3, 2022.
9. "Owned by the Burns family": Douglas Burns, telephone interview by Clegg, March 3, 2022.
10. Christopher R. Martin, "What Makes Iowa Newspapers Resilient?," Center for Journalism & Liberty, September 23, 2020, https://www.journalism liberty.org/publications/what-makes-iowa-newspapers-resilient.
11. Alex S. Jones, "*Des Moines Register* to Be Purchased by Gannett," *New York Times*, February 1, 1985, https://www.nytimes.com/1985/02/01 /business/des-moines-register-to-be-purchased-by-gannett.html.
12. Circulation figures for the six-month period ending March 31, 2022, as reported to the Alliance for Audited Media, https://auditedmedia.com/.
13. Martin, "What Makes Iowa Newspapers Resilient?"
14. Martin, "What Makes Iowa Newspapers Resilient?"

15. R. W. Apple, "Life in Iowa May Not Have Changed, but the Political Turf Is Another Story," *New York Times*, October 28, 1995, https://www.nytimes.com/1995/10/28/us/life-in-iowa-may-not-have-changed-but-the-political-turf-is-another-story.html.

16. Kyle Munson email message to Ellen Clegg, February 13, 2022.

17. Munson, video interview by Clegg, January 17, 2022

18. US Census Bureau QuickFacts: Denison, IA, July 1, 2021, https://www.census.gov/quickfacts/denisoncityiowa.

19. Lorena López, telephone interview by Clegg, August 12, 2021.

20. Art Cullen, "President Trump's Last Gasps," *Storm Lake Times*, November 25, 2020, https://www.stormlake.com/articles/art-cullen-editorial-president-trump-last-gasp.

21. 2022 Facebook Accelerator Program, August 23, 2022, https://www.facebook.com/community/whats-new/apply-now-2022-community-accelerator.

22. Clara Hendrickson, "Critical in a Public Health Crisis, COVID-19 Has Hit Local Newsrooms Hard," Brookings Institution, April 8, 2020, https://www.brookings.edu/blog/fixgov/2020/04/08/critical-in-a-public-health-crisis-covid-19-has-hit-local-newsrooms-hard.

23. Martin, "What Makes Iowa Newspapers Resilient?"

24. "Art Cullen of *The Storm Lake Times*, Storm Lake, IA," 2017 Pulitzer Prize Winner in Editorial Writing, Pulitzer Prizes, https://www.pulitzer.org/winners/art-cullen.

25. Cullen, 2017 Pulitzer Prize Winner in Editorial Writing.

26. Dave Davies, "*Storm Lake* Documentary Depicts the Triumph and Struggle of a Local Newspaper," *Fresh Air*, November 12, 2021, https://www.npr.org/2021/11/12/1055057480/storm-lake-documentary-depicts-the-triumph-and-struggle-of-a-local-newspaper.

27. Lee Enterprises Brands, https://lee.net/markets/, accessed February 23, 2022.

28. Jake Hansen, "Population Trends in Rural Iowa: Decline and Recovery," *Major Themes in Economics* 2 (2000): 21–31, https://scholarworks.uni.edu/cgi/viewcontent.cgi?article=1009&context=mtie.

29. Hansen, "Population Trends in Rural Iowa."

30. "*Storm Lake Times* Buys *Pilot-Tribune* and Ad Guide," *Storm Lake Times Pilot*, April 1, 2022, https://www.stormlake.com/articles/storm-lake-times-buys-pilot-tribune-and-ad-guide.

31. Michael Grabell and Bernice Yeung, "The Battle for Waterloo," *Storm Lake Times*, December 22, 2020, https://www.stormlake.com/articles/the-battle-for-waterloo.

32. "Our Latest Podcast Features an Interview with Art Cullen."

33. US Census Bureau QuickFacts, Storm Lake, IA, July 1, 2021, https://www.census.gov/quickfacts/stormlakecityiowa.

CHAPTER NINE: TEXAS

1. Eric Neugeboren, "El Paso Lawmakers Say That Despite Polarized Climate, Texas Legislature Must Act on Guns, Reproductive Rights," *Texas Tribune*, June 28, 2022, https://www.texastribune.org/2022/06/14/inside-the-interim-el-paso-22.

2. Evan Smith, in-person interview by Ellen Clegg, July 22, 2022.

3. Clark Hoyt, "Recession, Revolution and a Leaner *Times*," *New York Times*, October 31, 2009, https://www.nytimes.com/2009/11/01/opinion/01pubed.html.

4. Richard Pérez-Peña, "Web News Start-Up Has Its Eye on Texas," *New York Times*, July 17, 2009, https://www.nytimes.com/2009/07/18/business/media/18texas.html

5. "Emerging Nonprofit Models in Local News," Harvard Shorenstein Center for Media, Politics and Public Policy, July 3, 2019, https://shorensteincenter.org/landscape-local-news-models-nonprofit-models.

6. Evan Smith, "T-Squared: 2022 Will Be My Last Year as *The Texas Tribune*'s CEO," *Texas Tribune*, January 12, 2022, https://www.texastribune.org/2022/01/12/evan-smith-texas-tribune-ceo.

7. John Thornton biography, *Texas Tribune*, https://www.texastribune.org/about/staff/john-thornton, accessed August 17, 2022.

8. Smith, "T-Squared."

9. Ross Ramsey, LinkedIn profile, https://www.linkedin.com/in/ross-ramsey-84b50a, accessed August 17, 2022.

10. Jon Egan, "Revered Austin Journalist Evan Smith Exiting Post as CEO of *Texas Tribune*," *Culturemap Austin*, January 13, 2022, https://austin.culturemap.com/news/city-life/01–13–22-austin-journalist-evan-smith-exiting-ceo-texas-tribune.

11. Kevin Brass, "Eye of the Media Storm," *Austin Chronicle*, March 6, 2009, https://www.austinchronicle.com/news/2009–03–06/751675.

12. Smith interview.

13. 2021 Pulitzer Prize in National Reporting, Pulitzer Prizes, https://www.pulitzer.org/winners/staffs-marshall-project-alcom-birmingham-indystar-indianapolis-and-invisible-institute.

14. "About Us," *Texas Tribune*, https://www.texastribune.org/about, accessed August 16, 2022.

15. *The Texas Tribune 2021 Annual Report*, https://static.texastribune.org/media/files/14d6468ed89edb26db46a95949fd04b8/TT-2021-Annual-Report-Web_05–25–2022.pdf.

16. Emily Dresslar, telephone interview by Clegg, July 6, 2022.

17. Swenson: Kristen Hunter, "Meet the Guy Who Made Austin Cool," *DuJour*, https://dujour.com/news/roland-swenson-sxsw-austin, accessed August 17, 2022; Powers: University of Texas Office of the President, https://president.utexas.edu/past-presidents/william-powers-jr, accessed August 17, 2022.

18. Tanya Erlach, LinkedIn profile, https://www.linkedin.com/in/tanya-erlach-40a3813, accessed August 17, 2022.

19. "Our Team," The 19th, https://19thnews.org/team, accessed August 14, 2022.

20. Emily Ramshaw, telephone interview by Clegg, July 15, 2022.

21. Gregg Ramshaw profile, LinkedIn.com, https://www.linkedin.com/in/gregg-ramshaw-547729a, accessed August 17, 2022.

22. Ross Ramsey, telephone interview by Clegg, July 7, 2022.

23. Emily Ramshaw, telephone interview by Clegg, July 15, 2022.

24. "Census: American Internet Use Surges," *Austin Business Journal*, June 3, 2009, https://www.bizjournals.com/austin/stories/2009/06/01/daily32.html.

25. Sharon Strover , Joe Straubhaar, Karen Gustafson, Wenhong Chen, Alexis Schrubbe, and Paul Popiel, *Digital Inclusion in Austin: Results from a Citywide Survey*, University of Texas at Austin, Technology and Information Policy Institute, 2015, https://moody.utexas.edu/sites/default/files/sites/communication.utexas.edu/files/images/content/tipi/Digital_Inclusion_final_report_edited.pdf.

26. Matt Stiles, telephone interview by Clegg, July 13, 2022.

27. *The Blast*, https://www.texastribune.org/theblast/, accessed August 15, 2022.

28. James Henson biography, University of Texas Department of Government website, https://liberalarts.utexas.edu/government/faculty/hensonjr, accessed August 17, 2022.

29. Patrick Svitek, "Greg Abbott Leads Beto O'Rourke by 9 Percentage Points in Hypothetical Matchup, UT/TT Poll Finds," *Texas Tribune*, November 5, 2021, https://www.texastribune.org/2021/11/05/texas-poll-greg-abbott-beto-orourke.

30. James Henson, telephone interview by Clegg, July 12, 2022.

31. Ross Ramsey, "Meet the Flintstones," *Texas Tribune*, February 17, 2010, https://www.texastribune.org/2010/02/17/texans-dinosaurs-humans-walked-the-earth-at-same.

32. Sewell Chan, in-person interview by Clegg, July 22, 2022.

33. 2021 Pulitzer Prize in Editorial Writing, Pulitzer Prizes, https://www.pulitzer.org/prize-winners-by-category/214.

34. "Editorial: An Examination of the *Times*' Failures on Race, Our Apology, and a Path Forward," *Los Angeles Times*, September 27, 2020, https://www.latimes.com/opinion/story/2020–09–27/los-angeles-times-apology-racism.

35. Brian Lopez and Emily Hernandez, "Lt. Gov. Dan Patrick Wants Texas Version of Florida Law That Critics Dubbed 'Don't Say Gay,'" *Texas Tribune*, April 4, 2022, https://www.texastribune.org/2022/04/04/texas-dont-say-gay-dan-patrick.

EPILOGUE

1. "Congress Excludes JCPA and LJSA from Omnibus Bill," *America's Newspapers*, December 20, 2022, https://www.newspapers.org/stories/congress-excludes-jcpa-and-ljsa-from-omnibus-bill,4162083.

2. Chris Krewson, "A Letter to LION Members about the Journalism Competition Preservation Act and the Online News Act," LION Publishers, September 5, 2022, https://www.lionpublishers.com/a-letter-to-lion-members-about-the-journalism-competition-preservation-act-and-the-online-news-act.

3. Steven Waldman, "The Best Local News Bill," Rebuild Local News, June 16, 2021, https://www.rebuildlocalnews.org/commentary/the-best-local-news-bill.

4. Mary Yang, "Meta Reports Another Drop in Revenue, in a Rough Week for Tech Companies," NPR, October 26, 2022, https://www.npr.org/2022/10/26/1131590734/meta-earnings-slump.

5. "Breen Named *Independent* Editor," *New Haven Independent*, November 1, 2022, https://www.newhavenindependent.org/article/breen_named _independent_editor; Paul Bass, email messages to Dan Kennedy, November 30 and December 19, 2022; Tom Breen, email message to Kennedy, December 21, 2022.

6. Tanner Curl, "Elizabeth Dunbar Will Lead Our Newsroom as *MinnPost*'s Next Editor," *MinnPost*, June 8, 2022, https://www.minnpost.com/inside -minnpost/2022/06/elizabeth-dunbar-will-lead-our-newsroom-as-minnposts -next-editor; "Editor Andrew Putz Leaving *MinnPost*," *MinnPost*, February 15, 2022, https://www.minnpost.com/inside-minnpost/2022/02/editor -andrew-putz-leaving-minnpost; Laura Lindsay, "An Interview with *MinnPost* Editor Elizabeth Dunbar," *MinnPost*, August 30, 2022, https:// www.minnpost.com/inside-minnpost/2022/08/an-interview-with-minnpost -editor-elizabeth-dunbar.

7. Rick Edmonds, "After 13 Years at the Helm of the *Star Tribune*, Publisher Mike Klingensmith Is Retiring," *Poynter Online*, September 15, 2022, https://www.poynter.org/business-work/2022/after-13-years-at-the-helm -of-the-star-tribune-publisher-mike-klingensmith-is-retiring.

8. Katie Robertson, "*The Texas Tribune* Names a New CEO," *New York Times*, October 26, 2022, https://www.nytimes.com/2022/10/26/business /media/texas-tribune-ceo-sonal-shah.html; Ben Smith, "*Texas Tribune*'s Co-Founder Will Spread Local News Gospel," *Semafor*, October 30, 2022, https://www.semafor.com/article/10/30/2022/texas-tribune-evan-smith -laurene-powell-jobs.

9. Don Seiffert, "Gannett Shutters Real Estate Publication *Boston Homes* After 25 Years," *Boston Business Journal*, September 27, 2022, https:// www.bizjournals.com/boston/news/2022/09/27/gannett-shutters-real -estate-publication-boston-ho.html; Wayne Braverman, "A New Journey Begins . . .," *Bedford Citizen*, October 11, 2022, https://www.thebedford citizen.org/2022/10/a-new-journey-begins; Teri Morrow, email message to Kennedy, December 18, 2022.

10. Ben Badgikian interview, *Smoke in the Eye: Why Did CBS and ABC Back Off from Exposés on the Tobacco Industry?*, Frontline, PBS, 1999, https:// www.pbs.org/wgbh/pages/frontline/smoke/interviews/bagdikian.html.

11. Ben H. Bagdikian, *The New Media Monopoly* (Boston: Beacon Press, 2004), 185.

12. Robert D. Putnam, *Bowling Alone: The Collapse and Revival of American Community* (New York: Simon & Schuster, 2001), 218.

13. Pagan Kennedy, "William Gibson's Future Is Now," *New York Times Book Review*, January 13, 2012, https://www.nytimes.com/2012/01/15/books /review/distrust-that-particular-flavor-by-william-gibson-book-review.html.

INDEX